[ALTERNATIVE]
LITERARY PUBLISHING

SALLY DENNISON

[ALTERNATIVE] LITERARY PUBLISHING

Five Modern Histories

UNIVERSITY OF IOWA PRESS IOWA CITY

Drawings by Peter Nelson © *1984.*

University of Iowa Press, Iowa City 52242
© 1984 by The University of Iowa. All rights reserved
Printed in the United States of America

Library of Congress Cataloging in Publication Data

Dennison, Sally, 1946–
   Alternative literary publishing.

   Bibliography: p.
   Includes index.
   1. Little presses—History—20th century.
2. English literature—20th century—History and
criticism. 3. American literature—20th century—
History and criticism. I. Title.
Z231.5.L5D47 1984   070.5   84-8700
ISBN 0–87745–126–5
ISBN 0–87745–127–3 (pbk.)

To Winston Weathers and to Gene Dennison

CONTENTS

INTRODUCTION   1

1. T. S. ELIOT
   With a Little Help from His Friends   17

2. VIRGINIA WOOLF
   With a Press of One's Own   49

3. JAMES JOYCE
   From the Bookshop   77

4. ANAIS NIN
   The Book as a Work of Art   119

5. VLADIMIR NABOKOV
   The Work of Art as a Dirty Book   159

6. ALTERNATIVE PUBLISHING
   "The Handmaiden of Literature"   193

NOTES   201

BIBLIOGRAPHY   217

INDEX   223

INTRODUCTION

In the first decade of the twentieth century, the young poet Ezra Pound set out to foster an awakening in English-language literature that would, in his words, "make the Italian Renaissance look like a tempest in a teapot." A promoter by nature, Pound had the enthusiasm and drive to hurdle any obstacle. The most important obstacle he found was the commercial publishing establishment to which all young writers looked for access to a reading public. By 1912 he had learned there was a close connection between literary renaissance and literary publishing, for when Harriet Monroe wrote from Chicago asking Pound for advice about starting a poetry magazine subsidized by donations, Pound wrote back, "Your scheme . . . seems not only sound but the only possible method. There is no other magazine in America which is not an insult to the serious artist and to the dignity of his art."[1]

Pound had spent the past seven years writing poetry and bombarding editors with his work. He tried every kind of magazine from *Atlantic* to the *Ladies Home Journal* without much success. In 1908, impatient to get a volume of his poetry before the public, he paid for the printing of his own book. His success with that venture convinced him it was far better to publish his own work than to publish only what the commercial editors would accept. He would have begun his own literary magazine had people like Monroe not provided him

[1]

outlets for his writing. "I don't think it's any of the artist's business to see whether or no he circulates," Pound wrote her, "but I was . . . on the verge of starting a quarterly, and it's a great relief to know that your paper may manage what I had, without financial strength, been about to attempt rather forlornly."[2]

Not just for himself, but for the future of literature, Pound realized, new outlets would have to be found, ones which like Monroe's subsidized *Poetry* could afford to foster new writing at the expense of popularity. "If one is going to print opinions the public already agrees with," he reasoned, "what is the use of printing them at all? Good art can't possibly be palatable all at once." Publish the best poetry, he advised Monroe, solid work "directed toward the broadening and development of the Art of Poetry. And 'TO HELL WITH HARPERS AND THE MAGAZINE TOUCH'!"[3]

What Ezra Pound said in 1912 about literary publishing was to become even more evident with the passing of years. Commercial publishers, which have increasingly had to depend upon quick sales in order to survive in a mass-market society, have necessarily become less receptive to literature which has challenged all literary norms. Unconventional writing is inherently unpopular, for readers, like participants in a game, resent one's changing the rules without notice; yet the aesthetic sensibility of the twentieth century has fostered experimentation in all the arts.

The ideas about serious writing which Pound and his colleagues set forth in small magazines and privately published books during the first two decades of the century were indeed unpopular. "BLAST . . . from start to finish every form that the poetry of a former condition of life . . . has foisted upon us," they said in *BLAST*, a journal edited by Wyndham Lewis.[4] Destroy "politeness, standardization, and academic, that is civilized, vision."[5] Poetry was to be freed of end rhymes and strict rhythms. Ambiguity and uncertainty were to be virtues, and form was to be fluid to support a fluid content. In prose as well as verse, prudery was to be banished in

[2]

favor of honesty, while conventions were to be "trampled down," if they stood in the way of "the precise rendering of the impulse."[6] "Writing is an art," Pound wrote, "... an art that must be in constant flux, a constant change of manner, if it is to live."[7]

Confronted by radical changes in poetry and fiction, readers were confused, often outraged. The institutions of society—the church, the press, and the courts—were mustered to combat the revolution. They fought a losing battle. These radical, unconventional ideas, and the very spirit of anticonventionality, became the conventions of the art, determining the course of literature in the twentieth century.

This paradox is explained partly by the phenomenon of alternative publishing. Wherever new writing has flourished—in London of the pre-World War I era, in Paris between the wars, in Greenwich Village, San Francisco, London, and scattered outposts since World War II—small presses have appeared in writers' lofts and basements, in bookshops and back rooms. These new outlets were subsidized by writers, their friends and relatives, or by generous patrons of the arts who rarely expected or got any financial return. Many, like Harriet Weaver's Egoist Press, or Margaret Anderson's *Little Review*, existed on donations, were important outlets for some of the best writers of the day, and then folded. Despite the literary influence of these presses, their output wasn't popular enough to make them self-supporting. Although individual small presses have come and gone, the phenomenon of alternative publishing is a permanent part of the twentieth-century literary scene.

In this study the term "alternative publishing" is used to denote all methods of reaching an audience other than through commercial publishing. It includes self-publishing, small press and university press publishing, little magazine publishing, publishing through a bookstore, publishing through patrons, readings, *samizdat*, or any means other than through a large general trade publisher.

The largest and most prestigious category of alternative

[3]

publication has been university presses, which currently produce one in every twelve books published in the United States.[8] This category has grown phenomenally in the twentieth century, and has helped fill the gaps left by commercial presses in the areas of regional and scholarly publishing. Because they were developed and funded primarily as tools of higher education, however, university presses have published very few new literary works, and so have not been as useful to literary artists as other types of alternative presses.

Two terms sometimes misapplied to alternative publishing have contributed to a great deal of prejudice against it on the part of the general public, and sometimes even on the part of literary scholars. These terms are "vanity publishing" and "coterie publishing."

The first of these terms correctly applies only to one branch of commercial book production and not at all to alternative publishing. A "vanity" book is one produced through one of a handful of subsidy book publishers. These houses, usually quite large and profitable, will often advertise for manuscripts; they agree to publish a work only after the author pays all printing and binding costs. In addition, the writer is bound by a contract in which he or she gives up a percentage of the proceeds from book sales, as well as any control over how the work will be printed, bound, advertised, and distributed. Vanity, or subsidy, publishers offer writers the worst of both worlds, forcing them to pay the costs of publication and at the same time to give up all editorial control. Not surprisingly, none of the seven writers discussed here has ever been involved in vanity publishing.

Very often, as we will see in the following publishing histories, the editor/publisher is himself a writer, usually a friend of the author. A lot of mutual backscratching has gone on: Pound got Eliot published in *Poetry;* Eliot published Pound in *Egoist;* the Woolfs published Eliot at Hogarth Press, and Eliot published the Woolfs in *Criterion.* Because of these kinds of arrangements, alternative publishing has been frequently derogated as coterie publishing. What this

[4]

thinking ignores is that almost all commercial publishing is also coterie in the same sense. Commercial editors often publish each other's writing as well as that of friends. It is extremely rare for a manuscript to be picked out of the "slush pile" of unsolicited submissions and published by a commercial house.

The difference between the alternative "coterie" and the commercial "coterie" has been one of scale and of writer-control. Since alternative presses are often one- or two-person operations, the writer and his friendly publisher do not have to deal with the staff of readers, copyeditors, sales managers, and so on, all of whom have a hand in producing the typical commercial book. Special requests can more easily be granted and (as in the case of Joyce's *Ulysses*) alterations more easily made. As a result, the modern writers have gained a great deal of freedom to see their innovations into print, freedom from many of the forces which have tended to standardize commercial literature.

Throughout this century, alternative publishing has played a primary role in the development of all literary genres. By the first decade, poetry had become a "drug on the market" and a losing proposition for commercial book publishers. Most of them simply refused to publish books of poetry; others continued to bring out a few volumes each year, usually works by established poets. They were willing to lose money in order to keep a toe in the door of literary prestige. Popular magazines publishing poetry consistently chose the sort of verse they knew would be acceptable to the general public, rather than new forms. Gradually the general public came to prefer prose to poetry, and even these markets dried up.

Short fiction continued to flourish in the popular magazines and to a lesser extent in books until after World War II. Short stories by "literary" writers like Hemingway or Faulkner were widely sold and read along with the strictly "popular" stories by writers such as Daphne du Maurier and Erle Stanley Gardner. (Hemingway's first publishers, however,

[5]

were not the *Saturday Evening Post* or Scribners, but the *Double Dealer* of New Orleans and Contact Editions and Three Mountains Press, both operated by friends of Hemingway in Paris.) Following World War II, television began to compete with magazines for audiences and advertising dollars. One by one the general circulation magazines which published fiction went out of business, until finally the most popular short story writers, like the newcomers, had trouble getting published.

Even the novel, the one truly popular literary genre of our century, has faced constant pressure to conform to public tastes. Increasingly, commercial publishers have refused to read unsolicited or "unagented" manuscripts, while agents have considered representing only those writers with commercial potential. Nor has it been so easy for novelists to publish noncommercially as it has been for poets and short story writers. The cost of printing and binding a novel-length book has been prohibitive even for the most generous of patrons—about the same as a new Cadillac according to one estimate. An avant-garde writer has usually had to catch the eye of an editor at one of the few small presses which publish novels in order to get his or her experimental works into the hands of readers.

Of course commercial publishers have not always turned a cold shoulder to new writing. Shortly after World War I, several new publishers set up shop in New York and London and began to challenge the older houses by bringing out the "daring" poetry, stories, and novels of the literary moderns. Following World War II, a new generation of editors conducted a similar revival within established houses and literary magazines. The pattern, however, was for these publishers to pick up avant-garde writers whose careers were flourishing already in the writer-edited little magazines and presses. The commercial publishers would then throw their machinery of promotion behind these serious writers in an effort to make their works popular. In some cases, like that of Hemingway, these efforts succeeded; in other cases the publishers lost money in the short run, but gained prestige and a slow trickle of profits with the passing of years. Often the publishers simply lost money.

The story of commercial publishing, as detailed in Thomas Whiteside's three-part study in the *New Yorker* magazine (September 29, October 6 and 13, 1980),[9] has been one of cottage industries growing into public corporations, then being absorbed into giant conglomerates in order to survive financially. In such a climate, sales figures and popular appeal increasingly have become the primary consideration in nearly all editorial decisions. Such factors as potential for book club, paperback, and movie sales have come to mean the difference between profit and loss for publishers. In addition, there has been a steady decline in the popularity of fiction as nonfiction has been more and more in demand, and as a result nonfiction has all but crowded fiction out of the pages of general circulation magazines and has had a drastic effect upon book publishers' lists. In light of these facts, we can be amazed only at the extent to which editors do continue to back serious writers whose books they know ahead of time will lose money.

By and large, however, literary artists and the commercial publishers have had to part company because their interests have lain in opposite directions. For the artists, these publishers have played a secondary role, that of popularizer of literary trends developed elsewhere. It has been left to writers themselves to "see whether or no" they circulate as they follow the modern trend to defy the conventional. What this phenomenon of alternative publishing has meant—how it has affected the development of twentieth-century literature—is the subject of this book.

The five publishing histories which follow all demonstrate important literary developments. Several of the works, such as *Ulysses,* and *The Waste Land,* are recognized almost universally as landmarks; others are well known only to specialists in modern literature but are widely accepted by them as having contributed to the art. They have been chosen for

[7]

this study because of their importance, because they represent several literary periods both chronologically and stylistically, and because they represent three major literary genres—poetry, short fiction, and the novel.

All five works were published originally through alternative presses, and they are no different from many other important works in that respect. At least one work of fiction by almost every major twentieth-century writer has been published by a small press, as have most works of virtually all serious poets. Since these five works are typical of the way in which much new writing has reached audiences, their publishing histories should give us a clearer understanding of forces which have shaped writing in our times.

The year 1922 was one in which more than a decade of literary upheaval culminated in a bumper crop of modernism. T. S. Eliot's *The Waste Land*, Virginia Woolf's *Jacob's Room* and James Joyce's *Ulysses* were among the important works which appeared that year. Each was radically modern in form as well as content, and all took the shape they did partly because of these writers' experiences with alternative publishing.

Anaïs Nin began her career in the milieu of the Paris avant-garde during the early thirties, when small writer-operated presses abounded. When the outbreak of World War II forced her to flee to New York, Nin brought with her this tradition of self-publishing. Her beautiful editions of *Winter of Artifice* and *Under a Glass Bell* helped revitalize the idea of literature as a self-expressive art in the heyday of the proletarian writer.

The mid-fifties, like the early twenties, saw the development of new trends which challenged literary norms. Vladimir Nabokov's *Lolita* was somewhat radical in purpose as well as subject matter, and it helped to define the post-World War II era in the same way that the 1922 works had defined literary modernism a generation before. Like its predecessors, *Lolita* was originally published alternatively.

Some of these five writers entered into the alternative pub-

[8]

lication of their works as a last resort, only to find they had gained new freedom as artists by doing so. Others knowing they would be published alternatively wrote works much more daring in form or content than they could have with a commercial publisher in mind. Only in the case of Nabokov did the author who sought an alternative publisher have cause to regret it, and even he found such publication, despite its hazards, far better than none at all.

A literary history of our century might well begin in 1908 in Venice. Here an unknown young American paid for the publication of a book of his own poems. It was the beginning of a literary career—that of Ezra Pound—which would revolutionize Anglo-American letters. How Pound came to publish his own book and the effect this publication had on his later development is worth retelling here, for in many ways it introduces the relationship between publishing and literature which has existed since.

When the adolescent Pound began writing he believed his talent would be recognized and he would be published, if he wrote well enough. As a student at the University of Pennsylvania and as a teacher in Indiana he tried marketing his work to commercial journals which published poetry. The journals repeatedly rejected what he considered his best poetry, though several published his more banal verse. In 1908, declaring that American editors preferred the dull and diluted to art of "maximum intensity," he left for Europe.

Pound took with him a manuscript of forty poems which had been rejected by at least one American book publisher. The young writer first settled in Venice, where he tried vainly to stave off hunger by sending poetry and fiction to *Harper's* and the *Ladies Home Journal.* Unsuccessful, he grew impatient with the established literary press, and in 1908 decided to swallow his pride and publish his own book at his own expense. Adding a few new poems to the original forty, Pound took his manuscript to A. Antonini, a printer in Venice.

He was not content to sit back and let fame find him once

his book was out. While it was still being printed, he formulated a strategy for getting the book, and himself, noticed. "The American reprint," he wrote his mother, "has got to be worked by kicking up such a hell of a row with genuine and faked reviews that Scribner or somebody can be brought to see the sense of making a reprint. I shall write a few myself and get someone to sign 'em."[10] And just to make sure this notice wasn't lost on Scribner's et al., Pound planned to collect clippings of all his reviews and to send them to various American publishers.

Only one hundred copies of the book, *A Lume Spento*, were printed. They were seventy-two pages, bound in a green paper cover. Pound sent almost half of them to his father to be used as review copies in America. Antonini agreed to try to sell some at five lire in Venice. The rest of the edition Pound stuffed into his suitcase and took to London. Here, *A Lume Spento* became his calling card, for he knew no one in the entire city when he took up residence there in September 1908, with five dollars in his pocket. Introducing himself as the author of *A Lume Spento*, Pound succeeded in getting the *Evening Standard* and *St. James's Gazette* to publish his poem "Histrion" on October 26, just a month after his arrival. The *Evening Standard* also reviewed *A Lume Spento*, calling it "original, imaginative, passionate and spiritual. . . . Coming after the trite and decorous verse of most of our decorous poets, this poet seems like a minstrel of Provence at a suburban musical evening."[11]

The most important door opened for Pound by his little self-published booklet was the door to Elkin Mathews's bookshop in Vigo Street. In the 1880s Mathews, in partnership with John Lane, had operated the Bodley Head, bookshop and publisher of avant-garde poetry—the work of Yeats and the Rhymers Club poets. Mathews and Lane had quarreled in 1894, and Lane moved to new quarters down the street, taking the Bodley Head name with him. Mathews continued to sell and publish books on his own. When Pound arrived on the scene in September 1890, he considered these two shops in

[10]

Vigo Street "the two peaks of Parnassas." He soon visited both with copies of *A Lume Spento* and each took a few to sell.

Encouraged, Pound had another book printed up in time for the Christmas trade. The twenty-eight page *A Quinzaine For This Yule* contained seventeen poems and two prose pieces. Again Pound had a first printing of only a hundred, but this time all copies sold in a few days and Elkin Mathews quickly agreed to print a second edition. In January 1909, Pound took Mathews a new collection of poems, and Mathews decided to publish them, after some negotiation, as Pound reported later:

> Mr. E. M.: Ah, eh, do you care to contribute to the costs of publishing it?
> Mr. E. P.: I've got a shilling in my clothes if that's any use to you.
> Mr. E. M.: Oh well, I rather want to publish 'em anyhow.[12]

And so, with this third book, *Personae*, Pound finally found a publisher—not one of the big commercial houses, but a publisher nonetheless. As he wrote to Mathews's widow thirteen years later, "I certainly shall not forget that it was he who first accepted my work when I landed in London, *sans sous*. These beginnings count for more than the middle steps of the journey."[13]

Mathews introduced Pound to the London literary world. In February he took the newcomer to the Poet's Club, where he met the famous Bernard Shaw. Pound was also invited to tea by the novelist Olivia Shakespear, and met her daughter Dorothy, whom he later married. The Shakespears introduced him to friends of Yeats, and eventually to the man himself. By mid-1909 he was attending the regular Monday night meetings at Yeats's rooms near Euston Station. In April, Pound met with a newly formed group of poets, led by T. E. Hulme, that was dedicated to the renewal of English poetry. The publication of *Personae* that month brought praise from influential reviewers on both sides of the Atlantic.

In the midst of his growing fame, Pound wrote his friend from college days, William Carlos Williams, to thank him for a copy of Williams's first book (privately printed in Rutherford, New Jersey). In his letter Pound admitted that perhaps he had printed too much of his own early poetry. However, printing too much had been far better for his career than printing none at all. "After eight years' hammering against impenetrable adamant," Pound wrote, he had suddenly become "somewhat of a success."[14]

As it was for Ezra Pound, so it would be for others: years before they ever broke into print with the commercial literary press, they had already gained audiences, broken new literary ground, and become somewhat famous — all through alternative publishing means. Why was this so? And what has it meant for the development of literature? Some answers can be found in the cases of five twentieth-century writers.

T. S. ELIOT

. . . with a little help from his friends

1

As his fortunes rose, Ezra Pound was never hesitant to use his influence at the little magazines to promote the careers of others whose work he admired. No career owed more to Pound's sponsorship among the alternative presses than that of a fellow American, T. S. Eliot.

When the two men met in 1914, Eliot was a philosophy student on leave from Harvard, completing his doctoral dissertation at Oxford. He showed Pound a few poems he had written four years before, poems which had been rejected by the one editor who had seen them. Pound loved the poems and immediately recognized that Eliot was not just a graduate student dabbling in poetry. Here, he wrote Harriet Monroe at *Poetry*, was a promising young talent, unique in that he had "actually trained *and* modernized himself *on his own*."[1]

Pound took up Eliot's cause with great enthusiasm and promoted his work tirelessly to everyone he knew at commercial and alternative presses alike. The commercial presses remained uninterested; six years would pass before Eliot's work would be published by the daring young Alfred Knopf, and two more years would go by before the appearance of *The Waste Land* in alternative publications and a subsidized Boni & Liveright edition would gain him "instant" fame. The first decade of Eliot's career was spent largely in writing and editing for small presses and little magazines. In this lively world of alternative publishing the young writer first exercised the poetic and critical skills that would one day gain him the Nobel Prize.

Eliot had begun writing poetry as a boy and continued writing, with occasional appearances in student publications, even after he began graduate studies in philosophy at Harvard. There, in 1910 and 1911, he composed "The Love Song of J. Alfred Prufrock," the poem that was to impress Pound most favorably in 1914.

For three years following its composition, "Prufrock" sat in Eliot's desk drawer while he concentrated on his studies. Finally, in July 1914, he showed it to Harvard friend Conrad Aiken, who was impressed with the poem's "extraordinary quality" and asked Eliot to let him try to place it. Aiken's efforts, however, were unsuccessful:

> At a "poetry squash" I showed it to Harold Monro, who called it "absolutely insane" and practically threw it back at me, saying "I can't be bothered with this." He was then editing *Poetry and Drama.*
>
> Later . . . I began to wonder if Monro hadn't thought it was mine, so I mailed it to him with a note which said, "It's really by Mr. T. S. Eliot." It was again turned down.[2]

After this fiasco, Eliot put "Prufrock" and his other early poems back into his desk and there they stayed until the end of September when, at Aiken's suggestion, he showed them to Ezra Pound. Pound shared Aiken's enthusiasm. The poems confirmed his first impression of Eliot as a well-educated and serious poet who shared his own aesthetic views. Pound quickly sent "Prufrock" to several people, including H. L. Mencken, editor of the then influential literary magazine, the *Smart Set,* and Harriet Monroe at *Poetry.* To Mencken he wrote, "I enclose a poem by the last intelligent man I've found—a young American, T. S. Eliot. . . . I think him worth watching."[3] Since he was acting in the capacity of *Poetry's* foreign editor at the time, Pound was much more direct to Monroe: "Hope you'll get it *in* soon!"[4] But Monroe disliked the

[18]

poem and delayed its publication. She wanted it toned down before it appeared in *Poetry*, while Pound insisted it be published without revisions:

> No, most emphatically I will not ask Eliot to write down to any audience whatsoever. I dare say my instinct was sound enough when I volunteered to quit the magazine quietly about a year ago. Neither will I send you Eliot's address in order that he may be insulted.[5]

Two months later, he wrote to answer some of Monroe's objections, saying "'Mr. Prufrock' does not 'go off at the end.' . . . A portrait satire on futility can't end by turning that quintessence of futility, Mr. P., into a reformed character breathing out fire and ozone."[6] Still Monroe delayed. "*Do* get on with that Eliot," Pound nagged her in April 1915,[7] and when the poem didn't appear in the May issue he wrote her, "My gawddd! This is a ROTTEN number of Poetry."[8] It finally came out in July 1915. Eliot was greatly encouraged by this publication, especially since it occurred at one of the turning points of his life.

Eliot's fellowship at Oxford was up, yet he dreaded returning to Harvard, "and the people whom one fights against and who absorb one all the same."[9] He had been an outstanding philosophy student, a teaching assistant, and president of the Philosophy Club. Once he finished the Ph.D., Eliot was sure to be offered a teaching position at Harvard, where he had strong family as well as personal connections. Ezra Pound's enthusiasm for Eliot's poetry and his success in getting it published changed all that. Eliot began to think of himself as a poet.

With Pound's introduction Eliot had become a part of an exciting circle of writers, editors, and critics in London. In mid-1915 Pound began taking him to Thursday-night gatherings in Soho and Regent Street restaurants with Ford Maddox Hueffer, Wyndham Lewis, H.D., and Richard Aldington. It was a stimulating environment for the young man, who suddenly found himself regarded as a promising poet among a small but influential group of trend-setting intellectuals. By the summer of 1915, when "Prufrock" finally appeared in *Poetry*, he had married Vivienne Haigh-Wood and taken up permanent residence in London, thus burning the bridges which led back to his parents and the philosophy department at Harvard.

Meanwhile, Pound had found other outlets for Eliot's poetry. One was the second and final number of *BLAST*, a radical journal of the arts edited by Wyndham Lewis; it appeared in July 1915, a month after the *Poetry* publication of "Prufrock." *BLAST* contained Eliot's "Preludes," and "Rhapsody on a Windy Night." Another Eliot publisher in 1915 was a little magazine called *Others: A Magazine of New Verse*. Pound's poet friend from college days, William Carlos Williams, was assisting Alfred Kreymborg (publisher through the Boni brothers of Pound's *Des Imagistes* anthology in 1913) on *Others*, a monthly published in Grantwood, New Jersey. In September 1915, they printed Eliot's "Portrait of a Lady."

Not content with these successes, Pound put together a poetry anthology with the idea of "getting sixteen pages of Eliot into print at once."[10] This collection of new poetry, which Pound named *Catholic Anthology* over the objections of its publisher, Elkin Mathews, included nine Pound poems, and works of Pound's current publishers, protégés, and friends. Introducing the book was a poem by Yeats, referring to ". . . the lines / That young men, tossing on their beds, / Rhymed out in love's despair." It then led off with sixteen pages of Eliot's poetry, including "Prufrock," "Portrait of a Lady," "The Boston Evening Transcript," "Miss Helen Slingsby," and a paragraph entitled "Hysteria." This was the young poet's first appearance in a book.

Catholic Anthology was a commercial failure and apparently drew no reviews until the following October, when Arthur Waugh denounced it in *Quarterly Review*, likening Eliot and Pound to the drunken household slaves it was customary in ancient times to exhibit before the sons of the

[20]

household as a warning against such "ignominious folly."[11] Waugh's reaction and Pound's reply lauding Eliot in the June 1917 issue of the *Egoist* helped to spread Eliot's name in intellectual circles. Though he had no more than these few alternative press publications and had actually written only a handful of poems, he was already becoming a poet one must read in order to be up on the newest trends.

Eliot needed encouragement desperately in 1915 and 1916, for his parents were upset by the turn his life had taken and still hoped he might return to Harvard. During a visit in July 1915, they had extracted from Eliot a promise to finish his dissertation in exchange for a continuance of the small allowance he had gotten since his marriage. As 1915 drew to a close, these few publications were important to Eliot as tangible evidence that he had a future as a poet.

One of the most important people with whom Pound put Eliot in contact in the early years was Harriet Shaw Weaver, editor of the *Egoist: An Individualist Review.* An idealistic young heiress, Weaver had been disappointed when her favorite magazine, the *Freewoman,* had ceased publication in 1911, and so had contributed a large share of the funds needed to reactivate it as the *New Freewoman* in 1913. Almost by default, Weaver wound up editing the publication. Her assistant, Rebecca West, went in search of new contributors to the literary section of the publication and encountered Pound, who quickly appropriated it as an outlet for himself and his friends. Since the publication had no funds to pay contributors, Pound paid his friends himself.

Pound's friends, mostly men, didn't like having their work associated with a "suffragette" magazine. They urged the name be changed to suit this "organ in which men and women of intelligence can express themselves without regard to the public," as Allen Upward wrote in a letter to the magazine also signed by Pound and others.[12] So, beginning with the first issue in 1914, the *New Freewoman* became the *Egoist.* At the same time Pound's friend Richard Aldington became assistant editor, replacing Rebecca West.

[21]

Eliot probably first encountered Weaver sometime in 1915, at one of the weekly literary suppers in Soho to which Pound took him. Pound, however, often failed to introduce people at these gatherings, so that in April 1916, when Pound wrote Weaver urging that Eliot be called upon to write for the *Egoist,* she wrote back to ask about this Mr. Eliot—"What was his line?"[13] Pound answered:

> Eliot is very intelligent. He has a large education, writes a little very intelligent verse. (vide Catholic Anthology). His prose seems very good, though he has not yet had a chance to write it unhampered. Next to Lewis and Joyce he seems to me the best of the younger men. NOT weedy.[14]

In May 1917, Weaver offered Pound the position of assistant editor of the *Egoist* to replace Aldington, who had been called up by the military. Pound, however, had just completed an arrangement to become foreign editor of the American little magazine the *Little Review,* so suggested Eliot be given the job at the *Egoist.* In June 1917, Eliot began his first job as an editor with the *Egoist* at a salary of nine pounds ($45) a quarter, to which Pound personally contributed a total of twelve pounds ($60) in the two years Eliot was there.

Eliot's work on the *Egoist,* which like his other writing had to be squeezed in after his hours at Lloyd's Bank, was important to his development as a writer and critic. In a letter to *Encounter* written in October 1961, Eliot described his *Egoist* experience:

> As editor-in-chief, Miss Weaver limited her control to publishing instalments of a philosophical work by her friend Miss Dora Marsden. An instalment occupied the first half of each issue; and the assistant editor was allowed to fill up the remaining pages with whatever matter he liked or could obtain.... Two or three of my own early essays appeared there, notably *Tradition and the Individual Talent;* and at least once I filled a column with Letters to the Editor—of my own composition, and under fictitious names. I also enjoyed the use of the office, a small room in some

[22]

building in the Adelphi, occasionally visited, I believe, by a charwoman. It was all great fun, my first experience of editorship.[15]

Not only did Weaver give Eliot his start as a literary editor, she also published his first book of poetry. In April 1916, Eliot noted he had fifteen to twenty poems either published or ready for publication, and began to put together a book-length manuscript with Pound's help. It isn't clear what efforts were made to find a publisher for the book during the next year, but in the spring of 1917 Pound offered the manuscript to Elkin Mathews. It wasn't a very large collection, Mathews noted. By this time it contained only twelve poems, half of which had been written in Eliot's student days and half since his residence in London. Mathews didn't much want to take a chance on this little book of poetry, but said he would publish it if someone would help pay for the printing costs—in advance. Pound tired quickly of Mathews' attitude and took the book to Weaver, who by this time had set up as a book publisher under the Egoist Press imprint in order to bring out James Joyce's *A Portrait of the Artist as a Young Man*. Pound himself was prepared to foot the bill for printing costs. As he wrote New York art patron John Quinn on April 11, "I have borrowed the cost of the printing bill (very little) and am being the Egoist. But Eliot don't know it, nor does anyone save my wife, and Miss Weaver of The Egoist [the two lenders] and it is not for public knowledge."[16] Pound exaggerated his involvement in the project. He actually ended up contributing five pounds ($25) "towards expenses," money later repaid by Weaver.[17] The book was published early in June 1917, as *Prufrock and Other Observations*.

Prufrock's audience was too small for this 500-copy edition to show a great profit. It sold first at a shilling, then its price "was raised gradually to 5s., at which price the remaining copies were sold in 1920–1," according to bibliographer Donald Gallup.[18] Eliot received no royalties, at least at first.

The audience *Prufrock* had in 1917, though small, was influential. The alternative press volume was reviewed in at

[23]

least three leading journals of the day. It was ridiculed in the *Times Literary Supplement* of June 21 as a

> purely analytical treatment, verging on the catalogue, of personal relations and environments, uninspired by any genuine rush of feeling. As, even on this basis [Eliot] . . . remains frequently inarticulate, his "poems" will hardly be read by many with enjoyment. . . . Among reminiscences which pass through the rhapsodist's mind and which he thinks the public should know about, are "dust in crevices, smells of chestnuts in the streets, and female smells in shuttered rooms, and cigarettes in corridors, and cocktail smells in bars." The fact that these things occurred to the mind of Mr. Eliot is surely of the smallest importance to any one—even to himself. They certainly have no relation to "poetry."

Other periodicals, as Bernard Bergonzi notes in *T. S. Eliot,* were "kinder and more perceptive":

> The *Westminster Gazette* saw Eliot as "a poet who finds even poetry laughable, who views life with a dry derision and comments on it with the true disengagement of wit. He is not like any other poet, not even the Imagists, whom he seems at first sight to follow." . . . The *New Statesman* commented, "Mr. Eliot may possibly give us the quintessence of twenty-first century poetry."[19]

Bongonzi also notes that

> E. M. Forster, then living in Cairo somehow got hold of a copy, which he read with immense satisfaction while recovering from a sprained ankle; he found in Eliot's gestures of ironic diffidence a welcome contrast to the violent rhetoric of a world at war.[20]

Forster's friends in London, the Bloomsbury group of intellectuals, shared his enthusiasm for this new poetry. Clive Bell recalls having met Eliot in the summer of 1916, after Harvard professor Bertrand Russell had asked him to "look out for" Eliot in England.[21] When *Prufrock* came out the next year, Bell says he took ten or twelve copies to a Garsington Easter party and distributed them "hot from the press like so

[24]

many Good Friday buns"[22] to Philip and Lady Ottoline Morell, Mrs. St. John Hutchinson, Katherine Mansfield, Aldous Huxley, Middleton Murry, and perhaps Lytton Strachey. Katherine Mansfield read the poem aloud and "it caused a stir, much discussion, some perplexity." Bell remembers this edition as "bound in a trashy yellow jacket and badly printed on bad paper. Misprints, if I remember right, and letters turned upside-down are discoverable."[23]

Bell's recollections seem to be faulty, at least in part, because Easter was on April 8 in 1917, not in June when the book came out. Nor does the copy of the *Prufrock* first edition at the University of Tulsa's McFarlin Library seem to fit Bell's description. It is bound in buff index paper, and neatly printed on heavy wove paper. It does seem likely, however, that the Bloomsbury group would be intrigued by Eliot's poetry. Not only was it experimental, but its ironic tone was in keeping with their own attitudes.

Leonard Woolf, who with his wife Virginia had just started a small publishing venture, the Hogarth Press, recalls: "I bought a copy of *Prufrock* when it was published by the Egoist, Ltd. in 1917, and it has the following inscription on the cover: 'Inscribed for Leonard Woolf, my next/second publisher, with gratitude and affection, T. S. Eliot.'"[24] On the strength of *Prufrock's* reputation alone the Woolfs had agreed to publish Eliot's next book of poems.

In retrospect, the little Egoist Press *Prufrock* would seem to have been "the clarion call of modernism in English verse," according to John Quinn's biographer, B. L. Reid.[25] Certainly, by December 1917, when Mrs. Sybil Colefax invited "the author of Prufrock" to share the roster at a charity poetry reading with Aldous Huxley and other prominent poets, it was clear Eliot's reputation in England had been given a big boost by this forty-page booklet published by the "courageous" amateur Harriet Weaver. Eliot praised her in his 1961 eulogy letter, saying, "What other publisher in 1917 (the Hogarth Press was not yet in existence) would, I wonder, have taken *Prufrock?*"

[25]

As soon as *Prufrock* came off the press, on June 12, 1917, Pound sent a copy to Alfred Knopf, a New York commercial publisher who was bringing out the American edition of Pound's *Lustra*, and was fast making his name among the older commercial houses with his Borzoi Books.

Knopf was a young man in his mid-twenties. He had worked for Doubleday, Page & Company for two years and had encouraged them to publish Conrad's books. Here he became acquainted with Conrad's (and Pound's) patron, New York lawyer John Quinn. Then, in 1915, he and his wife Blanche had set up their own business with a stake of $3,000, at a desk in his father's office. A Jew with modern tastes in a trade dominated by staid Victorian Bible publishers, Knopf was not the average New York commercial publisher. Although extremely shy of the censors, he was daring in that he would gamble on new works he admired and, as Willa Cather said of him later, "he had set out to do something unusual and individual in publishing."[26] According to Reid:

> Quinn was trying to groom Alfred A. Knopf as the American publisher for Pound and Pound's stable of proteges, especially Eliot, Joyce, and Wyndham Lewis. By early January of 1917 Quinn had had two conversations with Knopf about Pound's poetry and prose, and he wrote on the twelfth to present Knopf formally to Pound as: "not a plunger," as "a man of his word," and one who was "in the business to stay." On the twenty-fourth Pound wrote back to say he was happy to be . . . "associated with a contemporary, a young man unbound to nineteenth century loyalties." Two days later Pound suggested that as soon as Knopf had his own work well in hand he "should undertake . . . Eliot's little vol. of poems."[27]

Early in August, Quinn sent Knopf another copy of *Prufrock*, commending it to his notice and commenting he liked everything about the volume but its title. Knopf wrote back on August 17:

> I have read Eliot's little book of poems with immense enjoyment. I do not know whether it is great poetry or not. I do know that it is great fun and I like it. I surely hope that he writes some more of it so that we can make a book of him over here.[28]

[26]

There was nothing he could do with a thirty-two page booklet, Knopf added, "except to give it away as an advertisement, and even that would be difficult."[29]

The news that Knopf had to have more poems before he could publish the book was discouraging to Eliot because he knew it would be some time before he could really expect to add enough to the size of the collection to make it of a suitable length for Knopf. As he wrote Quinn on March 1, 1918, "I have only written half a dozen small poems in the last year, and the last I have been unable to finish."[30]

That summer, however, Eliot and his wife vacationed in the country, and the relaxation of living away from London proved fruitful, for by September Eliot had a book "almost ready" for Knopf. He had decided to make his first American book a miscellany of prose and verse. Writes Valerie Eliot, "He would have preferred 'to keep the prose and verse apart. . . But it is time I had a volume in America, and this is the only way to do it.'"[31] Eliot sent the manuscript to Pound, who made final adjustments to it before sending it on to Knopf in October.

Then two months went by without so much as an acknowledgment that the publisher had received the manuscript. At the end of December, Pound cabled Knopf in Eliot's behalf to ask if he had received it. He still had no reply from Knopf a week later on January 6, 1919, so Eliot wrote Quinn expressing his concern for the book:

> . . . it is very important to me that it should be published for private reasons. I am coming to America to visit my family some time within the summer or autumn, and I should particularly like to have it appear first. You see I settled over here in the face of strong family opposition, on the claim that I found the environment more favourable to the production of literature. This book is all I have to show for my claim—it would go toward making my parents contented with conditions and toward satisfying them that I have not made a mess of my life as they are inclined to believe.[32]

[27]

Eliot's father, however, died that month, and Eliot, still not having heard from Knopf, wrote Quinn on January 26:

> ... this does not weaken the need for the book at all — it really reinforces it — my mother is still alive. .... If you could write or speak to Knopf and find out his definite intentions, I should be very grateful. If he intends to use the stuff I should like him to get busy on it; if not, I should like him to deliver it into your hands. Perhaps then you could look it over with a view to what publisher might be willing to take it? ... I hope you will not think me very cheeky in proposing it ... but a great deal hangs on it for me, and it was already a pressing matter several months ago![33]

At the end of January, Pound heard from Knopf and passed the bad news on to Eliot. As Eliot told his brother in February, "Knopf wrote to Pound that the success of his book *Pavannes and Divisions* had not been sufficient to warrent his undertaking any new contracts with him, Wyndham Lewis or myself."[34]

Quinn retrieved the manuscript from Knopf and immediately sent it to another new publisher in New York, Boni & Liveright. It took almost two months for Liveright to reply. Finally, on April 29, 1919, Quinn told Eliot that Liveright had agreed to publish Pound's book, but Eliot's was still under consideration. According to Valerie Eliot:

> Eliot wrote [to Quinn] on 25 May that he wished to alter the manuscript if possible, as he had two or three essays and a very few poems (including *Gerontion*) to add, and the essays, from the *Athenaeum,* were better than those submitted. Quinn cabled him to send what he had and on the same day, 30 June, expressed his anger with Liveright who, he believed, had delayed his answer because he knew the lawyer was about to go on holiday, and hoped to force him to accept his terms at the last minute: "Liveright expected me to put up a guarantee of $100 or $150 in connection with your book. If he had been decent about it, I should have been willing to do so."[35]

Eliot's first contact with Liveright thus ended unsuccessfully. Quinn retrieved the manuscript and arranged for it

[28]

to be offered to the British commercial firm John Lane with a guarantee of $150 to cover printing costs. In August the Lane editors wrote, politely rejecting the book, $150 and all. "Mr. Eliot's work is no doubt brilliant," they said, "but it is not exactly the kind of material we care to add to our list."[36]

Knopf, however, was still "willing and anxious to publish the poems in a volume by themselves." Now that "Gerontion" and a few others had been added, the manuscript was long enough for a book without the essays, and Knopf agreed to publish it under the title *Poems by T. S. Eliot.* On October 3, 1919, Quinn signed the contract with Knopf on Eliot's behalf, after having made a few amendments. The book was published on February 18, 1920, two years and eight months after the Egoist Press edition of *Prufrock and Other Observations.*

Eliot's first American book and first commercial "trade" publication seems not to have enhanced his reputation on this side of the Atlantic as much as he had hoped. The hardback, sixty-three page volume in its yellow dust wrapper apparently went almost totally unnoticed in America's mass-circulation newspapers and magazines. Harriet Monroe's *Poetry* mentioned *Poems* in its April issue and published a favorable review in June. Marion Strobel compared the experience of reading the collection to the ascent of a mountain peak. A newly revamped literary review, the *Dial,* edited by a long-time Eliot schoolmate, Schofield Thayer, published a favorable review by the then-unknown young poet E. E. Cummings, who seems to have been the first real student of Eliot's poetry to write a review of his work. Cummings praised Eliot's ability to create through his verse "the unique dimension of intensity," which is substituted for the "comfortable furniture of reality." No record exists of how well the Knopf edition sold, but it is perhaps indicative that Knopf declined to publish Eliot's next book of poetry, *The Waste Land,* when he was offered the opportunity two years later.

While Eliot was waiting to be published in America, his career had received another boost in England, this from the fledgling little press of Virginia and Leonard Woolf. In the spring of 1917, the Woolfs had purchased a small hand press, set it up on their dining room table at Hogarth House in Bloomsbury, and begun to publish small, hand-set editions of their own writing. These they sold by subscription to a list of their acquaintances. This enterprise proved a modest financial success, and by 1918 they began to look about for other writers to publish. As Anne Oliver Bell notes in *The Diary of Virginia Woolf*:

> In September Virginia Woolf, writing to Clive Bell, asked him to ask Mary Hutchinson to send her Eliot's address again, as she had lost it; thus it seems probable that she had now [October 28, 1918] written suggesting he should visit them and bring some of his poems. He wrote to her . . . on 12 November saying he should look forward to Friday with much pleasure.[37]

Friday, November 15, was the day Eliot had dinner with the Woolfs at Hogarth House, meeting Virginia face to face for the first time. "He produced 3 or 4 poems for us to look at," she wrote in her diary several days later, "—the fruit of two years, since he works all day in a Bank, & in his reasonable way thinks regular work to be good for people of nervous constitutions."[38]

It seems likely that Leonard Woolf had encountered Eliot before this dinner, because he recalls in *Beginning Again*[39] a conversation "at the end of 1917 or the beginning of 1918" in which Eliot had asked the Woolfs to meet with Harriet Weaver regarding the publication of James Joyce's *Ulysses*. And, probably on the basis of Eliot's *Prufrock* reputation, the Woolfs decided to publish his next volume of poetry even before seeing any of its contents. On October 15, 1918, a month before her first meeting with Eliot, Virginia wrote Roger Fry, "We are asking Eliot to let us print a poem."[40]

At the time, the Woolfs' Hogarth Press was still very much a cottage industry. They had published only two books—a slender booklet, *Two Stories*, containing a short story by Leonard and one by Virginia; and *Prelude*, a long story by their friend Katherine Mansfield. They were preparing to

[30]

bring out another Virginia Woolf story, *Kew Gardens*. All of these were typeset by hand by the Woolfs themselves and, except for *Prelude*, were printed on their hand press. The Woolfs produced Eliot's *Poems* the same way, setting the type one character at a time and printing the pages one sheet at a time. According to Leonard Woolf:

> The machine was small enough to stand on a kitchen table; it was an ordinary platen design; you worked it by pulling down the handle which brought the platen and paper up against the type in its chase. You could print one demy octavo page on it, and, I think, you could just squeeze in two crown octavo pages.[41]

They bound each copy themselves, hand-sewing the pages into paper covers of various types, some "left-overs" from the binding of the earlier Hogarth publications. The finished product had the look of having been manufactured by amateurs, at least on the outside. It was only sixteen pages long, and the title and author's name were printed on a label which was then pasted on the paper cover. Inside, however, the printing was clean and neat. There was only one typographical error, and that was corrected before the printing of the edition was finished.

In retrospect, the publication of Eliot's *Poems* seemed to Leonard Woolf to have been "a red letter day for the Press and for us, although at the time when I began to set the lines ... I could not, of course, foresee the remarkable future of the author."[42] Woolf recalls his enjoyment of reading the Eliot poems during the printing process: "I never tired and still do not tire of those lines which were a new note in poetry and came from the heart of the Eliot of those days."[43]

The reviewer for the *Times Literary Supplement* (June 12, 1919) did not agree with this assessment. Eliot's poetry was too self-consciously experimental, according to the critic. It was "novel and ingenious," but "fatally impoverished of subject matter." Eliot "seems to have a 'phobia' of sentimentality, like a small schoolboy who would rather die than kiss his sister in public." Unlike the *TLS* reviewer of *Prufrock* two

[31]

years before, this critic gave Eliot credit for "his remarkable talent" which "expresses itself in saying always, from line to line and word to word, what no one would expect." But he accused Eliot of burying his talent in trivialities:

> Mr. Eliot . . . likes to display out-of-the-way learning, he likes to surprise you by every trick he can think of. He has forgotten his emotions, his values, his sense of beauty, even his common-sense, in that one desire to surprise, to get further away from the obvious than any writer on record. . . . Mr. Eliot is fatally handicapping himself with his own inhibitions; he is in danger of becoming silly, and what will he do then?

Negative as it was, this review was significant. The *Times Literary Supplement* was then the single most influential organ for literary news in the English-speaking world. Unlike the established reviews of our day, *TLS* was willing to devote some space to assessments of books like *Prufrock* and the Hogarth pamphlets which were published privately and through small alternative presses. The review of *Poems* seems to have had a very great effect on Eliot's career, for the *TLS* reviewer had hit upon Eliot's greatest drawback as a poet, his extreme reserve. Eliot was stung. Months later he told Virginia Woolf, "The critics say I am learned and cold. The truth is I am neither."[44] Soon after the appearance of the *TLS* review, Eliot began to think in terms of completing some fragments of poetry he'd been witholding from publication—fragments which dealt with his private, emotional experience. That autumn he told John Quinn, "I hope to get started on a poem I have in mind," and to his mother he wrote that it was his resolution for 1920 "to write a long poem I have had on my mind for a long time."[45] These were Eliot's first references to what would become *The Waste Land*.

In the same month that Knopf published *Poems by T. S. Eliot* in the United States, the Ovid Press, operated in Paris by poet John Rodker, brought out what is the fanciest edition of Eliot's early poetry, a limited edition of 264 copies called *Ara Vos Prec*. This collection virtually reproduced the contents of the Knopf book except that "Ode" is substituted for "Hysteria," and "Le Directeur" is printed as "Le Spectateur," as it had been in the Hogarth Press *Poems*. It was a hardback edition covered in black paper and yellow cloth, with some copies stamped with the title in gold, others titled with a paper label. This publication indicates how Eliot's reputation had grown; Rodker apparently wanted the outstanding avant-garde poet of the day to inaugurate his new alternative press. The notice of *Ara Vos Prec* which appeared in the *TLS* on February 12, 1920, reflected Eliot's new respectability, and perhaps the fact that he had by now become a writer for the *Times;* the poetry was the same as that panned in the *TLS* in 1917 and 1919, but now the reviewer downplayed his negative reactions. "Verse by an able scholar and litterateur," he wrote, "whose poetical work, however, may be said to be the most challenging and bizarre of any of the younger bands [bards?] of the day."

Plagued by financial woes and declining readership, the *Egoist* ceased publication at the end of 1919. By this time Eliot was writing articles on literature for other literary magazines such as the *Athenaeum,* edited by Middleton Murry, as well as for the *Times.* He had accumulated a good deal of critical writing which had never been published in book form. During 1920, Eliot delayed work on *The Waste Land* in order to put together a book of the best of his literary essays; it would quickly become a classic of modern criticism. This book, *The Sacred Wood,* was his first writing to be accepted for publication by a commercial book publisher in England: Methuen & Company brought out a hardback trade edition on November 4, 1920. In the United States, Alfred Knopf imported the sheets printed in England—enough for 365 copies—and published *The Sacred Wood* under his Borzoi imprint in February 1921. Much of the material for *The Sacred Wood* had been developed for publication in little reviews, and with the book's publication Eliot established himself as a widely respected literary critic.

By 1921, Eliot had also become a well-known poet in British

[33]

intellectual circles, even though no verse of his had yet appeared from a British commercial press. The exposure and encouragement he received as a result of his publication by alternative presses were as vital to the development of Eliot's early poetry as they were to his critical writing. His status was soon to change, however. In 1922 an avant-garde literary monthly would publish Eliot's first major work, *The Waste Land,* and this small-press poet would suddenly find himself famous.

As has been detailed by Lyndall Gordon in *Eliot's Early Years,* "The manuscript of *The Waste Land* is a hoard of fragments accumulated slowly over seven and a half years," beginning when Eliot was still at Harvard in 1914. "Only in the seventh year were the fragments transformed into a major work."[46]

In the autumn of 1921 Eliot suffered a nervous breakdown and took three months' sick leave from the bank to recuperate. On October 22 he checked into the Albemarle Hotel, Cliftonville, Margate, where at last he had the leisure to write the poem which had germinated for so long. According to Gordon, "It is likely that it was during his three weeks there that a good deal of *The Waste Land,* almost certainly 'The Fire Sermon'—was written."[47]

Though Pound had by now grown disgusted with the London literary scene and moved to Paris, Eliot still depended upon his early mentor for editing and publication advice. In November, following his stay at Margate, Eliot visited Pound in Paris and showed him the first draft of the poem. Pound marked some suggestions for Eliot, who then took the poem with him to Lausanne, Switzerland. There Eliot worked on the poem and showed Pound the revised version, now about nineteen pages long. To say that Pound was impressed with the results would be an understatement. On Christmas Eve he wrote to Eliot, "Much improved. . . . Complimenti, you bitch. I am wracked by the seven jealousies." Pound dated this letter "24 Saturnus, An 1," and called Eliot's nineteen pages "the longest poem in the English langwidge."[48]

[34]

Pound's great admiration for this version of the poem did not deter him from making more suggestions concerning its revision, suggestions which Eliot acted upon almost without exception. Pound's editorial contributions to *The Waste Land* were extensive enough to substantiate his claim that "Ezra performed the Caesarean Operation"[49] which brought the poem into the world. Of the approximately 700 lines which Eliot showed his mentor, only 434 survived in the final poem. Pound's surgery did much to improve "The Waste Land" manuscript without altering its tone or technique. Even in its longest form, the poem was a series of fragments without the connections which would make a coherent narrative. (In letters written in early 1922, Pound referred to the work as a series of poems.) The passages and words cut were ones which had diffused the effect, without clarifying the meaning. Pound also suggested a few very effective word changes, and sometimes saved the poem from Eliot's tendency toward excess.

It seems likely that Pound and Eliot began discussing possibilities for publishing *The Waste Land* when Pound saw it for the first time on November 18. Early in January, while the poem was still undergoing revision, Eliot reported he had "writ to Thayer asking what he can offer for this."[50] "Thayer" was Schofield Thayer, former classmate of Eliot's, now editor of the New York literary magazine, the *Dial*.

The Waste Land's publication in the *Dial* marked a turning point for both the magazine and modern poetry. As told by William Wasserstrom in a 1962 *Sewanee Review* article, the *Dial*, now thirty-five years old, was floundering when it was purchased and moved to New York by "two wealthy young men," Thayer and James Sibley Watson, Jr., in 1919.[51] Thayer and Eliot had been acquaintances from prep school days; Thayer was younger and had followed Eliot through Milton Academy, Harvard, and Oxford. According to Wasserstrom, "Thayer had been impressed by the elder boy's genius."[52]

Thayer and Watson shared Pound's and Eliot's aspirations for a renaissance in poetry and were seeking through the *Dial*

[35]

to reform the tastes of the American reading public along modern lines. If their circulation figures can be trusted, they were having a great deal more success with this endeavor than had *Poetry* and the *Little Review* before them. By the end of 1922 they had 6,374 subscribers, according to Nicholas Joost, *Dial* historian. No sooner had Thayer taken over the *Dial* than he wrote to both Pound and Eliot, expressing an interest in their writing. Both became frequent contributors. Pound's "Paris Letter" appeared regularly starting in October 1920. Eliot sent critical essays to the publication, and his "Possibility of a Poetic Drama" appeared as the leading essay in November 1920. By May 1921, Eliot was contributing a regular "London Letter" to the *Dial*.

According to Joost, Eliot wrote Thayer on January 20, 1922, to offer *The Waste Land* for publication as soon as it was completed. Eliot apparently didn't send a copy of the work, only described it as "a poem of about 450 lines, in four parts." In the same letter, "he asked whether the *Dial* wished to print it (it would *not* appear in any periodical on his side of the water) and if so, approximately what the *Dial* would offer. He asked to know quickly as he would postpone all arrangements for publication until Thayer replied."[53]

Such was Thayer's belief in Eliot that he wrote back accepting the poem sight unseen and offering to pay $150, or about thirty pounds for the eleven pages of poetry. But Thayer's faith failed to impress Eliot:

> What must have been the Editor's amazement to receive from Eliot a wire stating that he could not accept under 856 pounds [about $4,300]! But Thayer treated the demand urbanely, presuming epistolarily that there was some error on the part of the telegraph service; nevertheless, in the meantime he told Eliot that he had had to notify *The Dial* "that we are apparently not to receive the poem."
>
> Of course there had been no mistake. Garrulous old George Moore had been boasting about how much *The Dial* had paid him for a short story—a hundred pounds [$500]—and, with the contempt they felt for Moore's work, Eliot and Pound agreed that $150 for a poem that had taken the poet a year to write and that he called his biggest work was a sum to be declined.[54]

[36]

Pound seems to have been responsible for Eliot's refusal of the *Dial* offer. At this same time he was busy with a scheme he called "Bel Esprit" to subsidize Eliot financially, enabling him to quit his bank job and devote all his energies to literature. This was necessary, he wrote, because "We want a better grade of work than present systems of publishing are willing to pay for."

Eliot himself had become persuaded he deserved more for his work, and he didn't back down. It was just as well the *Dial* didn't publish the poem, he wrote Thayer on March 16, because he didn't want it to come out in a journal first anyhow, certainly not if he were only to be offered thirty pounds for such a publication. Eliot reminded Thayer that he had asked Eliot several times for the first refusal of his new poem. Thayer wisely never answered this letter, though he scribbled notes in its margins to the effect that he couldn't refuse a poem which was never actually submitted.[55]

As usual, Ezra Pound launched a campaign to boost Eliot's poetry. On February 18, he wrote Thayer, enthusiastically recommending the work, and also sent word to Sibley Watson and to Gilbert Seldes, *Dial* managing editor in Thayer's absence, that "Eliot had composed an important sequence of poems." They began to pressure Thayer to get the poem, and Thayer reported that Eliot was hostile to the *Dial* but that he would continue to correspond with the poet concerning it. Thayer's admiration for Eliot, however, was wearing thin. "If Eliot's poem," he wrote his staff, "was anything like Pound's Cantos, perhaps we are unwillingly blessed" not to get it.[56]

Thayer stood firm in his insistence that he would not pay more than the *Dial*'s regular rate for poetry, ten dollars per page. On April 30 he wrote to Pound:

> I am too tired to discuss the matter further. What I have previously said to yourself and written to Eliot concerning The Dial rates is the truth. But I do not propose when conducting a journal for the benefit of contemporary writers at great expense to myself in time as well as money to waste further time answering letters such as that from Eliot in which he quite definitely implies that in my previous letter I lied to him.[57]

[37]

The editing of "The Waste Land" was now complete, and Eliot and Pound began negotiating for its publication in book form in the United States. Knopf was given first right of refusal and exercised that right, saying the poem came too late to be included in his autumn list. Next they turned to Horace Liveright, with happier results. As Eliot wrote Quinn on June 25, 1922, "Pound introduced me to Liveright in Paris, and Liveright made me the offer of 15% royalty and $150 in advance."[58]

Horace Liveright, who had been running a failing toilet-paper business in 1914 when Albert Boni had interested him in publishing, had by this time turned Boni's idea for the "Modern Library" of classics by European writers into a commercial success. Still, he was considered more an alternative publisher than part of the New York publishing establishment. According to historian John Tebbel, "Except for 'The Modern Library' the Boni [& Liveright] list was radical, and that was how the firm seemed to publishers uptown, particularly those of the old school like Holt and Scribner, who considered these newcomers a rowdy and perhaps dangerous crowd."[59] John Quinn always regarded Liveright with suspicion, and dealt with him only because he couldn't hope to place Pound's and Eliot's work with a "regular" publisher. Even Knopf "disliked and resented" Liveright, according to Bennett Cerf, because Knopf himself "didn't want to be considered in that class of 'fresh young Jews'" which Liveright typified.[60] Pound, however, appreciated Liveright's willingness not only to publish new work, but also to pay for it. On July 4, 1922, he wrote Quinn that Liveright was unique among publishers for innocently assuming that writers were worthy of their hire.[61]

Eliot, however, was not impressed by Liveright's generosity when he received a contract for *The Waste Land*. On June 25, 1922, he wrote Quinn complaining that the contract was "extremely vague . . . and tantamount to selling . . . the book outright for $150."[62] He asked Quinn to negotiate a contract such as he had arranged with Knopf for the 1920 *Poems*.

[38]

Liveright proved more willing than Thayer to negotiate terms. On July 19 Eliot reported to Quinn:

> I have yesterday a mild letter from Liveright which sounds as if he would come to terms. As it is now so late I am enclosing the typescript to hand to him when the contract is complete, or to hold if he does not complete.... This will do for him to get on with, and I shall rush forward the notes to go at the end. I only hope the printers are not allowed to bitch the punctuation and spelling, as that is very important for the sense.[63]

On July 28 Quinn wrote Eliot to say he had negotiated the new contract, and Liveright had signed it "without the change of a word."[64] He included his impressions of the poem:

> *Waste Land* is one of the best things you have done, though I imagine that Liveright may be a little disappointed [with the size], but I think he will go through with it. It is for the elect or the remnant or the select few or the superior guys, . . . for the small numbers of readers that it is certain to have.[65]

Eliot wrote back on August 21 that he was pleased with the contract, but by now the *Dial* was back in the picture with a new offer. According to Joost,[66] Sibley Watson had met with Pound during a summer visit to Paris and offered to sweeten the deal with Eliot by awarding him the *Dial*'s $2,000 annual prize for service to American letters. "By the middle of August a manuscript of *The Waste Land* was with Dr. Watson in Paris, and on August 16 he sent a copy he had had typed on Hotel Meurice stationery to Thayer in Vienna."

It seems Quinn was unaware of Pound's deal with Thayer, and Pound was unaware of Quinn's with Liveright. Eliot felt obligated to live up to the book contract Quinn had worked out for him. He wrote, "They [Thayer and the *Dial*] suggested getting Liveright to postpone the date of publication as a book, but I have written to them to say that it seemed to me too late to be proper to make any change now."[67]

The *Dial*, however, wanted badly to introduce what was shaping up to be the first major poem by the best-known

[39]

modern poet. Gilbert Seldes wrote Quinn on August 31 to see if a deal could be worked out with Liveright. According to Reid,[68] Seldes and Quinn met informally and worked out a proposal which they offered Liveright in a second meeting on September 7:

> The crux of the matter was not only the magazine's wish to publish the poem but also their wish to award to Eliot the annual *Dial* prize of $2,000 for service to letters in America; it was felt that the poem should appear in an American journal in advance of the award as one demonstrable validation of the award. Eliot's contract of July 29 with Liveright bound him to publish the book by November 1. Quinn and Seldes were able to persuade Liveright that publication of the poem in the *Dial*, would probably work to the advantage of his edition, with the date of that set a bit later. Details of the agreement were quickly settled.[69]

The agreement under which *The Waste Land* was finally published was, as Reid notes, "an ingenious and admirable scheme, in which everybody got what he wanted and everybody profited, but particularly T. S. Eliot."[70] It provided that

(1) The *Dial* would publish the poem, without notes, as soon as possible.

(2) They would copyright the poem in Eliot's name.

(3) They would pay Eliot for the poem at their standard rates for verse.

(4) They would announce that Boni & Liveright would soon publish the poem as a volume, with notes.

(5) They would award the $2,000 prize to Eliot, and announce it in advance of the book publication.

(6) They would buy 350 copies of the book when published, thus insuring Liveright against any possible loss on the book.

(7) Liveright would delay publication of the book until after the *Dial* publication, but accomplish it by January 31, 1923.

(8) He would pay Eliot $150 on publication and subsequent royalties, as stipulated in the existing contract.

According to Reid, "All these conditions were set down in

letters of agreement signed by Liveright and by Seldes as Managing Editor of the *Dial*, and Quinn sent copies on to Eliot."[71] Only the following year would Quinn reveal that this subsidy from the *Dial* probably saved the Liveright book publication. Apparently Liveright had begun to fear losing money on the little book of "difficult" poetry by a poet known only in elite circles, a book which Knopf had turned down. "Confidentially," Quinn wrote to Eliot on February 26, 1923, "the success of the book was rather a surprise to Liveright. He almost had cold feet about it before the *Dial* suggestion was made."[72]

Besides the deal between Liveright and Seldes, two other publications of *The Waste Land* were in the offing, these in England. With patronage from Lady Rothermere, Eliot was on the verge of inaugurating his own small literary quarterly, the *Criterion*. He included "The Waste Land" in the premiere issue. Although it bore the date of October 1922, and appeared at the end of October, about the same time as the November *Dial* that carried *The Waste Land*, he was careful to withhold it from America so as not to interfere with the *Dial*'s right to first publication there.

Leonard and Virginia Woolf had become closer friends with Eliot by 1922, and during a visit in March he told them about *The Waste Land*, which they agreed to publish sight unseen. Virginia wrote in her diary:

> He has written a poem of 40 pages, which we are to print in the autumn. This is his best work, he says. He is pleased with it; takes heart, I think, from the thought of that safe in his desk.[73]

Meanwhile Eliot was making plans for the *Criterion* and had invited them to submit their writing. In her answer on April 14, 1922, Virginia Woolf wrote, "When are we to see your poem [*The Waste Land*]? — and then I can have a fling at you."[74]

The Woolfs heard the poem before they saw it. As Virginia records in her diary on June 23:

[41]

> Eliot dined last Sunday & read his poem. He sang it & chanted it rhythmed it. It has great beauty & force of phrase: symmetry; & tensity. What connects it together I'm not so sure. But he read till he had to rush — ... & discussion was thus curtailed. One was left, however, with some strong emotion. The Waste Land, it is called; & Mary Hutch[inson], who has heard it more quietly, interprets it to be Tom's autobiography—a melancholy one.[75]

"It was not until the end of 1922 that Tom gave us *The Waste Land* to read," recalls Leonard Woolf. "We agreed to publish it; printed it ourselves and published it on September 12, 1923."[76] This Hogarth edition was bound in blue, marbled paperboards, with a paper label bearing the title pasted on the front cover. According to Bergonzi, it was "not without a quantity of misprints."[77]

Scholars and poets are agreed generally that the publication of *The Waste Land* is the watershed event in the history of modern poetry. Typical, if overstated, is William Carlos Williams's recollection in his *Autobiography* that the poem "wiped out our world as if an atomic bomb had been dropped on it."

The flurry of *The Waste Land* republications contributed to the poem's impact, especially in the United States. Americans had been reading about Eliot in the various "London Letters" in literary publications here, and now they learned he had written his first major work. In the April 1922 issue of *Vanity Fair*, they learned from Aldous Huxley's "London Letter" that Eliot's poem would probably be published in the United States soon by the *Dial*. Those who had been reading Eliot's own London Letters in the *Dial* were no doubt curious to see the creative work of this erudite critic, especially since his already published poems were so radical. In late October the poem appeared simultaneously as the lead article in both the *Criterion* in London and the *Dial* in the U.S. It must have mystified readers then, even as it does first-time readers today. In late November, the December *Dial* appeared with the announcement that Eliot had won the *Dial* award for outstanding service to American letters for

[42]

1922, along with a lengthy explication of *The Waste Land* by Edmund Wilson.

This review, the first of many assessments of *The Waste Land*, was carefully planned to support the *Dial*'s choice of Eliot for the award. According to Wasserstrom:

> ... the Editors ... tried to find a critic whose opinion would help readers to decide in the poet's favor. They wanted a man of reputation who would write a notice.... Early in October Seldes wrote to George Saintsbury about their plan to publish the poem and confer the Award. "Because Eliot's poetry is not widely known," he said, "we plan to present an essay upon his work. We would like this essay to come from you." Saintsbury refused.[78]

By this time it was too late to contact their second choice, Padraic Colum, so they decided to take a chance on the then little known Edmund Wilson, who had already offered to write the review.

Wilson's review, "The Poetry of Drouth," interpreted *The Waste Land* for readers as a portrayal of "our whole world of strained nerves and shattered institutions." According to Wilson, Eliot spoke "not only for personal distress, but for the starvation of a whole civilization." His praise of Eliot was unqualified. Here, he declared, was a poet who had "brought a new personal rhythm into the language and who has lent even to the words of his great predecessors a new music and a new meaning."

The Liveright hardback edition of *The Waste Land* appeared on December 19, and was publicized in the pages of the *Dial*, which of course had a financial stake in the success of the book. Nor was the *Dial*'s publicity campaign confined to its own pages. Gilbert Seldes contributed a three-page article to the December 22 *Nation* in which he extolled Eliot as critic and poet, and gave an explanation of the poem, defending its form as having been dictated by the theme of the work.

Comments about *The Waste Land* continued to appear during 1923 in publications such as *Forum*, the *Literary Review*, and the *New York Times;* and Eliot "floated if not precisely on

[43]

an ocean at least on a small inland sea of publicity."[79] "Newsstand sales [of the *Dial*] jumped from just over 4,500 in November to 6,261 in December perhaps as a result of the publication of Eliot's 'The Waste Land' in the November issue."[80] Liveright's first edition sold out so quickly that by early 1923 he came out with a second edition of a thousand copies.

In England, the publication of the Hogarth edition was greeted with a lengthy analysis of the poem which might well have been written by the same individual who attacked Eliot's lack of emotion in earlier reviews of his work. "There is," the *Times Literary Supplement* reviewer laments, "a disinclination to awake in us a direct emotional response." Calling the poem an "ambitious experiment," the reviewer scolds Eliot:

> Here is a poet capable of a style more refined than that of any of his generation parodying without taste or skill.... Here is a writer to whom originality is almost an inspiration borrowing the greater number of his best lines, creating hardly any himself. It seems to us as if "The Waste Land" exists in the greater part in the state of notes.... Mr. Eliot ... has reached a stage at which he can no longer refuse to recognize the limitations of his medium; he is sometimes walking very near the limits of coherency.[81]

This review is indicative of the "generation gap" which seems to have developed regarding *The Waste Land*. According to Bergonzi:

> Some reviewers of *The Waste Land* regarded it as a hoax, but there were others who responded positively, like Edmund Wilson, Conrad Aiken, and Gilbert Seldes. ... as Edmund Wilson wrote in *Axel's Castle*, "where some of even the finest intelligences of the elder generation read *The Waste Land* with blankness or laughter, the young had recognized a poet." In 1928 E. M. Forster echoed this judgment, remarking on Eliot's influence on readers aged between eighteen and thirty: "Mr. Eliot's work, particularly *The Waste Land*, has made a profound impression on them, and given them precisely the food they needed. ... He is the most important author of their day."[82]

[44]

That Eliot was an experimental poet, misunderstood by critics for established reviews, and published mostly by alternative presses, only added to his allure for the young. As this younger generation aged and its members began to assume positions of greater influence in the literary culture, their admiration of *The Waste Land* became the majority opinion. More than any other work, Eliot's poem popularized the modern voice in poetry, which heretofore had been heard mostly in publications of the alternative press, so that *The Waste Land* soon gained its present status as a literary classic. Eliot, who himself had gone from obscurity to fame as a poet and critic through alternative publications, was now on his way to becoming the foremost voice of a literary establishment which would hold sway in England and the United States for a generation.

VIRGINIA WOOLF
. . . with a press of one's own

2

T. S. Eliot was an innovative writer who relied on friends at small presses and little magazines for publication; this allowed him to get his unconventional poetry published without tailoring it to popular tastes and commercial needs. Another important writer worked hard on her fiction to make it conventional and commercial, until she tried another form of alternative publication, self-publishing. This freed her to find her own unconventional voice in fiction, and as a result she became one of the great innovators of the modern era.

When Virginia Woolf's experimental novel *Jacob's Room* was published in 1922, it marked a radical shift in her writing. A successful author of two novels in the traditional mode with an established commercial press, Woolf in her third book introduced a new technique of narrative which she was to perfect in *Mrs. Dalloway* and *To The Lighthouse*. This technique, sometimes called "stream of consciousness," changed the English-language novel in a fundamental way. One literary scholar writes of Woolf and other moderns who helped develop stream of consciousness narrative:

> What these writers have contributed to fiction is broadly one thing: they have opened up for it a new area of life. They have added mental functioning and psychic existence to the already established domain of motive and action. They have created a fiction centered on the core of human experience.[1]

[49]

It was no coincidence that *Jacob's Room* was the first of Woolf's novels to be published by her own Hogarth Press. Through her success in publishing her own fiction, Woolf gained a small but influential audience for this radical kind of narrative, and with it the self-confidence she needed to do her greatest work.

The daughter of the distinguished Victorian scholar Leslie Stephen, Virginia Woolf decided to be a writer at an early age and began to practice the craft seriously in her teen years. Throughout her life, Woolf's writing career was interrupted periodically by severe nervous illnesses. The first came a few weeks after the death of her mother when the writer was thirteen. With this sad event, the secure world she had known as a child disappeared. Not only was she plunged into her own grief at the loss of her mother, but she had to endure the atmosphere of gloom which her bereaved father enforced upon the household:

> At meals he sat miserable and bewildered, too unhappy and too deaf to know what was being said, until at length, in one scene after another all through that dreadful summer, he broke down utterly and, while his embarrassed children sat in awkward silence, groaned, wept and wished that he were dead.[2]

Probably more devastating than her father's grieving, however, were the actions of her twenty-six-year-old half-brother, George Duckworth. Under the guise of comforting his little sisters, he began a pattern of sexual molestation of Virginia and her elder sister Vanessa which would continue throughout their teen years. With their mother dead and their father absorbed in his grief, Virginia and Vanessa had no safe person to whom they could turn for help. George took charge of his sisters' lives. He acted as their chaperone, forced them to attend salons and parties with him once they were old enough, and objected self-righteously to any breach of Victorian convention. All of this no doubt aggravated Woolf's already nervous disposition. She was plagued with recurrences of mental illness all of her life, and in 1940,

[50]

facing yet another breakdown, she committed suicide.

Between intervals of illness, Virginia Woolf enjoyed years of comparative health during which she worked seriously at the craft of writing and made great contributions to literature. The spectre of nervous breakdown was always present, however, and part of her illness was an excessive fear of failure in her writing career. Yet she was able to take great risks artistically, to follow untried paths in literature. There are several reasons for the courage, even audacity, with which Woolf pursued literary innovation.

First, Woolf was able to search for new forms confidently because she early grounded herself in regular literary modes through constant reading and practice. In addition, she had a great desire not only to find her own literary voice, but also to produce work which would be quite new, thus breaking free of the Victorian literary practices of her day. This desire could have been rooted in her experiences with George Duckworth, but was no doubt strongly reinforced by the Bloomsbury milieu of which she was a part.

The primary reason Virginia Woolf was able to find the courage she needed to break away from literary norms, however, was that she did not have to submit her innovations to commercial publishers for approval. She was free to write and publish exactly as she chose from the time she first began to experiment with new forms of narrative; Woolf—along with her husband Leonard—operated her own press and published her own books.

Before the advent of the Hogarth Press, Virginia Woolf had made herself a successful novelist in the accepted mode of the day by first giving herself a thorough education in her craft, then by taking advantage of the many contacts she had among London publishers. Of her education, her biographer Quentin Bell writes:

> Her journals during these [early] years consist, almost always, of careful essays written as though for publication . . . [which] attest to the high seriousness and immense thoroughness with which

[51]

Virginia prepared herself for the profession of letters. Her constant, almost compulsive reading and writing were intended to compensate for the fact that she had not had what she called "a real education," by which she meant a University education.[3]

Woolf's first published work was an essay which appeared in the *Guardian*, a London weekly newspaper catering to a clerical public. The editor of the *Guardian*'s women's supplement was a friend of Woolf's friend Violet Dickinson, and it was through Dickinson's introduction that Virginia Woolf's work first reached print on December 14, 1904. She was twenty-two at the time. "From now on," writes Bell, "Virginia was regularly employed as a writer of short articles and reviews. She would turn her hand to almost anything."[4]

By this time, Leslie Stephen had died, George Duckworth had married, and the Stephen children had taken up residence, over George's strenuous objections, at 46 Gordon Square in the less-than-fasionable neighborhood of Bloomsbury. Here, in February of 1905, Virginia's brother Thoby Stephen began holding a regular Thursday evening "At Home" for his friends from Cambridge. Virginia and her sister Vanessa joined in the lively intellectual discussions among the radical young economists, artists, and writers who came to be referred to as the "Bloomsbury Group."

The group, which met at ten in the evening for talk over whiskey, buns, and cocoa, included, in addition to the Stephens, Saxon Sydney-Turner, Duncan Grant, Clive Bell, Lytton Strachey, John Maynard Keynes, and others. Leonard Woolf, who had been part of this group at Cambridge, returned from Ceylon in 1911 and joined the circle. The young men, while at Cambridge, had sat at the feet of the philosopher G. E. Moore, and believed like him that the Victorian notion of morality was a sham. There were no such things as moral or immoral deeds they felt, only moral or immoral states of mind. The highest morality was truth based not on scripture or convention but solely upon rationality. Sex was openly discussed at these gatherings, along with literature, art, religion, and politics.

[52]

For two young unmarried women to sit up late at night with a group of young men indulging in frank discussions of sex and other taboo topics was shocking to George Duckworth and others of the social circle in which the Stephens had been brought up. But the young women found such conversation exhilarating. The social gatherings George had forced her to attend had been terrifying to Virginia, but this intellectual coming out was far more congenial. As Vanessa would later recall of the Bloomsbury evenings, "There was very little self-consciousness I think in these early gatherings . . . but life was exciting, terrible and amusing and one had to explore it thankful that one could do so freely."[5] At last the Stephen sisters were being exposed to the kind of intellectual environment they had been denied by their lack of a university education.

> Here they were being asked to do something that had not been required of them before — to use their brains. The rest of them didn't much matter. For whereas the tacit purpose of a party in Belgravia was the pursuit of matrimony, the purpose of a party in Bloomsbury was to exchange ideas. It was this purely cerebral attitude of Thoby's Cambridge friends, or at least of most of them, which made them interesting to Virginia, and she was glad to be free of the marriage market.[6]

Through 1905 and the first half of 1906, Woolf continued to write, review books, and teach history at Morley College. Then in September 1906 she toured Greece with her brothers and sisters. By the time they returned in late October, both Thoby and Vanessa were ill. On November 20 Thoby died of typhoid fever. With the loss of their brother, one might expect the other Stephen children to lose touch with his Cambridge friends. Instead, their friendships grew stronger, and two days after Thoby's death, Vanessa agreed to marry Clive Bell. After Vanessa's departure, Virginia and her younger brother Adrian moved to a small house at 29 Fitzroy Square, where they resumed the Thursday night-gatherings in the autumn of 1907.

[53]

At about this time Virginia began working on a novel she referred to as *Melymbrosia*. She worked for five years on the book, which was published eventually as *The Voyage Out*. In the process, according to Bell, she burned seven different versions of the book. During these years Virginia published no other fiction. "She was still terrified of the world, terrified of exposing herself. But with this was united another and nobler emotion—a high regard for the seriousness of her profession."[7] She did show her writing to Clive Bell, however, and found his comments encouraging and helpful.

Virginia continued writing journalism during that time. By 1909, the "*Times Literary Supplement* had become her chief employer."[8] She was also reviewing books for the *Cornhill*, and it was to the editor that she submitted an essay which was actually a piece of fiction in the guise of a book review, "Memoirs of a Novelist." This spoof, which purported to be a critique of Miss Linsett's *Life* of Miss Willatt, was rejected at the *Cornhill* in a polite note. Virginia, always hypersensitive about her work, found it hard to take the rejection in stride: "She never published or, I think, tried to publish in *The Cornhill* again," reports Bell.[9]

Indeed, fear that her writing would be rejected would be a central part of Woolf's recurrent illness. In March 1910, just as an early draft of *Melymbrosia* was nearing completion, Virginia suffered another nervous breakdown, the first of several, each of which would accompany the completion of a novel. In April 1911, she wrote to Clive about her fears, "If I thought 'There! thats solid and done with' I'm sure I should have the palsy." One day when her writing didn't go smoothly she wrote to Vanessa, "I could not write, & all the devils came out—hairy black ones. To be 29 & unmarried—to be a failure—Childless—insane too, no writer."[10]

In 1912 one reason for Virginia to think herself a failure was removed by her marriage to Leonard Woolf on August 10. Leonard now replaced Clive Bell as the person to whom Virginia Woolf turned for a reaction to her writing, so that when *The Voyage Out* was finished in February 1913, he was the first

[54]

to read the book. He apparently liked it very much, and no doubt the Woolfs discussed together possibilities for its publication.

In addition to George, Woolf had another half brother, Gerald Duckworth, who owned a successful commercial publishing house. On March 9 Leonard took the manuscript to Gerald; would Duckworth's like to publish it? Gerald turned it over to a reader, Edward Garnett. As she waited for a decision, Woolf's fears of rejection came to the fore again. "I expect to have it rejected," she wrote Violet Dickinson.[11] But Garnett gave the book an enthusiastic report, and on April 12 Woolf went to Gerald's office to receive the good news; he would be happy to publish his little sister's book.

One wonders at this point what would have happened to Virginia Woolf's writing career had she not had a brother in the publishing business. Would she have been able psychologically to weather the repeated rejections which normally greet a writer's first novel? As it was, the prospect of her fiction finally appearing in print for all to see seems to have helped precipitate the longest and most serious breakdown of Woolf's life. Why this was so, one can perhaps speculate.

Her prolonged victimization by George Duckworth when she was a teenager no doubt did much to destroy Woolf's sense of self-worth. It was perhaps to regain this sense that she poured so much effort into learning the craft of writing. She would make herself a respected writer, and thus be worthwhile in her own right. As she grew up, this manner of thinking seems to have become a pattern. With her first real work completed, all she could see were its flaws, and the prospect that her friends and critics would also see them terrified her. If *The Voyage Out* failed, she was a failure, for she had poured all her best efforts into it for five years.

The reception of Woolf's books was of grave concern to her throughout her life, and became an obsession during recurrences of her illness. *The Voyage Out* was no sooner in Gerald Duckworth's hands than Woolf began to experience severe headaches, a sense of guilt, an aversion to eating, and sleep-

[55]

less nights. She began to talk of suicide, at the same time insisting that nothing was wrong with her, that her problems were the fault of her own lack of character. On July 24, her doctor sent her to a rest home for women in Twickenham which was operated by Jean Thomas. Thomas, like Leonard and most others close to Woolf at the time, attributed Woolf's illness to her writing:

> It is the novel which has broken her up. She finished it and got the proof back for correction . . . couldnt sleep & thought everyone would jeer at her. Then they did the wrong thing & teased her about it and she got desperate—and came here a wreck.[12]

On September 9, after visiting two doctors, Woolf took an overdose of veronal and, despite being rushed to the hospital to have her stomach pumped, she came very close to death. Her recovery from this illness came very slowly. She began to realize that she was indeed quite ill, but with this realization came a new fear, the fear that she would never return to sanity. This fear grew with each new relapse, of which there were several during the next two years. Still, she did improve, and that gave both Virginia and Leonard a new lease on life. They began to shop for a new house together and to make plans for the future.

One idea Leonard hit upon, and shared with his wife during one of her more healthy intervals in January of 1915, was to buy their own printing press. On her thirty-third birthday, January 25, 1915, they went into the city to a movie. Woolf reported in her diary:

> I dont know when I have enjoyed a birthday so much—not since I was a child anyhow. Sitting at tea we decided three things: in the first place to take Hogarth, if we can get it [they had been negotiating to buy Hogarth House in Richmond]; second, to buy a Printing press; in the third to buy a Bull dog, probably called John. I am very much excited at the idea of all three—particularly the press.[13]

A few weeks later, while in town at the dentist's, they began shopping for the press. But now the publication of *The Voyage Out* was imminent, and Woolf suffered a severe relapse, becoming manic, talking wildly and incessantly, until she finally sank into a coma. On March 25, the day before the publication of *The Voyage Out,* she was taken to a nursing home while her husband moved their belongings to Hogarth House, for which they had finally negotiated the lease.

At this point those close to Woolf, and probably even Woolf herself, began to despair that she would never be sane again. She had now been quite ill off and on for two years, and Vanessa wrote that summer after comparing her sister's current letters with those of earlier years, "The early ones are so brilliant, better than her novel . . . & the later ones during the last year or two are so dull by comparison—it looks as it she had simply worn out her brains."[14]

When the novel finally did appear it received almost universal praise from friends and critics alike, and this recognition, by laying to rest both her fear of failure and of insanity, seems to have brought about Woolf's gradual return to health. Bell wrote:

> Her dread of the ruthless mockery of the world contained within it the deeper fear that her art, and therefore her self, was a kind of sham, an idiot's dream of no value to anyone. [f. "Suppose one woke and found oneself a fraud? It was part of my madness that horror." *AWD (Berg),* 16 May 1927.] For her, therefore, favourable notice was more valuable than mere praise; it was a kind of certificate of sanity.[15]

By October 1916 Woolf was well enough that the idea of buying the press was revived. Not only would the manual occupation of typesetting provide a good escape for Virginia when the pressures of writing began to threaten her stability, but both Woolfs liked the prospect of being able to publish their own work. The wait for *The Voyage Out* to be published at Duckworths had contributed to Woolf's breakdown, but with her own press, she would presumably be so busy printing her fictions she wouldn't have time to worry so much about their reception.

[57]

Another motivation for having their own press was perhaps financial. That Woolf was his sister apparently did not prompt Gerald Duckworth to offer her more generous terms on her first novel than were offered other writers. In fact, he seems to have expected her to take less. According to Leonard Woolf, Duckworth contracted to pay his sister royalties on only twelve out of every thirteen copies sold. Nor did he sell an impressive number of the books, despite the universally favorable reviews:

> They printed 2,000 copies, and 14 years later, when in 1929 the Hogarth Press acquired the rights from Duckworth, there were still a few copies unsold. In the ten years before the Hogarth Press took the book over, 1919–1929, Duckworth sold 479 copies for which Virginia received in royalties £26.2s.10d.[16]

The Woolfs perhaps reasoned that they could do that well on their own, considering the contacts they had in the London literary establishment, and they wouldn't have to give up control of the books to Duckworth's or settle for a small royalty.

In 1916, however, they were a long way away from having the expertise to publish a manuscript the length of Woolf's novel. In the first place, they didn't know how to print, but decided to take printing lessons. In the second, they couldn't afford to buy a press, but were expecting a tax refund that would give them the necessary sum of twenty pounds.

> When we went to the St. Bride's school of printing . . . we learned that the social engine and machinery made it impossible to teach the art of printing to two middle-aged middle-class persons. Printing could only be taught to union apprentices, the number of whom was strictly limited.[17]

The tax refund turned out to be fifteen pounds, instead of the thirty-five they had expected, delaying purchase of the press still further. Finally, on March 23, 1917, they were able to pay for a small hand-operated press complete with type chases, cases, and all the tools of the printing trade. According to

[58]

Leonard, the proprietor of the Excelsior Printing Supply Company who sold them the equipment encouraged them to teach themselves the printing craft, with the help of a sixteen-page booklet which came with the press:

> When the stuff was delivered to us in Richmond, we set it all up in the dining-room and started to teach ourselves to print. The Excelsior man proved to be right; by following the directions in the pamphlet we found that we could pretty soon set the type, locking it up in the chase, ink the rollers, and machine a fairly legible printed page. After a month we thought we had become sufficiently proficient to print a page of a book or pamphlet.[18]

The press, as hoped, occupied Woolf immediately to such an extent she had little time for worry. She wrote Vanessa on April 26:

> Our press arrived on Tuesday. We unpacked it with enormous excitement, finally with Nelly's help, carried it into the drawing room, set it on its stand—and discovered it was smashed in half! It is a great weight, and they never screwed it down; but the shop has probably got a spare part. Anyhow the arrangement of the type is such a business that we shant be ready to start printing directly. One has great blocks of type, which have to be divided into their separate letters, and founts, and then put into the right partitions. The work of ages, especially when you mix the h's with the ns, as I did yesterday. We get so absorbed we can't stop; I see that real printing will devour one's entire life.[19]

The initial item the Woolfs set in type was a handbill advertising their first publication:

Hogarth House
Richmond

THE HOGARTH PRESS

It is proposed to issue shortly a pamphlet containing two short stories by Leonard Woolf and Virginia Woolf, (price, including postage 1/2).

If you desire a copy to be sent to you, please fill up the form below

[59]

and send it with P.O. to L. S. Woolf at the above address before June

A limited edition only will be issued.

Please send   copy of Publication No. 1 to

for which I enclose P.O. for

Name
Address[20]

The advertisement was more the product of enthusiasm than sound business sense, for the press was still broken, and so incapable of printing the handbill itself, much less a book. And although Leonard's contribution to Publication No. 1, "The Three Jews," was ready for publication, Virginia Woolf's contribution was not even written yet.

They printed the handbills without use of the press in early May and sent them out to fifty friends, apparently everyone they could think of, for they also requested names and addresses from others. On May 22, Woolf wrote Vanessa:

> We've got about 60 orders already, which shows a trusting spirit, especially as most of them come from old ladies and poets in the North, recommended by Bob Trevelyan, whom we've never heard of.[21]

They were just starting to print Leonard's story, Woolf admitted; "I haven't produced mine yet, but there's nothing in writing compared with printing."[22]

The writing of her contribution to *Two Stories* came quite easily. For the past two months she had been working on her second book, *Night and Day*, which was to be "a perfectly orthodox and conventional novel." The exercise had quickly become a bore, and the writing of her story for Hogarth Press's Publication No. 1 was a welcome chance to break free. She wrote to Ethel Smyth years later, "I shall never forget the day I wrote the *Mark on the Wall*—all in a flash, as if flying, after being kept stone-breaking for months."[23]

[60]

"The Mark on the Wall" was a product of the freedom and enthusiasm which came with having a press of her own, and was a departure from the sort of fiction she had produced up to that time. The entire "story" was of a single instant's perception of a single mark on a wall, with the action taking place entirely inside the perceiving mind. It was her first experiment with the sort of narrative, sometimes called stream of consciousness, which would be her greatest achievement as a writer.

The little booklet, *Two Stories*, was bound by the Woolfs themselves, and hand-stitched into paper covers. "We took a good deal of trouble to find some rather unusual, gay Japanese paper for the covers," Leonard recalled years later in *Beginning Again*.[24] "We printed a circular . . . explaining that we in The Hogarth Press proposed to print and publish in the same way from time to time paper-covered pamphlets or small books, printed entirely by our two selves, which would have little or no chance of being published by ordinary publishers."

The book appeared in July in an edition of 150:

> . . . and by the end of the month we had practically sold out the edition for we had sold 124 copies. (The total number finally sold was 134.) I still have a list of the 87 people who bought the 134 copies and all but five or six of them were friends or acquaintances. . . . The total cost of production was £3. 7s. 0d. [about $16], which included the noble sum of 15s. to Carrington for woodcuts, 12s. 6d. for paper, and 10s for the cover paper. The two authors were not paid any royalty. The total receipts were £10. 8s. 0d., so the net profit was £7 1s. 0d. [about $35].[25]

The Woolfs, perhaps because their book appeared in such a small edition, did not send copies to the reviewing media. No notice of it appeared in the *Times Literary Supplement*, despite the fact that Virginia Woolf was regularly writing reviews for the *TLS* at this time. They did, however, get notes from their friends—polite congratulations for Leonard and

[61]

rave reviews for Virginia. These reactions were especially gratifying for Woolf because they came from all the people she had always wanted most to impress. On July 17, just days after publication, Lytton Strachey wrote to Leonard Woolf:

> The *Two Stories* was a most cheering production. I could never have believed it possible. My only criticism is that there doesn't seem to be quite enough ink. Virginia's is, I consider, a work of genius. The liquidity of the style fills me with envy: really some of the sentences!—How on earth does she make the English language float and float? And then the wonderful way in which the modern point of view is suggested. *Tiens!*[26]

Violet Dickinson wrote to say she liked the book and to ask for four more copies. Clive Bell, like Strachey, praised the experimental form of the story, and Woolf's reply showed these reactions had encouraged her to think about experimenting further. "I should like to discuss this with you, and see *why* you think it good—Its an absorbing thing (I mean writing is) and its high time we found some new shapes, don't you think so?"[27]

When she answered David Garnett's letter two days later, it was evident she had been giving even more thought to her future writing career:

> I'm very glad you liked the story. In a way its easier to do a short thing, all in one flight than a novel. Novels are frightfully clumsy and overpowering of course; still if one could only get hold of them it would be superb. I daresay one ought to invent a completely new form. Anyhow its very amusing to try with these short things, and the greatest mercy to be able to do what one likes—no editors, or publishers, and only people to read who more or less like that sort of thing. We've been seeing a writer named Kotelian-sky who says that to write for a small public is damnation. However, I dont like writing for my half brother George [Ed. corrects "George" to "Gerald"].[28]

The experience with "The Mark on the Wall," which was published within a few weeks of its composition (instead of months or years later as was—and is—almost always the

[62]

case when short stories are submitted to commercial magazines) and immediately praised as a successful experiment in fiction, apparently opened up a whole new world for Woolf. That Woolf confused Gerald with George in this letter perhaps indicates the extent to which she resented Duckworth's control over her career. Writing "for my brother George" might also have been a reference to the sort of audience George Duckworth represented—Victorian, conventional, and unwilling to accept anything new—for this was the audience her books would need to please if they were to be viable for a large press. She and Leonard began to discuss the possibility of expanding the scope of the Hogarth Press so they could publish her novels themselves.

Already, the printing of *Two Stories* had convinced the Woolfs they would need a larger press if they were seriously going to go into the publishing business. On June 27 Woolf wrote Vanessa: "We have just got a handsome sum back on our income tax, which we mean to spend on a press (I need hardly say) which will print 8 pages at a time, and then we shall be very professional."[29] "We ... mean to take it [printing] up seriously and produce novels with it," she told Violet Dickinson about the press on July 21.

During the year following *Two Stories,* the Woolfs hired an assistant, ordered a larger press, then had to cope with the frustration of waiting for the press's delivery. Meanwhile they published Katherine Mansfield's *Prelude,* setting the type themselves, then using a larger press at a print shop to have it run off. Woolf was working on what would be her last conventional—and conventionally published—novel, *Night and Day,* but experimental narrative continued to intrigue her, especially in light of the favorable reaction "The Mark on the Wall" had received. In 1918 she wrote a short story in the same vein called "Kew Gardens." However, she was still far from confident of the new form she was in the process of discovering. When her sister urged the writer to send her a copy of "Kew Gardens" so she might illustrate it with woodcuts as Carrington had done *Two Stories,* Woolf was hesitant.

[63]

"The story seems to me very bad now, and not worth printing, but I'll send it you if you like—I thought perhaps I could rewrite it."[30]

Woolf did go ahead and send the story, apparently without revising it, and by July 15 she received a drawing her sister had done as illustration for the book. Woolf wrote Vanessa to thank her: "I think your drawing is a most successful piece; and just in the mood I wanted." But she still had her doubts about the story: "the difficulty is, suppose we decide not to print that story after all?" Vanessa apparently liked the story, however, and overcame Woolf's doubts by continuing to do illustrations for it. By November 7, when the Woolfs began to set type on the story, they had already had proofs taken of Vanessa's woodcuts, and Woolf was enthusiastic about the forthcoming publication. "I think the book will be a great success—owing to you," she wrote Vanessa.[31]

A success it would be when it finally appeared in May 1919. This five-month gap was due in part to a delay in getting the larger press delivered and in part to the Woolfs' having decided to issue their next three books—Middleton Murry's *The Critic In Judgement*, Eliot's *Poems*, and Woolf's *Kew Gardens*—all at once. Meanwhile Woolf's mind was occupied with publishing decisions about the size of the edition, the price of the books, choices of paper and ink, and proper payments to Vanessa for the illustrations. If she had her usual prepublication jitters, they were obscured by the business of being her own publisher.

On publication day, May 12, 1919, the depression hit her, but not so forcefully that she was unable to analyze it to herself in her diary:

> I read a bound copy of Kew Gardens through; having put off the evil task until it was complete. The result is vague. It seems to me slight & short; I dont see how the reading of it impressed Leonard so much. . . . As Sydney Waterlow once said, the worst of writing is that one depends so much upon praise. I feel rather sure that I shall get none for this story; & I shall mind a little. Unpraised, I find it hard to start writing in the morning; but the dejection lasts

[64]

only 30 minutes, & once I start I forget all about it. One should aim, seriously, at disregarding ups & downs; ... the central fact remains stable, which is the fact of my own pleasure in the art.[32]

On May 16, she was feeling better about the book, because Roger Fry had praised it, but was disappointed in its slow sales. "It looks as though the market for such commodities is a small one—infinitesimal; we shan't even pay our expenses it seems."[33] By May 22, however, she was beginning to receive "a surfeit of praise for Kew Gardens,"[34] and the next day Lytton Stachey dubbed her "the inventor of a new prose style, & the creator of a new version of the sentence."[35]

Then the next week an enthusiastic review of *Kew Gardens* appeared in the *Times Literary Supplement*, which ended Woolf's fears of losing money on the book. The review, written by Harold Child, showed his appreciation for this very special small-press production:

> What in the world, one asks, on picking up this volume, can be the connexion between Kew Gardens and this odd Fitzroy-square looking cover? ... What are Mrs. Woolf and Mrs. Bell going to find in Kew Gardens worth writing about, and engraving on wood [sic. The book was illustrated with woodcuts, not wood engravings] and binding in a cover that suggests the tulips in a famous Dutch-English catalogue—"blotched, spotted, streaked, speckled, and flushed"?
> When we have read these pages, we are firmly convinced of the truth of "Kew Gardens" . . . a thing of original and therefore strange beauty, with its own "athmosphere," its own vital force. ... we should like to tempt others into "Kew Gardens" ... the more one gloats over "Kew Gardens" the more beauty shines out of it; and the fitter to it seems this cover that is like no other cover.

As a result of this publicity, the Hogarth Press was innundated with orders—"150 about, from shops & private people"—for the book. "We came back from Asheham to find the hall table stacked, littered, with orders for Kew Gardens. ... And 10 days ago I was stoically facing complete failure!"[36] The work of filling these orders consumed most of the

[65]

Woolfs' time for days. Ninety more copies were ordered than they had on hand, so they had to bind and mail that many as quickly as possible. It was becoming obvious that they could make better use of their time if they hired out some of this work to commercial printers and binders. The Hogarth Press had outgrown its "loving hands at home" beginnings.

Even as it pushed the press farther toward professionalism, the surprise success of this experimental story pushed Woolf farther in the direction of innovation in her writing. *Night and Day* had been accepted for publication by Duckworth on May 7, 1919, just before *Kew Gardens* was published. By the time it appeared on October 20, Woolf had a reputation as an innovator in fiction, based on the little books she had published herself through Hogarth. She was being compared to James Joyce by those who knew of his innovations, and many people who had never read "Mark on the Wall" and *Kew Gardens* had heard that Mrs. Woolf was a writer one must read to be "up" on the new fiction, in the same sense that Eliot was the poet one must read for the new poetry. Conventional reviewers, such as the critic who reviewed the book for the *Times Literary Supplement*, had high praise for *Night and Day*, but to those who admired her innovations, this book was a disappointment. According to Bell:

> Clive . . . Violet and Vanessa were eulogistic, Lytton enthusiastic. . . . But Morgan [Forster] wrote to say that he preferred *The Voyage Out*. . . . Katherine Mansfield hated *Night and Day*. Her private opinion was that it was "a lie in the soul." "The war never has been: that is what its message is. . . . I feel in the *profoundest* sense that nothing can ever be the same—that, as artists, we are traitors if we feel otherwise: we have to take it into account and find new expressions, new moulds for our new thoughts and feelings." . . . Thus Katherine to Middleton Murry. . . . Writing in the *Athenaeum* Katherine Mansfield was discreet; but she said enough to inflict pain.[37]

The *Athenaeum* review appeared on November 26, 1919, and the criticism hit home. In her diary two days later Woolf grumbled, "A decorous elderly dullard she describes me."[38]

[66]

Not surprisingly, Woolf's next story was another experiment, and she revealed her ambition to expand these innovations in the title she gave it—"An Unwritten Novel." Until this time the experimental narratives had been "treats I allowed myself when I had done my exercise in the conventional style." With this story, however, Woolf recognized that the new narrative she was developing freed her from a form which had imprisoned her novels. Years later she told Ethel Smyth, "The Unwritten Novel was the great discovery . . . [that] in one second showed me how I could embody all my deposit of experience in a shape that fitted it . . . *Jacob's Room* . . . *Mrs. Dalloway* &c. How I trembled with excitement."[39] "An Unwritten Novel" was published in the *London Mercury* in July 1920.

In 1920 Woolf began to prepare a collection of her experimental stories for her first full-length Hogarth book, to be called *Monday or Tuesday,* which appeared the following year. At the same time she was seriously considering the new form of novel she had been contemplating since the success of "The Mark on the Wall" nearly three years before. The concept seems to have taken shape suddenly after these years of germination. On January 26, 1920, the day after her thirty-eighth birthday, she told her diary:

This afternoon [I] arrived at some idea of a new form for a new novel. Suppose one thing should open out of another—as in An Unwritten novel—only not for 10 pages but 200 or so—doesn't that give the looseness and lightness I want; doesn't that get closer and yet keep form and speed, and enclose everything, everything? My doubt is how far it will enclose the human heart—Am I sufficiently mistress of my dialogue to net it there? For I figure that the approach will be entirely different this time: no scaffolding; scarcely a brick to be seen; all crepuscular, but the heart, the passion, humour, everything as bright as fire in the mist . . . . Conceive *Mark on the Wall, K [ew] G [ardens]* and *Unwritten Novel* taking hands and dancing in unity. Anyhow I must still grope and experiment but this afternoon I had a gleam of light. Indeed, I think from the ease with which I'm developing the unwritten novel there must be a path for me there.[40]

[67]

The "unwritten novel" in this last sentence seems not to refer to the story by that name, but to a new work she was just beginning, her first experimental novel and her first self-published novel, *Jacob's Room*.

After the initial flashes of inspiration, Woolf seems to have had a difficult time settling down to the task of actually writing the book. Jitters over the publication of "An Unwritten Novel" and a great demand for her reviewing kept her from it, but she finally got underway on April 16. By May 11 she was far enough into the book to tell her diary:

> ... the creative power which bubbles so pleasantly on beginning a new book quiets down after a time, & one goes on more steadily. Doubts creep in. Then one becomes resigned. Determination not to give in, & the sense of an impending shape keep one at it more than anything. I'm a little anxious. How am I to bring off this conception? ... I want to write nothing in this book that I dont enjoy writing. Yet writing is always difficult.[41]

But nine days later she found *Jacob* "the most amusing novel writing I've done . . . ."[42] By August she was writing daily, with few interruptions, and expecting to finish by Christmas. By the last week of September she was half finished with the book and had been writing steadily for two months.

Several things now caused Woolf to doubt her writing, throwing her off her pace. There was a visit from Eliot during which "he completely neglected my claims to be a writer."[43] James Joyce (to whom Woolf was often compared) was discussed, and Eliot called his novel *Ulysses* "extremely brilliant." She found herself disagreeing with Eliot's pronouncements about literature, yet unable to hold her own in the discussion. "Now in all this L [eonard] showed up much better than I did."

Bigotry against women chiseled away at her self-confidence. It was implicit in Eliot's attitude and in the way her husband seemed to overshadow her even during discussions about her field of endeavor, literature. Meanwhile, there was much discussion in the popular press about Arnold Bennett's

[68]

new book of essays, *Our Women*, in which he studied "women of the top class and of those classes which . . . imitate the top . . . class," and reached the conclusion that "intellectually and creatively man is the superior of woman."[44]

Woolf, as perhaps the foremost example of the class of woman to which Bennett was referring, took exception and issued a counterblast, but the fact that she had to defend herself did nothing to restore her self-confidence after Eliot's visit. A week later she was still thinking about it: "He [Eliot] said nothing, but I reflected how what I'm doing is probably being better done by Mr. Joyce. . . . Perhaps at the bottom of my mind, I feel that I'm distanced by L[eonard] in every respect." The next day Woolf was threatened by one of the headaches which were usually a prelude to a breakdown, and so her writing was delayed further. This lapse would continue for two months, as she took additional time off to complete her collection of experimental short stories, *Monday or Tuesday*, and ready it for publication by the Hogarth Press.

On her thirty-ninth birthday, January 25, 1921, Woolf resolved to finish *Jacob* "in 20,000 words, written straight off in a frenzy."[45] She set out on this task and did well until April 7, when a half-column review of *Monday or Tuesday*, just published by the Hogarth Press, appeared in the *Times Literary Supplement*. Woolf was unable to write, and took to her diary to analyze, sanely, the "question of praise & fame," or "praise & blame" as she sometimes called it.

> I'm a failure as a writer. I'm out of fashion; old; shan't do any better. . . . Ralph sent my book [*Monday or Tuesday*] to the Times for review without date of publication in it. Thus a short notice is scrambled through, . . . put in an obscure place, rather scrappy, complimentary enough, but quite unintelligent. I mean by that they don't see that I'm after something interesting. So that makes me suspect that I'm not. And thus I can't get on with Jacob.[46]

The rejection of *Monday or Tuesday* by George H. Doran Company in New York caused Virginia to reflect on advantages and disadvantages of self-publishing. "How much dif-

[69]

ference does popularity make?" she wrote. "One wants ... to be kept up to the mark; that people should be interested, & watch one's work." She wondered if "the feeling that I'm writing for half a dozen instead of 1500" would make her writing eccentric. Still, the security of self-publishing had freed her to experiment and find her own voice. "What depresses me is the thought that I have ceased to interest people—at the very moment when, by the help of the [Hogarth] press, I thought I was becoming more myself."[47]

During the following month, as reviews, comments, and orders for the book began to pour in, Woolf's fears of being "dismissed as negligible" were eased, and a "slow trickle" of work began on Jacob. Despite the disappointment of the *TLS* review, her reputation as an important writer seems to have been increased greatly by *Monday or Tuesday*. Articles about her book and the Hogarth Press appeared in the *New Statesman*, the *British Weekly*, the *Daily News*, and the *Dial* in New York.

In the case of the *Dial* review, Woolf found it "4 pages of sneer & condescending praise." But the Hogarth Press gave her power over such hurts. "Oddly enough, I have drawn the sting of it by deciding to print it among my puffs [at the back of *Jacob's Room*], where it will come in beautifully."[48]

The praises which meant the most to Woolf, however, came from her friends, or rather from those among them whom she liked to call "the 6 or so people whose opinions I respect." The "astonishing news" that Lytton Strachey had praised one of the *Monday or Tuesday* stories was enough to "flood every nerve with pleasure," and Roger Fry pleased her immensely by telling her she was "on the track of real discoveries, & certainly not a fake."[49] Even Eliot, who had made her feel insignificant, "astounded" Woolf "by praising Monday & Tuesday!" It was, she declared, pleasing "to think I could discuss my writing openly with him."[50]

Three days after she wrote these happy words, however, Woolf suffered a sleepless night which was the beginning of a severe nervous breakdown, "all the horrors of the dark cup-

[70]

board of illness once more displayed for my diversion."[51] Unlike her earlier bouts with illness, however, this one lasted only two months. Its origin is hard to pinpoint; Woolf herself had begun to suspect that her "insanity" was at least partly due to physical causes, and the suddenness with which this particular malady struck in the midst of a period of saneness lends credence to that view. Leonard, however, continued to believe that her periods of "insanity" were caused by the strain of writing and worries about the reception of her work. Not taking any chances, Woolf quit work on *Jacob*, as well as all reviewing, until the autumn.

Finally, on Friday November 4, 1921, she finished the first draft of *Jacob's Room*. She was still suffering the aftereffects of her summer breakdown, and apparently put off the revision for several months, while she did some nonfiction writing. On February 14, 1922, she wrote, "I have to hold over [the publication of] Jacob's Room till October; & I somehow fear that by that time it will appear to me sterile acrobatics."[52] Beginning in March 1922 she apparently worked steadily on the revision, and by June was finishing up a fair copy for the typist.

No sooner had she turned it over to be typed than she began to worry about its reception—and her own reaction to that reception. Her only defense, she decided, was to have so much other work out she could defend herself against any kind of criticism. "Now what *will* they say about Jacob? Mad, I suppose: a disconnected rhapsody: I don't know."[53]

On July 23, Woolf got her first reaction to the novel. Leonard read it and declared it her best work:

> He calls it a work of genius; he thinks it unlike any other novel.... I am on the whole pleased. Neither of us knows what the public will think. There's no doubt in my mind that I have found out how to begin (at 40) to say something in my own voice; & that interests me so that I feel I can go ahead without praise.[54]

Finally, in October 1922, *Jacob's Room* was printed, bound,

[71]

and ready for publication. Unlike the earliest publications of the Hogarth Press, the novel looked much like those being issued from commercial houses. It was hard-bound and covered in yellow cloth, with a white label on the spine bearing its title and author. It even had a dust wrapper, cream paper printed in cinnamon and black. A first edition of 1,200 copies was produced at R&R Clark Printers.

Woolf seems to have had no embarrassment about publishing her own novel. Beneath her name as the author on the title page was the inscription "Published by Leonard and Virginia Woolf at the Hogarth Press, Hogarth House, Richmond." And when Violet Dickinson wrote Woolf to ask why Gerald Duckworth wasn't bringing out *Jacob's Room* as he had her first two novels, Woolf answered simply, "I didn't send my book to Gerald, as I thought he wouldn't like it."[55]

Still, to publish one's own novel is risky business, both financially and artistically. On the eve of *Jacob's* publication, Woolf recorded her predictions for its success:

> I think we shall sell 500: it will then go on slowly, & reach 800 by June. It will be highly praised in some places for 'beauty'; will be crabbed by people who want human character. The only review I am anxious about is the one in the Sup [plemen]t.: not that it will be the most intelligent, but it will be the most read & I cant bear people to see me downed in public. . . .Nothing budges me from my determination to go on.[56]

The review in the *Times Literary Supplement* was a full column long, and generally complimentary. As predicted, the reviewer lamented that the new narrative style Woolf had created did not give the reader a psychological analysis of the characters. "We should have to say that it does not create persons and characters as we secretly desire to know them." But he relished the adventurousness of the new method. "What she has undoubtedly done is to give a quickened sense of the promise and pity in a single destiny, seen against those wilful, intersecting lines of chance and nature."[57]

Woolf wasn't entirely happy with this review, and never

[72]

forgot the criticism that the book only gave its reader an external view of the character. That flaw she would tackle successfully when she took up her newly discovered narrative technique again to begin *Mrs. Dalloway.* Still, in most ways the experiment of *Jacob's Room* was a great success. Sales easily exceeded her predictions, and within two weeks a second edition was ordered. "This time the reviews are against me and the private people enthusiastic," Woolf recorded in her diary on October 29. A month later she wrote: "People — my friends I mean — seem agreed that it is *my* masterpiece, & the starting point for fresh adventures. Last night we dined with Roger and I was praised whole-heartedly by him for the first time."[58] By the middle of December the sales had become sluggish, but the praises continued to arrive in each day's mail, as Woolf began work on her next book, *Mrs. Dalloway.*

It is now generally recognized that with the publication of *Jacob's Room* by the Hogarth Press in 1922, Virginia Woolf came into her own as a novelist. The later novels, for which she gained the reputation of a great writer, are outgrowths of this experimental work, in the same way that it is an outgrowth of her first experimental short stories, "The Mark on the Wall," "Kew Gardens," and "An Unwritten Novel."

Self-publishing had not only been a therapeutic occupation; it had been her salvation as an artist — the means by which she had been freed to write in her own unorthodox way. In so doing, she enriched the genre of the novel and helped to create literary modernism. The role that the Hogarth Press played in all this is generally ignored by contemporary scholars but it was clearly recognized by Virginia Woolf herself. On September 22, 1925, she would write in her diary, "How my handwriting goes down hill! Another sacrifice to the Hogarth Press. Yet what I owe the Hogarth Press is barely paid by the whole of my handwriting. . . . I'm the only woman in England free to write what I like."

[73]

JAMES JOYCE
. . . from the bookshop

3

In the early days of printing there were no publishing houses. Books were usually brought out by booksellers — printed in a room at the back of the shop in order to stock the shelves out front. Milton's *Paradise Lost*, Bunyan's *Pilgrims Progress*, and all of Shakespeare's works were originally published by booksellers. During the eighteenth century, however, publishing became a specialized trade. Bookstore publishing gradually died out, and since the mid-nineteenth century it has been practiced only on a very small scale, usually as an alternative when the commercial houses cannot take a risk on a book in which the bookseller is interested.

Publication by a bookstore, though it has usually been a last resort for the writer, has proved to have several advantages. It is the publishing alternative most likely to succeed financially for the writer, because a bookseller, like a commercial publisher, has a ready-made means of distribution for the books he or she publishes. The prospective buyers are already customers; often they are themselves interested in the writer's career. If this is not the case, the bookseller is in the position to promote the book to his or her customers personally, giving this alternative publication an edge on commercially published books, at least in this one bookstore. In addition, publication by a bookseller often gives a writer greater control over the publishing process than he would have with a commercial publisher. The bookseller may be more interested in seeing the book published for its own sake, rather than as an investment, and so may be more concerned that the writer's vision be reproduced as the writer wants it.

The most famous case of this form of alternative publishing in modern times involves one of the most influential English-language novels of our century, James Joyce's *Ulysses*. In April 1921, when Joyce's book had been rejected repeatedly by publishers and printers in the United States and England, his bookseller friend Sylvia Beach agreed to publish it for him in Paris through her little Left Bank bookshop, Shakespeare and Company.

This arrangement would make Sylvia Beach something of a legend among people interested in modern literature. The effect on Joyce and his book, however, has generally been overlooked. The freedom Beach allowed Joyce in the publication of his work enhanced *Ulysses* by making possible extensive revisions which moved the work further in the direction of experimentation.

Joyce had a great deal of confidence in his own writing abilities and concepts, and a sense of mission as a literary seer. It never bothered him to ask others for money; he felt such support was his due as a "priest" of the art. In exchange, he worked hard at his writing, and it infuriated him when some editor or publisher who had not worked and sacrificed wanted to change or censor his work. But Joyce's writing inevitably provoked censorship. One of his goals was to depict "with scrupulous meanness" the decayed spirit of his Irish homeland. In doing so, Joyce never scrupled to use the explicit language of the everyday man, nor to depict the seamier aspects of everyday life.

Joyce's works were not only sordid and frank by the standards of his day; they were also different in narrative form from the fiction being published in the first two decades of the twentieth century. Even his early short stories presented readers with a strange new technique, one many readers

[78]

would not be prepared to accept. Joyce biographer Richard Ellmann writes of this technique:

> Arrogant yet humble too, it claims importance by claiming nothing; it seeks a presentation so sharp that comment by the author would be an interference. It leaves off the veneer of gracious intimacy with the reader, of concern that he should be taken into the author's confidence, and instead makes the reader feel uneasy and culpable if he misses the intended but always unstated meaning, as if he were being arraigned rather than entertained. The artist abandons himself and his reader to the material.[1]

Not surprisingly, Joyce was plagued with publishing troubles through most of his career. In a letter to John Quinn in 1917, he summarized what had happened in the years 1905 to 1915 as he tried to get publishers for his short story collection, *Dubliners*, and for his first novel, *A Portrait of the Artist as a Young Man:*

> Ten years of my life have been consumed in correspondence and litigation about my book *Dubliners*. It was rejected by 40 publishers; three times set up, and once burnt. It cost me about 3,000 francs in postage, fees, train and boat fare, for I was in correspondence with 110 newspapers, 7 solicitors, 3 societies, 40 publishers and several men of letters about it. All refused to aid me, except Mr. Ezra Pound. In the end it was published, in 1914, word for word as I wrote it in 1905. My novel [*Portrait*] was refused by every publisher in London to whom it was offered—refused (as Mr Pound informed me) with offensive comments. When a review decided to publish it, it was impossible to find in the United Kingdom a printer to print it.[2]

A Dublin native, Joyce spent most of his early writing career in Trieste, having eloped there with Nora Barnacle in 1904. From Trieste, he began looking for a publisher for *Dubliners* in December 1905. Though London publisher Grant Richards had just rejected Joyce's collection of poetry, *Chamber Music*, Joyce sent him *Dubliners*, hoping he would accept a collection of fiction. Richards did, and in March 1906

[79]

the contract was signed. As the book was being prepared, however, Richards's printer found several passages objectionable.

Under English law at the time, printers were legally liable for printing material considered immoral, as were publishers. In addition, printers generally cared nothing for the development of the art of literature or for the prestige of the works that came off their presses. Examining each word as they set it in type, the printers had ample opportunity to detect even the most subtle allusions to human sexuality and other topics that might offend a reader and thus invite prosecution. This quirk of the law would cause Joyce trouble with British publications for the rest of his life. Printers had everything to lose and nothing to gain by setting in type stories that were even the slightest bit questionable.

A month after Joyce had signed the contract, Richards wrote to tell him that many passages would have to be changed. Joyce wrote back in protest—he couldn't understand the printer's objections; and besides, it was not his writing but English literary taste that needed to be changed. Joyce, however, discovered that he was in a very poor position to defend his art. He could either make the deletions Richards demanded of him or take his chances on finding another publisher. The more concessions Joyce made to Richards and the printer, the more they demanded. On July 9, Joyce resubmitted the manuscript with the objectionable passages deleted or rewritten. "I will not conceal from you that I think I have injured these stories by these deletions but I sincerely trust you will recognize that I have tried to meet your wishes and scruples fairly."[3]

When publication of *Dubliners* had seemed assured, Joyce had gone forward with his writing full steam. Now that problems arose, his self-confidence was shaken to the point that he was unable to write. His novel *Stephen Hero* bogged down in the twenty-fifth chapter. He began to have doubts about the troublesome collection of short stories, wondering if he had not been too harsh on his native land in them.

[80]

Word reached him in September that Grant Richards could not now publish *Dubliners*, despite all the deletions and revisions, and despite the contract he had signed to do so six months before. To mollify Joyce, Richards offered to consider his novel, then perhaps do the stories later. Joyce was furious. He went to the British consul in Rome to get the name of a lawyer who might represent him in a breach of contract suit. The lawyer he got did not think much of Joyce's case, however. He advised the writer to offer further revisons, and Joyce did, but still Richards rejected the book. Nor could the Society of Authors do anything. Finally, in November he gave up and submitted his book to another publisher, John Long.

Now he began to work on another story for *Dubliners*, one which would modify the harshness of the collection by showing Irish society in a more sympathetic light. This story, "The Dead," had just begun to take shape when Joyce learned in February 1907 that John Long was rejecting the book. "My mouth is full of decayed teeth and my soul of decayed ambitions," he wrote his brother.[4]

There was one bright spot in the writer's career that winter, for in January 1907 Elkin Mathews, whom Arthur Symons had contacted in the writer's behalf, agreed to publish *Chamber Music*. The book of poems—Joyce's first book publication—appeared in May. "The publication of *Chamber Music* brought no financial change. Royalties were not to be paid until three hundred copies were sold, and by July 24, 1908, only 127 out of 507 were gone; by 1913 the number was still less than 200."[5]

Joyce submitted *Dubliners* to Mathews, who rejected it in November 1907, then offered to show it to Hutchinson and Company. They didn't want to see it. Alston Rivers rejected it in February 1908, and Edward Arnold in July. There was, however, a Dublin publishing firm which was interested in the book, Maunsel & Company. Joyce was reluctant to send it there for several reasons. He believed a London publisher would be able to give his book a wider audience, one less pro-

[81]

vincial and thus more sympathetic to this portrait of Dublin's "paralysis" of spirit. Also, the managing director of this firm was George Roberts, a man to whom Joyce owed money and not one to whom he wished to give the power of publishing his work. Rather than do so, Joyce put the book aside for a year.

During this time, Joyce came into contact with a writer whose work had been so neglected as to convince him to give up writing altogether. Ten years earlier, Ettore Schmitz had written and published two novels which had gone completely unnoticed, perhaps because they were published at his own expense, instead of through a regular publisher. "There is no unaninimity so perfect as the unanimity of silence," he told Joyce. The experience destroyed Schmitz's confidence in his own talent, and he had written nothing for a decade. "I could come to only one conclusion, that I was not a writer." Joyce read Schmitz's books and was greatly impressed. "Do you know that you are a neglected writer?" he told Schmitz. Greatly encouraged by Joyce's confidence in him, Schmitz began to write again, using his earlier pen name, Italo Svevo, and eventually gained the respect of literary critics.

Schmitz's experience no doubt impressed Joyce with the importance of continuing to write despite the treatment one's work received from publishers and from the public. In addition, Schmitz read Joyce's fiction and expressed his enthusiasm. Encouraged, Joyce sent *Dubliners* to Maunsel & Co. in April 1909, and went back to work on his autobiographical novel with renewed energy.

That summer Joyce decided to return to Dublin. He had left with a great deal of resentment toward those in the literary establishment who had slighted him in 1904 and 1905. By sending *Dubliners* to Maunsel & Co., Joyce signalled a softening in his attitude toward his homeland. He returned to Dublin with his four-year-old son to come to terms with Maunsel & Co. and to look into the possibility of a professorship at the Royal University, where he had been graduated.

First he met with George Roberts, then with Roberts and

Joseph Hone, who was financing some of the firm's operations. The meetings resulted in a contract on August 19: Maunsel would publish *Dubliners* on better terms than those Grant Richards had agreed to, then withdrawn. Joyce was beginning to feel accepted in his homeland. The teaching post did not materialize, however, and he returned to Nora in Trieste.

After Joyce left Dublin, troubles began to arise with *Dubliners*. According to Ellmann, "As word of the book's contents leaked out, the subtle pressures that exist in Dublin . . . were slowly brought to bear."[6] Unlike Grant Richards, however, the Irish firm seemed more concerned about Joyce's negative portrayal of his homeland than about any possible allusions to sexuality.

Roberts wrote, expressing concern about a passage from "Ivy Day in the Committee Room," in which Queen Victoria was referred to as King Edward's "bloody old bitch of a mother." When Joyce deleted "bloody old bitch" and substituted "old mother," Roberts said this change was not effective and asked him to rewrite the whole passage. Joyce refused. After all, he pointed out, Grant Richards in London hadn't even objected to this particular passage. Roberts didn't reply. Joyce suspected Roberts of trying to get out of his contract, and he threatened to take legal action and to publicize the matter in the Irish press. Roberts did nothing but sit on the manuscript and delay publication month after month.

Finally, in December 1910, Roberts wrote that he was sending proofs of "Ivy Day" and planned to publish on January 20. Then he had second thoughts. Publication was delayed, and in February Roberts asked Joyce to remove all references to the English king. Joyce consulted a Dublin solicitor and was told he should do what his publisher asked, since legal action would be risky and expensive.

This new round of troubles so embittered and discouraged the writer he was unable to work on his novel, which he had begun to rewrite under the new title *A Portrait of the Artist as A Young Man*. In August, Joyce hit upon a desperate plan. He

[83]

wrote His Majesty George V for help, enclosing a proof of the disputed passage and asking if it should be withheld from publication as "offensive to the memory of his father."[7] King George's secretary replied that His Majesty could not express an opinion in such a case.

Finally, on August 17, Joyce gave in completely and granted permission to Maunsel to publish the story "with what changes and deletions they may please to make,"[8] but he did so only after making a public protest. He wrote up a history of his troubles with publishers over *Dubliners* and sent it as an open letter to the Irish press. "May I ask you to print this letter which throws some light on the present conditions of authorship in England and Ireland?" He included the disputed passage about King Edward and said of Maunsel & Co., "Their attitude as an Irish publishing firm may be judged by Irish public opinion."

Joyce's letter was published in Trieste newspapers, *Sinn Fein* in Dublin, and the *Northern Whig* in Belfast. Also, Joyce sent copies of his open letter to Roberts and Grant Richards. Roberts did not respond, but Richards wrote to thank Joyce for his copy and added, "I don't think you quite understand a publisher's difficulties."[9]

Nora was now planning a trip home to Galway, and Joyce sent her via Dublin so she could meet with Roberts in person. Roberts refused to discuss the matter with her, saying he was too busy. Joyce followed her, and confronted Roberts himself. The result of the meeting was not encouraging, as Joyce wrote his brother Stanislaus on July 17, 1912:

> The new proposals are: either the passage in *Ivy Day* and a passage in *An Encounter* are to be deleted, replaced by asterisks and with a note of preface by me or the book is to be bought over by me, bound and printed, on my note of hand for the cost amount and issued by Simpkin Marshall of London who will spread it on commission, the profits being mine.[10]

The idea of publishing the book himself was not new to Joyce, for Stanislaus had often urged his brother to take such a

[84]

course. The writer could have saved himself much frustration by publishing *Dubliners* himself in 1912, but he apparently did not feel up to the task, or perhaps he felt a self-published volume would not gain the attention this book deserved.

Roberts continued to sit on the manuscript, not publishing but not refusing to publish. Joyce wrote the publishers, begging them to live up to their contract. Roberts answered coldly:

> He [Roberts] pretended to have slowly come to realize the book's implications were anti-Irish and therefore out of keeping with his aims as an Irish publisher. . . . He may also have had a private reason: one Dublin rumor of the time said he had promised his fiancee, out of regard for her honor, that he would not publish a questionable book. Joseph Hone suggested later, though Roberts denied it, that the Vigilance Committee . . . had exerted pressure on the firm.[11]

Still Roberts did not return the manuscript or tell Joyce he was not going to publish it. One reason was perhaps the money he had already invested in printing it, but this was a relatively small sum. It seemed instead that the publisher was actually enjoying these "negotiations" and prolonging them on purpose. Each new concession on Joyce's part reminded Roberts that he had almost total control over the proud young man's career; this power gave him such satisfaction, apparently, that he hated to relinquish it simply by returning the manuscript:

> He [Roberts] was by nature incapable of being altogether straightforward in dealing with any of his writers. He specialized in adding new conditions after the first had been accepted. . . . [George Russell] gives an account of Roberts's dealing with Katherine Tynan which sound extremely like his dealings with Joyce.[12]

At last Roberts suggested that Joyce try to get Grant Richards to take over the sheets of *Dubliners*. This sugges-

[85]

tion, hinting as it did that Roberts, like Richards, was going to back out of his contract, moved Joyce to call his solicitor. He also went to Roberts's office in person and confronted him in a heated meeting. Roberts only became more demanding. Joyce would now have to omit "An Encounter" entirely, delete more passages from "Ivy Day," and substitute fictitious names for the public houses in "Counterparts" and other stories. Joyce agreed to the changes, on the condition that Roberts promise to publish the book before October 1912. Roberts hedged. He would consult his solicitor.

In the meantime, Joyce kept up the pressure. He asked his own solicitor, George Lidwell, to write an opinion that the book was not libelous, hoping this would leave Roberts with no excuse for not publishing it. When Lidwell wrote the opinion, the publisher read it, then told Joyce that the letter would have to be addressed to him to carry any weight. Lidwell refused to write an opinion addressed to Roberts on the grounds that the publisher was not his client. Joyce reported the meeting in a letter to his wife on August 21:

> I went to Roberts and told him this. Roberts said that Lidwell should write him a long letter on the whole case saying what I could do, as he could not endanger the firm. I said I would sign an agreement to pay him . . . sixty pounds the cost of a 1st edition if the book was seized by the Crown. He said that was no use and asked could I get two securities for . . . a thousand pounds each . . . to indemnify the firm for its loss over publishing my book. I said no person admired me so much as that and in any case it could never be proved that the loss (if any) of the firm was due to my book. He said then that he would act on his solicitor's advice and not publish the book.[13]

Faced with this refusal, Joyce came to a painful decision. He would allow Roberts to omit "An Encounter" entirely on four conditions:

> I). That the following note be placed by me before the first story: *This book in this form is incomplete. The scheme of the book as framed by me includes a story entitled An Encounter which stands*

[86]

between the first and second story in this edition. J.J.
II). That no further changes be asked of me.
III). That I reserve the right to publish the said story elsewhere before or after the publication of the book by your firm.
IV). That the book be published by you not later than the 6th of October 1912.[14]

Roberts agreed only to consult with his solicitors about this new offer. But he did talk with Joyce about binding and other publishing details, and expressed interest in the still-unfinished novel, so that Joyce went away feeling hopeful. That night he fantasized about the book, how it would look, and the reviews it would receive, but the next morning these hopes and dreams were dashed.

Roberts's solicitors advised him that he should not publish the book. He had agreed to meet with Joyce at noon, but when the writer went to the publisher's office, he found only a letter saying that the "publication of the book by Maunsel & Co. is out of the question. . . ." The lawyer had advised Roberts

that in practically every case where any going concern (e.g. public house, restaurant, railway company or other existing person, firm or body corporate with vested interests) is mentioned by actual name, then, having regard to the events described as taking place in connection with them, there is no doubt that actions in libel would lie. . . . They advised me that the author has committed a breach of the guarantee contained in Clause 11 of the agreement by offering for publication a book which, as he should know, is clearly libellous; and they recommend, if I so desire, that Maunsel & Co. proceed against you in order to recover all costs, charges and expenses for time, labour and materials expended on the book. . . . I must ask you to make a substantial offer towards covering our loss.

Failing your doing that, I shall have, most reluctantly, to put the matter in other hands.[15]

Joyce was devastated, and furious. He wrote Nora: "For a long time today I thought of spending the last money I have on a revolver and using it on the scoundrels who have tortured my mind with false hopes for so many years. . . . Every-

[87]

thing seems to have melted away from me, money, hope and youth."[16] Instead of buying a revolver, Joyce offered to make more deletions and changes in the book. "I have consented to omit *Encounter,* delete and change passage in *Ivy Day,* change names of public houses in *Counterparts* . . . , change name of pawnbroker Terry Kelly to Mickey Grundy, change name of Sydney Parade in *Painful Case* to White Church! on the condition that book is published before October 6, 1912," Joyce wrote Stanislaus on August 26.[17]

But when Roberts demanded many more changes, Joyce balked. "I refused to destroy my book," he wrote Stanislaus.

> Roberts asked me then to give him 30 pounds for the sheets (which cost 57 pounds) and look for a publisher: and asked me to come in tomorrow. . . . I went then to Griffith [editor of *Sinn Fein*] who received me very kindly and remembered my letter. He says I am not the first person from whom he has heard this story. He says Roberts has been playing that game for years. He says the idea of Maunsel sueing me is simple bluff.[18]

As September became August, Joyce at last began to accept the fact that Roberts was not going to publish his book. He did get from the publisher a verbal agreement to distribute *Dubliners,* however, if Joyce would publish it himself; so he set about arranging to become a Dublin publisher, finding office space and choosing a name for his new firm. Roberts, despite his threats of a few days before, was now co-operative. He agreed to have his printer go ahead and run a thousand copies of the book, if Joyce would agree to pay the thirty pounds in printing costs and sign a document freeing Maunsel from all responsibility in the publication of the book.

Now, however, the printer began to raise objections. He had read the book during the past few days and found it very objectionable. He claimed to have been tricked by Maunsel & Co., that he had somehow set the entire thing in type without any idea of its contents. Now he didn't want his name connected with it, didn't want to deal with Joyce directly, and

[88]

would deliver the first 104 copies only through a series of mysterious carriers so that it could never be traced back to him. Joyce agreed.

Relieved to have the book published at last, he set about choosing the binding materials and designing a cover. The next day, however, Roberts informed him the printer had refused to deliver the printed sheets. Joyce went to the printer's and begged to be given the sheets, promising he would list himself as both printer and publisher. The printer refused. What, then, where they planning to do with his book, Joyce asked. Destroy it, the printer replied. Burn the printed sheets and break up the type. If they did, they could never recover the printing costs, Joyce warned. The printer didn't care; they had learned their lesson and would not be so easily fooled again.

Joyce had learned a lesson too. Taking the one surviving proof copy of *Dubliners*, he left Ireland, never to return. The bitterness he now felt toward his native land would affect everything he wrote from this point on, solidifying his determination to depict with "scrupulous meanness" her decayed spirit, and convincing him he must forge in his imagination "a conscience in the soul of this wretched race," as he had written Nora a few days before. "Even if Dublin rejected *Dubliners*, he would still be able to conquer Ireland, in the artist's traditional way, by setting up the criteria by which it must judge and be judged."[19]

A stop in London to offer the book to other publishers proved fruitless, and he returned to Trieste, where he did actually become his own publisher long enough to print up and distribute a broadside, "Gas from a Burner," in which he mocked the self-righteous attitude of Roberts and his printer.

At "home" in Trieste, Joyce began to look with renewed vigor for another publisher for *Dubliners*. He sent it off to Martin Secker in London and asked Yeats to intercede there in his behalf. Secker rejected the book. Joyce immediately wrote to Elkin Mathews, offering the "famous book Dub-

[89]

liners" for publication, offering to have it printed in Trieste or in London at his own expense (paid in advance, if necessary) if Mathews would distribute it. "I intend to write a preface for it, narrating its eight years of adventure and final burning—a unique story out of which a publisher could make a great advertisement for it."[20] Joyce even offered to buy the first 110 copies. Despite these generous terms, Mathews too rejected the book, saying it would not be "in harmony" with his usual publications.

Not until late 1913 did Joyce's luck begin to change. On November 23 Joyce wrote Grant Richards, updating him on the hapless publishing career of *Dubliners,* and offering it to him for publication, along with the preface. "As there are 100 orders ready for it in this city I am prepared, if need be, to contribute towards the expenses of publication—expenses which I presume will be lighter as the book will be set up from printed proofs."[21]

Richards answered by return mail that, yes, he would be interested in seeing *Dubliners* again. On January 26, 1914, Richards agreed, for the second time, to publish the book. The contract took Joyce up on his offer to help defray the costs of printing. In fact, the terms Richards offered made it certain the writer would underwrite the publication of his book, for he was to waive his royalties on the first 500 copies sold and agree to buy 120 copies himself at the trade price. Joyce of course agreed, and on June 15, 1914, *Dubliners* at last appeared.

It was printed on cream-white laid paper, hard-bound in red cloth with a green dustwrapper.[22] Of the 746 copies bound and printed, 120 went to Joyce and 117 went out as review copies. The remaining 509 were to be sold at a price of 3s.6d.

After all the fuss printers and publishers had made about the book's suggestiveness, after all the fears of libel suits and the Vigilance Committee, its publication was carried off without any legal difficulties whatever. Reviews were generally good, although most reviewers had reservations. The

[90]

Times Literary Supplement recommended the book "to the large class of readers to whom the drab makes an appeal, for it is admirably written." They felt Joyce's unusual narrative technique was only partly successful:

> Shunning the emphatic, Mr. Joyce is less concerned with the episode than with the mood it suggests. Perhaps for this reason he is more successful with his shorter stories. When he writes at greater length the issue seems trivial, and the connecting thread becomes so tenuous as to be scarcely perceptible.[23]

Other reviewers had much the same reaction to the book. According to Ellmann: "Most of them found the stories cynical or pointless or both. . . . Gerald Gould, in *New Statesman*, found in the stories evidence of the emergence of a man of genius, but perhaps of a sterile order."[24]

Dubliners did, however, gain the unqualified admiration of one influential critic. Ezra Pound, writing in the *Egoist*,[25] enthusiastically greeted Joyce's "freedom from sloppiness" and "clear hard prose":

> He presents his people swiftly and vividly, he does not sentimentalize over them, he does not weave convolutions. He is a realist. . . . He is not bound by the tiresome convention that any part of life, to be interesting, must be shaped into the conventional form of a "story."

Pound recognized that Joyce was more than simply another member of the Irish movement. "It is surprising that Mr. Joyce is Irish," he wrote. "One is so tired of the Irish or "Celtic" imagination . . . flopping about. Mr. Joyce does not flop about. He defines." Joyce's portrayal of Dublin was not provincial but universal, and Pound publicly "adopted" Joyce in the review, saying,

> Mr. Joyce's more rigorous selection of the presented detail marks him, I think, as belonging to my own generation, that is, to the "nineteen-tens," not to the decade between "the nineties" and today.

[91]

Joyce had first heard of Pound when the poet wrote him a letter on December 15, 1914. Pound had heard about Joyce's plight from Yeats, and had immediately empathized with his problems with publishers. He wrote Joyce that he was connected with two American and two British journals, and would be glad to read anything Joyce could send him. Joyce sent *Dubliners* to Pound, along with the first chapter of his still-unfinished novel, *A Portrait of the Artist as a Young Man*, which he finished revising under the stimulus of Pound's invitation. Pound read the novel chapter and was enthusiastic. He sent it off immediately to Harriet Weaver at the *Egoist*, thus putting Joyce in contact for the first time with the remarkable woman who would become his patroness and do so much to further his career.

Pound read *Dubliners*, too, liked it immediately, and sent three of the stories off to H. L. Mencken at the *Smart Set* in the United States. They were published there in May 1915, partly at the urging of publisher B. W. Huebsch, who would later publish the book.

During the years of uncertainty about the publication of *Dubliners*, Joyce had been unable to complete his first novel, which he had been writing in one form or another for ten years. When Pound sent *Portrait* to Weaver in January 1914, Joyce still had no publisher for *Dubliners*, but Weaver liked the first chapter of the novel and agreed to publish the entire book in serial form in the *Egoist*, beginning with the February 2, 1914, issue. Joyce found himself in the position of having to work to finish each chapter of his book in time for its publication deadline. As the book was being written, he sent it chapter by chapter to Ezra Pound, who read and sometimes even edited it, then sent it to the *Egoist*, where it was published in installments.

Suddenly, with the publications of both *Dubliners* and *Portrait* in 1914, Joyce had readers, critics, even enthusiasts; and his writing, which had almost dried up completely during the years of waiting for publication, now flowered. Joyce had even acquired an agent, J. B. Pinker, who had been told about the writer by H. G. Wells. Pinker took over negotiations for the publication of *Portrait* in book form. However, British publishers seemed unimpressed by the book's appearance in the *Egoist*, which after all had a very small reading audience. No commercial publisher was willing to take a chance on the book:

> Grant Richards rejected it on May 18, 1915, on the grounds that it was not possible to get hold of an intelligent audience in wartime. Pinker, beset by Joyce, offered the book in July to Martin Secker. ... When Secker turned it down, Pinker offered it to Duckworth, who held the manuscript for several months.[26]

During the long wait for Duckworth's decision, Harriet Weaver offered to set the *Egoist* up as a book publisher and bring out the book, if all else failed. "Of course this would be nothing like so satisfactory as if the book were brought out by a proper book-publisher in London with his regular machinery for advertisement etc," she wrote Joyce. The writer fired back an enthusiastic approval of the plan. "As for the advantages of a regular publisher I have not seen them till now," he said. "I have never received any money from either of my two publishers and I dislike the prospect of waiting another nine years for the same result."[27]

All else did indeed fail. Duckworth's reader, Edward Garnett, not understanding Joyce's innovative narrative, rejected *A Portrait* on the ground that it was "a little sordid," "too 'unconventional,'" and needed "going through carefully from start to finish" to get rid of excess verbiage and give the book some semblance of form. It was clear from the reader's report that Joyce's growing reputation as a literary genius had not reached the commercial publishing district of London, for Garnett wrote of Joyce as if he were a talented but inexperienced beginner. "The author shows us he has art, strength and originality, but this MS. wants time and trouble spent on it, to make it a more finished piece of work, to shape it more carefully as the product of the craftsmanship, mind and imagination of an artist."[28]

[93]

Pound was livid when he read the report. "Hark to his [the reader's] puling squeek. Too 'unconventional,'" he fumed.

> It is with difficulty that I manage to write to you at all on being presented with the Duckworthian muck, the dungminded dung-bearded, penny a line, please the mediocre-at-all-cost doctrine. You English will get no prose till you exterminate this breed.[29]

Next, Pinker submitted the book to T. Werner Laurie, who rejected it, saying it was "a very clever book but too naughty for me to publish,"[30] then to Duckworths again, whom Jonathan Cape had urged to reconsider it. This time they offered to publish the book if Joyce would completely rewrite it along the lines suggested in Garnett's report. Pound's response to that was, "as for altering Joyce to suit Duckworth's reader—it would [be] like trying to fit the Venus de Milo into a piss-pot."[31]

At last, at Joyce's insistence, the manuscript was sent to Weaver, who immediately set about having it printed. She was soon dismayed to discover that although the book had already been printed and published in the *Egoist*, no printer would now take a chance on setting it in type again. By March 25, 1916, a succession of seven printers, alarmed by the recent prosecution of D. H. Lawrence's *The Rainbow*, refused to print the text as it stood. At this point Pound came up with the idea of leaving big holes in the text where questionable passages were deleted, "then the excisions can be manifolded ... by typewriter on good paper, and if necessary I will paste them in myself."[32]

Finally, in July 1916, a deal was struck with a new American publisher, B. W. Huebsch, to bring out the book in New York, with Weaver's purchase of 750 copies for English publication subsidizing his costs. Huebsch, the first of the "daring young Jews" to break into the puritan stronghold of American publishing, was to make his reputation by being the earliest on this side of the Atlantic to publish the controversial genius, James Joyce. In December 1916 he brought out not only *Portrait*, but also *Dubliners*, using sheets imported from Grant

[94]

Richards. Weaver's 750-copy edition of *Portrait* appeared in England on February 12, 1917.

Through the efforts of both Pound and Weaver, *Portrait* was widely reviewed not only in the United States and England, but also in Ireland. Many of the reviews were favorable, but many others denounced the book as offensive. Of a selection of the reviews published in the *Egoist* of June 1917, almost all were negative. The Irish papers accused Joyce of giving a distored picture of Irish life and ignoring the country's good features. It was, they agreed, far from the best example of fiction being written by an Irishman. These comments were typified by a statement attributed to the *Irish Book Lover* that, "No clean-minded person could possibly allow it to remain within reach of his wife, his sons or daughters."[33]

Huebsch and Weaver were much more generous than Richards with royalty payments, and also managed to sell more books. Huebsch's first edition of *Portrait* went into its second printing within four months of publication, and in August 1917 he paid Joyce an advance of fifty-four pounds on future royalties.

A decade of fruitless negotiations with commercial publishers had stymied Joyce's writing, but by subsidizing the publication of one book and placing the other with a small alternative press, he was now rejuvenated, and could go on to write his greatest work.

This lesson in artistic survival was not lost on Joyce. When it came time to find a publisher for his next book, *Ulysses*, he refused to wait around in hopes of finding a commercial publisher willing to take a chance on a controversial work. As soon as it became apparent that even the most forward of the new American and British publishers would not or could not bring out *Ulysses*, he found a bookseller to publish it for him. This choice of a publisher allowed Joyce to tinker with the text during the publication process, a freedom he used to alter *Ulysses* substantially, and to experiment with the new forms he would later develop in *Finnegans Wake*.

[95]

The idea for *Ulysses* had first occurred in 1907 when Joyce was adding stories to the *Dubliners* collection and planned one about a Jewish man whose wife had been unfaithful. The story had not developed as planned, and Joyce dropped it from the book, but the idea grew steadily in his mind until he determined to write his next novel around it. The writing began in 1914 as *Portrait* was nearing completion, and went on steadily for the next eight years, right up until the book's publication in 1922.

By mid-1917 the early chapters of the new book were nearing completion, and Joyce began to think in terms of publication. Pound had written him a few months earlier to suggest that the book be published as a serial, as *Portrait* had been. The *Egoist* would surely do it in England, and in the United States Pound had found a new outlet in which to carry on the literary renaissance, a magazine called the *Little Review*, published by two women, the eccentric Margaret Anderson and her assistant Jane Heap.

Margaret Anderson had started the magazine in Chicago in 1914, and had since had to go to every extreme to keep the magazine going financially. For instance, she moved out of her rented room and lived in a tent on the shores of Lake Michigan to save expenses. She threw a party for subscribers and charged admission. When merchants wouldn't advertise she published "non-ads," little notices where ads might have been, telling her readers, "Mandel Brothers might have taken this page to feature their library furnishings, desk sets, and accessories," or, "Carson Pirie, Scott and Company ought to advertise something, though I don't know just what. The man I interviewed made such a face when I told him we were 'radical' that I haven't had the courage to go back and pester him for the desired full-page."[34]

Pound was attracted to Anderson's review by another such stunt, done not so much to save money as to express her disappointment with the lack of good writing to fill her pages. In the August 1916 issue she announced, "If there is only one really beautiful thing for the September number it shall go in

[96]

and the other pages will be left blank."[35] She made good on her threat; the September issue was made up of blank pages, the only printed matter being two pages of cartoons showing Margaret Anderson and Jane Heap on vacation. Pound immediately recognized a publisher with something like his own spunk and determination to foster real art.

Though he had been corresponding with Anderson for several years, Pound now wrote to her offering to solve her lack of good material by becoming her foreign editor. "I want a place where I and T. S. Eliot can appear once a month (or once an 'issue') and where Joyce can appear when he likes, and where Wyndham Lewis can appear if he comes back from the war," Pound wrote Anderson early in 1917.[36] Anderson was more than willing, and later would write, "When he [Pound] wrote suggesting that the *Little Review* employ his talents as a foreign editor we hailed the occasion."[37] They were even happier, no doubt, when Pound enlisted John Quinn to help out the magazine financially, because Anderson and Heap, who had just moved their magazine to New York, had literally been going without food to keep it afloat.

Pound began asking Joyce to contribute whatever writing he could to the *Little Review*, and suggested that he might serialize *Ulysses* there. Joyce answered on August 20, 1917, that he was prepared to consign *Ulysses* "serially from 1 January next, instalments of about 6000 words."[38] In December he sent Pound the first chapters, the *Telemachia*, and Pound, after reading them with appreciation, forwarded them to Margaret Anderson in New York. "He recommended [*Ulysses*] highly," Anderson later recounted,[39] "saying he had no idea if we would care to print it as it would probably involve us in difficulties with the censors." But Anderson read the material and was impressed. "This is the most beautiful thing we'll ever have, I cried. We'll print it if it's the last effort of our lives."[40]

The *Little Review* began to serialize *Ulysses* in March 1918, printing the first chapter, and continued regular publication in the face of official persecution and critical indifference:

We ran it month after month for three years and four times the issues containing it were burned by order of the United States Post Office, because of alleged obscenity.

. . . Besides, for many months—for years, to be exact—we had a minimum response from the world's intellectuals about the masterpiece. Almost nobody seemed to like it. A desultory appreciation came in from time to time—usually from the far west! New York was particularly cold. The *New York Times* was the worst. We could never insert a word of publicity about "Ulysses" in its literary columns. . . . The *Herald-Tribune* was almost as bad. Its literary section was directed at that time by Burton Rascoe. To excuse his utter negligence of "Ulysses" . . . he announced (two years later) that we published it incompletely, spasmodically, in a version unrelated to Joyce's original text.[41]

Joyce's book appeared regularly and faithfully in the *Little Review* until late 1920, when Anderson and Heap were finally hauled into court by the New York Society for the Suppression of Vice, fined, and ordered to stop. But despite snubs from the New York papers, the book did get occasional attention because of its serialization in the United States. On August 25, 1918, Joyce wrote Harriet Weaver, 'If you have occasion to write to my New York publisher [Huebsch] will you please thank him for the interesting controversial cuttings from American press about *Ulysses* and ask him to convey my thanks to Mr Hecht [Ben Hecht, Chicago poet and critic] for his article in defense of the book?"[42]

Meanwhile, the planned British serialization in the *Egoist* ran into difficulties in finding a printer. The *Egoist* had planned to begin with the first chapter ("Telemachus") in the March 1918 issue, but its regular printer, the Complete Press, got cold feet after setting it up and refused to print it, even with deletions. "In an attempt to break the deadlock, James Joyce persuaded a Paris firm, Georges Cres, to place their printer at her [Weaver's] disposal," but Weaver felt this arrangement would be impossible because of the distance between Paris and London.[43] Her next idea was to have the serial printed privately and to issue it as a supplement to the magazine, then later to issue it as an Egoist Press book.

[98]

T. S. Eliot, who was now Weaver's associate editor, suggested that Leonard and Virginia Woolf might set it up for him on their press. The Woolfs, who were in the midst of setting the type for their second publication, Katherine Mansfield's long story *Prelude*, were already realizing the limited capacity of their small hand press. When Weaver visited them in April 1918 with a "large brown paper parcel" containing the manuscript of the first chapters, they put it away in the top drawer of a cabinet for a month, then had the servants send it back. From their country house in Sussex, Virginia Woolf wrote Weaver a kind letter of rejection:

> We have read the chapters of Mr Joyce's novel with great interest, and we wish that we could offer to print it. But the length is an insuperable difficulty to us at present. We can get no one to help us, and at our present rate of progress a book of 300 pages would take at least two years to produce—which is, of course, out of the question for you or Mr Joyce.
>
> We very much regret this as it is our aim to produce writing of merit which the ordinary publisher refuses. Our equipment is so small, however, that we are finding it difficult to bring out a book of less than 100 pages.[44]

Woolf, however, had other reasons for her rejection, as she had already written Lytton Strachey on April 23:

> We've been asked to print Mr Joyce's new novel, every printer in London and most in the provinces having refused. First there's a dog that p's—then there's a man that forths, and one can be monotonous even on that subject—moreover, I don't believe that his method, which is highly developed, means much more than cutting out the explanations and putting in the thoughts between dashes. So I don't think we shall do it.[45]

After submitting the manuscript to a printer in Southport who refused it, Weaver gave up entirely on the idea of the supplement and decided she would simply publish in the *Egoist* whatever chapters she could get set in type. She took the manuscript back to the magazine's regular printer, the

[99]

Complete Press, and got the printer to agree to set up the second and third episodes. "Nestor" (the second chapter) appeared in the January-February 1919 *Egoist*, and "Proteus" (the third chapter), slightly expurgated, appeared in the *Egoist* for March-April 1919. Then the Complete Press resigned as the magazine's printer.

On July 6, 1919, Weaver wrote to Joyce:

> I have since made arrangements with another firm and they are bringing out the next number this week. Half of the sixth episode will appear in it; the other half in the following number. After that the paper is probably to be suspended for a time, . . . partly in order to develop our book publishing venture. I remember mentioning this new firm [the Pelican Press] in a previous letter: the manager, a Roman Catholic Irishman, had been much interested in your first novel. He has now seen the first ten chapters of *Ulysses* and so far as he can judge from these will be willing to print the complete text.[46]

In the waning months of the *Egoist*, two more episodes appeared, "Hades" (the sixth), and "Wandering Rocks" (the tenth). In the final *Egoist*, December 1919, Weaver announced that there would be "no issues of The Egoist in journalistic form in 1920." She also editorialized against the British laws which gave a "printing-works foreman" power to deny existence to the work of a literary craftsman through prior censorship. And with that the *Egoist* folded, after having done more in its few years of publication to foster the development of English-language literature than perhaps all the commercial magazines of its day put together.

Early in 1920, Joyce had his agent Pinker draw up a publication contract for the book and send it to Weaver. The contract provided for "a royalty of 25 per cent, an advance of 25 pounds and publication at 6 s. unless otherwise agreed. Harriet signed it, though she added a note of warning . . . about the price at which the book might have to be published."[47]

In mid-1920, Joyce moved with his family to Paris, where he would live for the next twenty years. Ezra Pound had con-

[100]

vinced Joyce he would be better able to arrange for the publication of *Ulysses* if he were to join Pound and other English and American writers in Paris, which was becoming an important center for the literary avant-garde. One Pound friend, the American poet John Rodker, was living there, after having set up as a book publisher and printing Eliot's *Ara Vos Prec*. When he learned of the difficulties *Ulysses* had been running into, Rodker suggested having it printed in France and published under his Ovid Press imprint. All that was needed was for the Egoist Press to finance his scheme.

Rodker's proposal would be worth considering only if all other avenues of getting the book printed were closed to Weaver. From Paris, Joyce wrote to ask her if the printer who had done the last installments of the *Egoist* would still be willing to print the complete book without asking for changes. Harriet went to this printer but he now firmly refused to print the controversial book. Weaver, after years of trying printer after printer to no avail, was now convinced it would be useless to try another shop. Then, Rodker backed out of publishing *Ulysses*, no doubt because he knew the book would prove too long to be printed on his hand press.

At the same time, however, Pound felt sure he could get it printed in the United States, if not actually published there in book form. Huebsch had expressed an interest in the book not once but many times during the years since he had published *Dubliners, Portrait, Exiles,* and *Chamber Music.* The Paris agent for Boni & Liveright, Leon Fleischman, had also expressed an interest in publishing the book in the U.S. With the prosecution of the *Little Review,* however, prospects for a regular trade edition became doubtful. In December 1920, John Quinn suggested to Huebsch that the American edition be privately printed and limited to 1,500 copies, of which half would be sold in Europe.

Huebsch waited to see how the obscenity trial of the *Little Review* turned out before he made his decision. Anderson and Heap went to court on February 14, 1921, with John Quinn as their lawyer. Scofield Thayer, Philip Moeller of the

[101]

Theatre Guild, and John Cowper Powys testified for the defense. Thayer didn't help the defense any when he admitted under cross-examination that he wouldn't have published *Ulysses* in the *Dial* for fear of prosecution. At one point, according to Anderson,[48] one of the judges refused to allow a passage from the book to be read in the lady's presence. "But she is the publisher, said John Quinn smiling."

The *Little Review* lost, and Anderson and Heap were fined $100 for publishing obscenity. On Quinn's advice they promised to publish no more of *Ulysses,* and so avoided a jail sentence, something Anderson later regretted:

> It is always a mistake to allow the persuasions of your friends or your lawyer to keep you out of jail. . . . I might have circulated some intelligent propaganda about "Ulysses" from my cell.[49]

With the suppression of *Ulysses* in February 1921, all hopes of having it published in book form in the U.S. ended. On March 24, 1921, Huebsch wrote Quinn that he could not publish *Ulysses,* even in the contemplated private edition, without alterations. On learning this, Joyce cabled Quinn to withdraw the manuscript from Huebsch immediately. He was determined not to give in to such demands from publishers after his disastrous experience with *Dubliners.*

Horace Liveright was willing to take a chance on a private edition, provided he be given first right of refusal to Joyce's next three novels. Quinn disliked such agreements and had repeatedly castigated Joyce for so binding himself to Grant Richards in the *Dubliners* contract (as if the writer had had a choice!). For this reason, Quinn hesitated to accept the Liveright offer, and while he was hesitating, received two more episodes from Joyce. A quick reading of "Circe" and "Eumaeus," in which Stephen and Bloom visit a brothel and then stumble drunkenly home, convinced Quinn he would be wasting time to try to make a better deal with Liveright. The book would not be published without the certainty of prosecution and conviction, he admitted to Liveright as he turned down the offer.

[102]

The loss of any possible American publication was a fatal blow to Joyce's hopes, for it also killed Weaver's plans to import the sheets for a British edition. Joyce, absolutely devastated, went to share the bad news with a friend at a little bookshop in the Left Bank neighborhood where he was living, a shop specializing in English-language books, called Shakespeare and Company. The shop had been opened the year before by an American, Sylvia Beach. The daughter of a Princeton clergyman, she had come to Paris to study literature. She and Joyce had met at a party not long after Joyce's arrival in Paris, and Joyce had become a frequent visitor at Shakespeare and Company.

Beach's friendship with Joyce and her respect for his work were perhaps in part due to what she had heard from Valéry Larbaud. Larbaud was an influential man of letters in Paris, a member of the board of editors for the *Nouvelle Review Français*, a committeeman of the Prix Goncourt, and a member of the judging board for awarding the Legion of Honor. According to Joyce scholar Richard Sullivan, Larbaud

> had a keen sense for recognizing what Pound would call "permanent books," and he considered his position as a mover in literary affairs as equally important with his own creative work. Moreover, he was an astute social politician.[50]

Larbaud had read Joyce's *Ulysses* excerpts in the *Little Review* early in 1921 and was so impressed by what he read that he was unable to write or sleep, and had written to Sylvia Beach expressing his enthusiasm. Predisposed by Larbaud's enthusiasm to take Joyce and his work seriously, Beach now listened with sympathy as the writer told her the bad news about his beleaguered book:

> In a tone of complete discouragement he said, "My book will never come out now." . . .
> It occurred to me that something might be done, and I asked: "Would you let Shakespeare and Company have the honor of bringing out your *Ulysses?*"

[103]

He accepted my offer immediately and joyfully. I thought it rash of him to entrust his great *Ulysses* to such a funny little publisher.[51]

Beach immediately consulted her good friend and fellow bookshop proprietress Adrienne Monnier about the plan, and Monnier "thoroughly approved." She had done some publishing herself and recommended Beach take the project to her printer, Maurice Darantière, in the nearby town of Dijon:

> Darantière was much interested in what I told him about the banning of *Ulysses* in the English-speaking countries. I announced my intention of bringing out this work in France, and asked him if he would print it. At the same time I . . . warned him that there could be no question of paying for the printing till the money from the subscriptions came in—if it did come in. . . . M. Darantière agreed to take on the printing of *Ulysses* on these terms. Very . . . sporting of him, I must say![52]

On April 10, 1981, Joyce wrote Weaver with the good news:

> The proposal is to publish here in October an edition (complete) of the book so made up:
>
> | | |
> |---|---:|
> | 100 copies on Holland handmade paper (signed) | at 350 frs |
> | 150 copies on verge d'arches | at 250 frs |
> | 750 copies on linen | at 150 frs |
>
> that is, 1000 copies with 20 copies extra for libraries and press. A prospectus will be sent out next week inviting subscriptions. There are many already in advance with shops here, I am told. They offer me 66% of the net profit.[53]

Joyce also wrote, "This does not cover the English edition but I think it would be to your advantage if that were amalgamated with the Paris one." Weaver was unsure what he meant by "amalgamated," but wrote back immediately for a clarification, offering to import the sheets for an Egoist edition after Beach's limited edition was sold out. Weaver also drew up a contract which she sent off to Paris. The terms she offered were even more generous than those Beach had given

[104]

Joyce. He would receive 25 percent royalties on the English edition until expenses had been covered, when he would receive 90 percent of the profits. In the meantime, she offered an advance of two hundred pounds. Joyce telegraphed his acceptance of her offer immediately, and Beach agreed to have the printer keep up the type for the Egoist edition.

Beach quickly put together a four-page "prospectus" or advertisement for the upcoming book. In what has been called a "masterpiece of promotional construction," Beach played up the "themes of avant-garde and modern art which could be evoked in the book and to which the Parisian literary public was enthusiastically responsive."[54] She included not only an announcement of the book and an order form, but also a picture of Joyce looking very much the avant-garde artist, and a page of excerpts from reviews of the *Little Review* serial version of *Ulysses*, which read "like a collection of slogans promoting avant-garde and experimental art."[55]

Beach mailed the prospectus to several hundred people, names supplied by Larbaud, André Gide, Pound, and Sherwood Anderson. Weaver also mailed out hundreds of copies of the prospectus to *Egoist* subscribers and Irish and American bookshops, while "in Paris, copies were posted in strategic locations, and Pound and Robert McAlmon were delegated to canvass on foot."[56]

Meanwhile, Joyce sent typescripts of the first chapters out to Darantière. He had been having the novel typed chapter by chapter as he wrote it, both for the serializations and because he was selling the manuscripts to John Quinn. Troubles with his typists plagued him, however. One lady was well into the typing of "Circe" when her husband chanced to read the page she was typing from and, scandalized, he threw the rest of the chapter into the fire. Joyce was forced to rewrite the burned pages and to find another typist.

He was writing the first drafts of the last two chapters when the first set of galley proofs arrived from Darantière on June 10, 1921. For the next three months he pored over the galleys, not just correcting, but revising them. According to Ellmann:

[105]

With Joyce the reading of proof was a creative act; he insisted on five sets, and made innumerable changes, almost always additions, in the text, complicating the interior monologue with more and more interconnecting details. Darantière's characteristic gesture, throwing up his hands in despair, became almost constant when the type had to be recast time after time.[57]

Beach gave the printer orders to send Joyce "all the proofs he wanted, and he was insatiable."

Every proof was covered with additional text. . . . They were all adorned with the Joycean rockets and myriads of stars guiding the printers to words and phrases all along the margins. Joyce told me he had written a third of *Ulysses* on the proofs.

M. Darantière warned me that I was going to have a lot of extra expense with these proofs. He suggested that I call Joyce's attention to the danger of going beyond my depth; perhaps his appetite for proofs might be curbed.[58]

Beach, however, refused to put such a damper on Joyce's creative genius; and so Joyce kept elaborating on the page proofs, getting new proofs of the revisions, revising the revisions, and so on, up until the "last minute" before the book went to press early in 1922.

The changes became progressively more extensive as Joyce went through the proofs. The *Telemachia* received relatively few minor alterations (ten or fewer on the average page), but by "Aoelus" (the seventh chapter), Joyce was beginning to include many new ideas which occurred to him for the first time as he was reading the printed text. Harry Levin, who analyzed some of the proof alterations in his critical introduction to *James Joyce's Ulysses: A Facsimile of the Manuscript*, stated:

Despite his failing eyesight, he cherished a Mallarméan feeling for the appearance of type upon a page. Those headlines which intersperse the chapter located in a newspaper office were written afterward [after the mansucript had been set in type], and so were the opening paragraphs, as if in conformity with the journalistic procedures they illustrate. Moreover, Joyce transposed italics to

[106]

roman capitals, and experimented with the phrasing [of the headlines] from proof to proof.[59]

The climactic chapter of *Ulysses* was changed substantially on the proofs, to become "what it is by intensive reworking," according to Levin.[60] The importance of the alterations is perhaps most clearly shown in what Levin calls "the culminating epiphany, Bloom's vision, as he leans down over the prostrate Stephen, of his lost son Rudy":

> Here the manuscript contains the bare core of the human situation, to which it adds one bathetic detail, the white lambkin. The rich development came at a late stage in the proofs: the fragments of the Masonic oath with which Bloom swears himself to secrecy, the sentimentalized lineaments of the boy that might have been had he lived to eleven instead of dying in infancy. And though the manuscript tells us that Rudy is reading, it is not until the proof that he "reads from right to left," apprising this wonderstruck father that the book he reads is in Hebrew.[61]

By the time he got to the last chapters, Joyce was clearly thinking of the original text as a bare outline upon which he would elaborate in set after set of proofs. As Clive Driver reports in his bibliographical preface to *James Joyce's Ulysses: A Facsimile of the Manuscript*:

> At this time Joyce made a slight alteration in his normal working procedure. With 'Circe' the printer had caught up to what Joyce had ready in typescript. He then began to send the printer typescripts of segments of the last episodes as they were being written, and used the galley proofs to an even greater extent for addition and revision.[62]

Such additions would not have been possible had Joyce's book been published by Huebsch or Liveright. The standard commercial publishing contract allows the author a limited number of changes in the text. Usually the author is required to pay the cost of reprinting for any author's alterations beyond the few allowed. Under such an arrangement, costs to

[107]

Joyce would have quickly become prohibitive, so that he simply could not have made the extensive changes he did. Yet these changes made *Ulysses* a far more effective book than it could have been without them. Joseph Prescott, in *Exploring James Joyce*, shows how the additions on the proofs intensified the book by adding a myriad of new details, actions, spoken words, and clues. All of this had the effect of enhancing Joyce's characterizations and making his picture of Dublin more realistic.

Levin shows how the alterations also helped to make the book a more unified narrative. He writes, "All of them [the chapters] are meaningfully extended here and there, with new sidelights and unexpected linkages, as among funeral guests in 'Hades' or the assortment of pedestrianism in 'Wandering Rocks.'"[63] Such "trains of thematic association help to unify the heterogeneous subject matter after it has been set down and put together."[64]

In addition to making *Ulysses* a better work the process of rewriting the book in proof led Joyce further and further toward the highly experimental writing that would characterize *Finnegans Wake*. The freedom to revise at will encouraged the author to give his mind free play, and the result was the addition of more and more word games, puns, and coinages of the sort that make up the "nighttime" language of the *Wake*. In "Cyclops," for instance, he "enlarged the easy flow of pub talk by repeated extensions in the guise of epic catalogues or ecclesiastical litanies: a list of prominent clergymen, a roll call of the saints, a survey of the natural beauties of Ireland, a fashionable wedding of trees, a well-attended public execution."[65]

In "Circe," at the point where Corney Kellerher (who was earlier humming "toolaroom") departs, Joyce adds the coined words "assuralooms" and "reassuralooms" to the proof. In "Penelope," according to Levin, "his [added] pun on Beerbohn Tree and Trilby's 'barebum' adumbrates the sort of word play that would soon be engulfing him in *Finnegans Wake*."[66] Joyce's delight with this play is evident in the remark he

[108]

made to the translator of "Penelope": "I've put in so many enigmas and puzzles that it will keep the professors busy for centuries arguing over what I meant."[67]

As Joyce drafted and revised the book in the waning months of 1921, anticipation in literary circles grew. Word of the prosecution of the *Little Review* was being spread in Paris by visiting Americans, and Joyce himself was becoming known as something of a mystery figure, somebody one ought to know more about, who was completing an avant-garde masterpiece. According to Sullivan, "By fall anticipation of the event was strong enough for *Le Figaro* to begin carrying daily accounts of the state of affairs at Shakespeare and Company."[68]

Meanwhile, Beach made further plans to boost advance sales of the book, and she was helped by her friends Adrienne Monnier and Valéry Larbaud, both of whom had more experience than Beach in the ways of the Paris cultural world. Monnier was the proprietess of a French bookshop around the corner from Shakespeare and Company, called La Maison des Amis des Livres. Here, literary evenings featuring readings from new works were commonplace occurrences, and these events were well attended by Parisians interested in avant-garde literature. Perhaps it was the idea of Larbaud, "a seasoned veteran of the inevitable wars attending the introduction of new works to the inbred circles of the Parisian cultural world,"[69] to launch *Ulysses* with just such a *séance*, carefully staged so as to play upon the excitement already beginning to build around the book.

The event staged to launch *Ulysses* was a reading of excerpts from the book in a French translation, which took place December 7, 1921, at Adrienne Monner's bookshop. Larbaud himself prepared a lecture about Joyce and *Ulysses* to preceed the reading, and announcements of the event were published in the Paris newspapers. Only a hundred seats were available for the *séance*, but 250 people turned out, some enticed, no doubt, by advertised warnings that Joyce's prose might very well prove shocking.

[109]

Larbaud presented Joyce as a man of extraordinary notoriety who had been persecuted and suppressed as had Flaubert and Baudelaire. He called Joyce "the greatest currently living writer of English," and stressed the experimental narrative technique, which stationed readers inside the characters' minds. Through this technique, he added, "all the elements are constantly melting into each other, and the illusion of life, of the thing in the act, is complete: the whole is movement."[70] "This reading was a triumph for Joyce," Beach would recall later.[71] "It was a tribute that just at that most critical moment in his career meant much to him."

Even after the "publication" by reading in Monnier's bookshop, Joyce continued to revise the proofs, and might have continued doing so indefinitely, had not his own superstition intervened. He had always believed his birthday, February 2, to be a lucky day, and now had decided that his masterpiece must be published on that day. With this in mind, he forced himself to cut off his revisions at the end of January, making it possible for Darantière to get two copies printed, bound, and on the express train to Paris by Joyce's fortieth birthday, February 2, 1922.

Shortly after 7 A.M., Beach delivered one of the copies to Joyce's door, then took the other back to Shakespeare and Company to be displayed in the window. As Beach tells the story, "The news spread rapidly in Montparnasse and outlying districts, and the next day, before the bookshop was open, subscribers were lining up in front of it, pointing to *Ulysses*." Beach recalls she was forced to remove the book from the window until the bulk of the first edition began to arrive a few days later.[72]

The edition was special in many ways. It was bound in paper covers, for which Darantière had gone to much trouble mixing inks to achieve a nonstandard color, the blue of the Greek flag. There was a briefly worded apology for the many typographical errors, which were "unavoidable in the exceptional circumstances." As agreed, it was a limited edition of a thousand copies, the cheapest of which sold for 150 francs.

[110]

For a month no reviews of the book appeared, and Joyce feared rumors of a critical boycott against *Ulysses* were true. Then, on March 5, Sisley Huddleston praised the book in the *Observer*, calling Joyce a genius and calling the *monologue intérieur* "the vilest, according to ordinary standards, in all literature. And yet its very obscurity is somehow beautiful and wrings the soul to pity."[73] The next review was in the *Sporting Times*, which used a banner headline on its front page and a placard advertising "THE SCANDAL OF JAMES JOYCE'S ULYSSES." Inside the "reviewer" castigated Joyce as a man of talent who had ruled out "all the elementary decencies of life" to dwell "appreciatively on things that sniggering louts of schoolboys guffaw about."[74] Joyce was perversely delighted with this publicity and had his picture made with one of the "SCANDAL" placards.

In April, an outstanding review appeared which Joyce would later credit with breaking "the blockade" against *Ulysses*. Middleton Murry, an influential member of the Bloomsbury group in London, wrote an impassioned review in the *Nation*, calling, *Ulysses* "the work of an intensely serious man . . . indisputably the mind of an artist, abnormally sensitive to the secret individuality of emotions and things."[75]

This was followed late in May by a diatribe against "the most infamously obscene book" in all literature, in a *Sunday Express* review by its editor, James Douglas. The review, titled "Beauty—and the Beast," also denounced *Ulysses* as blasphemous. "Mr. Joyce is a rebel against the social morality of Europe," Douglas said, and he issued a call to fight "the devil's disciples" to a "clean finish."[76] In August, Arnold Bennett's review called parts of the book superb, and even magical.[77] And so it went. The more some critics denounced the book, the more the others felt called upon to praise it.

By the summer of 1922 the first edition was exhausted. Harriet Weaver bought Darantière's plates from Beach and paid Darantière to print from them, changing the title page to read, "Published for the Egoist Press, London, by John

Rodker, Paris." According to Weaver, who reported the tale in a letter years later,[78] Rodker took delivery on the books in Paris and mailed them to those who had ordered them from Weaver. The second edition of 2,000 copies, which appeared in October 1922, managed to go through the mails without trouble at first. Then in the last weeks of 1922, the U.S. Post Office began to confiscate whatever copies came into its hands, and a batch of 400 copies was burned in December 1922. To replace the burned books, Weaver had Darantière print 500 more in January 1923. Some 400 of these were confiscated by the English Customs authorities at Folkestone, after which the book was banned in England.

By this time *Ulysses* was famous throughout the English-speaking world. Visitors to Paris were constantly stopping in at Shakespeare and Company to buy as many copies as they could smuggle home to friends. Between January 1924 and May 1930 Beach issued eight more printings of the book. In July 1927, a self-proclaimed admirer of Joyce, Samuel Roth, pirated the Shakespeare and Company's ninth edition of *Ulysses*, printed it in New York, and sold it to booksellers for five dollars. The dealers, selling under the counter, could name their own price, and one copy went for fifteen dollars in 1930. According to Slocum, "Copies of this pirated ninth edition reached Paris and were imported into the United States as genuine copies."[79] As always in his wars with publishers, Joyce sought legal recourse and was told there was little he could do. A petition protesting the piracy was circulated and signed by scores of Joyce's friends and fellow writers.

It was 1934 before an authorized edition of *Ulysses* was published by a standard commercial house. Bennett Cerf of Random House, then a relative newcomer in the publishing trade, was encouraged to try to publish the controversial book when he heard "a very high-powered lawyer," Morris Ernst, say that he would like to wage a fight to legalize it. Cerf couldn't afford to hire Ernst, so he offered him a lifetime royalty on the book if he could get it declared admissible in the U.S. Ernst agreed, and Cerf approached Joyce, offering a

[112]

$1,500 advance. Joyce, of course, was "delighted with that."[80] He had had his agent, Pinker, seeking offers in the United States for the past year and had gotten only one from a reputable firm—Huebsch—and that only for an expurgated edition.

Sylvia Beach, however, was not so happy with Cerf's offer. Joyce had given her a contract in which he had assigned Shakespeare and Company all foreign rights, but now he was acting as if he were offering an unpublished manuscript for sale instead of a "book that had been published by somebody else for almost ten years."[81] Peeved at Joyce, at Pinker, and at the commercial publishers, all of whom seemed to be completely ignoring her, Beach demanded $25,000 for her rights to *Ulysses*. "This of course made him [Joyce] and everybody who saw it . . . burst out laughing," Beach admitted. Joyce sent a friend around to shame her for "standing in the way of Joyce's interests." Angry, Beach telephoned the writer and told him to go ahead with the American sale, for she would make no further claims on it.[82]

Before Cerf would risk actually publishing the book, however, he had to get it cleared legally. The best hope of doing this was to show that *Ulysses* was an important literary work, but current judicial rules would not allow reviews of the book to be used as evidence. Ernst and Cerf found a way to get around this:

> The only way we could do it was to make them [the reviews] part of the book, since anything that was in the book could be used as evidence. So we took one of the Paris paperbound editions of *Ulysses* and pasted in it every opinion we wanted to use—dozens of them in several languages. . . . Since that copy had to be the one that would be used as evidence, we got somebody to take it over to Europe and bring it back on the *Aquitania,* and had our agent down at the dock when it landed. It was one of the hottest days in the history of New York. . . . When our man arrived, the customs inspector started to stamp his suitcase without even looking at it. Our agent, frantic, said, "I insist you open that bag and search it." The inspector looked at him as though he were an absolute lunatic, and said, "It's too hot."

[113]

"I think there's something in there that's contraband," our agent said, "and I insist it be searched."

So, furiously, the fellow had to open the suitcase. And the agent said "Aha!" as he produced our copy of *Ulysses*. The customs man said, "Oh, for God's sake, everybody brings that in. We don't pay any attention to it." But the agent persisted, "I demand that you seize this book."[83]

After much argument the book was seized. Ernst delayed the case until Judge John M. Woolsey was sitting on the bench, because he knew Woolsey was a well-read man, the one justice most likely to be sympathetic to literary freedom. The trial was over in two days, and Random House was certain of victory even before Woolsey issued his decision in their favor. Describing *Ulysses* as a "sincere and serious attempt to devise a new literary method for the observation and description of mankind,"[84] Woolsey ruled it was not obscene and could be admitted to the United States.

After an appeal was denied, the Random House edition of *Ulysses* was published in January 1934, twelve years after the book's original publication. By this time it was not just famous; it was a fad—"one of those books that are considered smart to own," and the Random House edition sold extremely well. *Ulysses* seems to have launched Random House, rather than the other way around. Reports Cerf, "*Ulysses* was our first really important trade publication."[85]

The success of the American edition no doubt prompted John Lane to try to break the English ban on *Ulysses* which had existed since the second Egoist printing was confiscated in 1924. In October 1936, Lane published a limited edition of a thousand copies, and this was followed in 1937 by an ordinary trade edition. To a friend, Joyce remarked, "The war between England and me is over, and I am the conqueror."[86]

Joyce was also the conqueror in his lifelong struggle with commercial publishers. His early frontal assaults on them had failed, but he refused to be silenced. Instead, he found alternatives for the publication of his works: he subsidized Richards's printing of *Dubliners*, got Weaver to subsidize

[114]

Huebsch's printing of *Portrait*, and got his friendly book-seller to publish *Ulysses*. The freedom he gained through these alternatives more than repaid his earlier sufferings at the hands of commercial publishers. He was able to experiment, to develop *Ulysses* out of *Dubliners* and *Portrait*, and *Finnegans Wake* out of *Ulysses*. At the same time, his fame spread, not just because of his genius but also because he was persecuted by the "old fashioned" publishers, critics, and legal authorities. Through alternative publishing, Joyce became both a best-selling novelist and a hero of the avant-garde, and he gained a sympathetic audience, so that he was assured his works would receive the serious attention of scholars and critics for years to come.

ANAIS NIN

. . . the book as a work of art

4

In the heyday of literary modernism during the 1910s and 1920s, writers thought of themselves as artists. Their works—novels, short stories, and poems—were works of art in the same way a painting or sculpture is a work of art. This idea was accompanied by a great deal of experimentation with language and narrative structure, a concern with the individual psyche rather than with society, and it contributed to a "new" critical theory that sought to judge each literary text as a self-contained artifact.

During the 1930s, with the western world in the grip of economic depression and threatened by the growth of fascism, this "writer as artist" idea became quite unpopular. The most important aspect of a writer's work became not its aesthetic soundness, but its social or political stance, and the writer's artistic role was secondary to his role as social historian. Writers who refused to shoulder this burden were labeled "effete" by literary critics and fellow writers alike. To be considered "important," a novel had to present itself as a sociological document.

In the cafes where writers gathered, and in the journals where they published literary criticism, politics replaced aesthetics as the central topic of discussion. Writers took sides. Some went to Spain to fight on the side of the Republicans in the civil war, while others devoted their energies to writing and publishing propaganda supporting a cause.

Literary modernism, which flowered in the 1920s, was all but dead by the end of the thirties. Ezra Pound allied himself with the Fascist cause in Italy, where he moved from Paris; the Bloomsbury group was dismissed as elitist; Harriet Weaver joined the Communist party; the Nobel Prize for literature went to Pearl Buck, the author of a "proletarian" novel, *The Good Earth.* Writers who ignored the spirit of the times, who continued to write experimental poetry and fiction which had nothing to do with social issues or the plight of the common people, had trouble getting their work published in the thirties and forties.

Yet it was during this period that one experimental writer, Anaïs Nin, established her career. For years, though admired by a number of well-known writers, her work was repeatedly rejected by commercial publishers. At last Nin bought herself a little press and produced her own books. Though handprinted, Nin's books were not amateurish in appearance. Instead, they were works of art, their physical form so well suited to their artistic content that they won the attention of the established critics and helped reassert the idea that literature is, above all else, an art.

Anaïs Nin was born in Paris in 1903, the daughter of a French-Danish singer and a Spanish concert pianist. From childhood she began to think of herself as a writer, and to practice her craft by composing little stories and poems. In 1914, when she was eleven, her father deserted the family and she was taken with her mother and two brothers to live in New York. The experience was traumatic for Nin.

During the voyage to America, she began keeping a diary in which she would write faithfully until her death sixty-three years later. The diary, begun as a letter to her father in hopes of luring him back to the family, became for her a commitment to her own life. By writing it down, as she would a story, she made of the trauma a grand adventure; she broke out of her isolation, confronted and worked through her pain. "When a child is uprooted," she would write later, " it seeks to

[120]

make a center from which it cannot be uprooted."[1] The diary was this center, and later it would be in the diary that most of her fiction would find its roots.

Like Joyce, Nin was raised in a strict Roman Catholic environment, but unlike him she attended public rather than church-sponsored schools. Her formal schooling ended at the age of sixteen. She dropped out of Wadleigh High School in New York, where she had been class president, because the public high school experience had taken all the joy out of education for her. Nin continued her education independently, and much more successfully.

In 1920, at the age of seventeen, she married Hugh Guiler, a banker who later, under the name of Ian Hugo, would become a film maker and an illustrator of Nin's books. Rose Marie Cutting wrote in her introduction to *Anaïs Nin: A Reference Guide:*

> Aside from a few professional collaborations—her acting in his films, and his designs which illustrate her novels—little is known about their relationship. All mention of her husband has been omitted from the published portions of Nin's diary, and Nin refused to discuss her marriage or even name her husband in interviews.[2]

In the mid-1920s, Nin moved back to France with her mother, brothers, and apparently her husband. The family settled in Louveciennes, near Paris, where they bought a two-hundred-year-old house, and Nin set about restoring it. "I had a sense of preparation for a love to come," she wrote in her diary late in 1931, ". . . as if I must first create a marvelous world in which to . . . receive adequately this guest of honor."[3] This "marvelous world," however, soon came to feel more like a "beautiful prison, from which I can only escape by writing":

> Ordinary life does not interest me. I seek only the high moments. I am in accord with the surrealists, searching for the marvelous.
> I want to be a writer who reminds others that these moments

[121]

exist; I want to prove that there is infinite space, infinite meaning, infinite dimension.

But I am not always in what I call a state of grace. I have days of illuminations and fevers. I have days when the music in my head stops. Then I mend socks, prune trees, can fruits, polish furniture. But while I am doing this I feel I am not living.[4]

Nin made frequent trips to Paris and began to read the fiction of D. H. Lawrence. Lawrence "awakened me," she told her diary, and in gratitude and enthusiasm, she sat down and wrote what would be her first published book, *D. H. Lawrence: An Unprofessional Study*. Having dashed off this appreciation in sixteen days, Nin took it "hot out of the oven" to a small Left Bank publisher in Paris, Edward Titus.

She chose Titus, perhaps, because he had published Lawrence's *Lady Chatterley's Lover* two years before, and was also publisher of the literary magazine which had been hospitable to new writers, *This Quarter*. These ventures of Titus into the literary avant-garde were not profitable enough to be self-supporting, and were subsidized by his wife, Helena Rubenstein, who had made a fortune with her line of cosmetics in the 1920s.

D. H. Lawrence had come to Titus with his *Lady Chatterley* after having had the work printed at his own expense in Florence, only to find it was immediately pirated in both the United States and Canada. Titus was happy to publish the book, and agreed to split the profits evenly with Lawrence if the writer would share the production costs. He did not, however, give *Lady Chatterley* his Black Manikin imprint, but marked the title page simply "Privately Printed 1929." Still, Titus gained prestige as Lawrence's publisher, and was pleased to put the Black Manikin imprint upon Nin's essay about Lawrence and his work.

Although she was an experienced writer, having kept her diary almost daily for the past seventeen years, Nin was a novice at getting her work published. "It will not be published and out by tomorrow, which is what a writer would like when the book is hot out of the oven, when it is alive

[122]

within one's self," she complained. "He gave it to his assistant to revise."[5]

Even though it was "delayed," however, this publication changed Nin's life. She had always kept the contents of her diary secret and been hesitant to show any of her writing to anyone. The process of publishing brought her into contact with the Montparnasse literary community, that aggregate of writers, intellectuals and hangers-on who had gathered on the Left Bank to wine, dine, and carry on a modern literary renaissance together. Added to the French artists and writers were many expatriates from England and the United States who had come to live and work in Paris in the atmosphere of freedom and intellectual stimulation found there.

Nin would later describe the Paris life as a "café life" which had value and beauty:

> The home and the studio were private. No one visited during the day. . . . But one was sure never to be lonely, for in the evening after work, one could always walk into certain cafes and find friends gathered there. There was an element of surprise. One never knew who would be there, or who would come with a new friend, a visitor or a disciple. If there was a party, one would hear about it at the cafe, and would go in a group. Or if a need of intimate talk was felt, one left the group and walked to some small, unknown cafe. It was unplanned, free, casual.[6]

Literary experimentation was very much in the air at these café gatherings, and the latest "movement" in writing when Nin began her career was surrealism. Surrealism had developed in the late 1920s among French poet André Breton's circle of disciples. In his memoir, *Life Among the Surrealists*, published thirty years later, Matthew Josephson writes, "They would try to 'change life' . . . by escaping from everyday realities to the zone of the 'super-real' and the occult."[7] When the movement began, the writers would meet in cafés to tell each other their dreams. Josephson reports:

> Were they going to practice therapy on each other I wondered? Or would they treat their recorded dreams as so much 'literature'?

[123]

Breton explained that their object was to explore the world of the undirected subconscious mind in 'scientific spirit,' thus to learn something of that surréalité which men of prosaic and rational ways were unable to enjoy.[8]

By late 1931, the heyday of the expatriate community was over. Pound, Hemingway, Fitzgerald, and others who had made the Paris scene what it was in 1922, were now gone. With the crash of the American stock market and the onset of the depression, many Americans whose freedom had been financed by checks and stock dividends from the United States were forced to return home. Others who had come to escape the commercialism of New York's literary world had by now been embraced by that establishment and were successful commercially published writers.

Although the well-heeled American toursists were gone, there were still plenty of struggling writers who had come to Paris to find freedom to live and write as they chose. One such writer was the American from Brooklyn, Henry Miller. The son of a tailor and grandson of a German immigrant, Miller had drifted from job to job in New York while writing poems, stories, and novels for which he could not find a publisher. Once he had a collection of his prose poems printed on tinted cardboard and his wife had gone door to door in Greenwich Village selling them.

At the age of forty, a "failure" with no money and four unpublished novels to his credit, Miller decided to move to Paris. In March 1930, using money his wife June had come by in some mysterious way, Miller emigrated to France. He left June behind, but took with him his latest novel, *Crazy Cock*, and went to Paris to find himself "as a man and as an artist."[9]

Miller was "desperately hungry not only for the physical and sensual, for human warmth and understanding, but also for inspiration and illumination" when he arrived in Paris.

Alfred Perles, whom Miller and June had first met in 1928, . . . and

[124]

who was working for the Paris edition of the Chicago *Tribune*, met Miller again and, realizing that he was "down and out," sneaked him into his own room at the Hotel Central. . . . Richard Osborn, a young lawyer from Bridgeport, Connecticut, who worked for the Paris branch of the National City Bank by day and led a bohemian life at night, offered Miller shelter during the winter of 1930, in his spacious apartment at 2 rue Auguste-Bartholdi, near the Champ de Mars.[10]

It was Osborn who introduced Nin to Miller. She had gone to the lawyer to consult him about the copyright on *D. H. Lawrence: An Unprofessional Study,* and he had told her about his "roommate." Nin reported Osborn's conversation in her diary:

Henry Miller is writing a book one thousand pages long which has everything in it which is left out of other novels. He has now taken refuge in Richard's hotel room. "Every morning when I leave he is still asleep. I leave ten francs on the table, and when I return there is another batch of writing done."[11]

Miller had begun to sell articles to the various English-language newspapers and journals which still flourished in Paris, and Osborn showed Nin one of these, an essay about Luis Buñuel's surrealist film, "L'Age d'Or." The article impressed Nin with its "primitive, savage quality." While preparing contracts of Nin's book about Lawrence, Osborn showed it to Miller, who commented, "I have never read such strong truths told with such delicacy."

"I would like to bring him to dinner," said Richard. And I said yes.

So delicacy and violence are about to meet and challenge each other.[12]

The two writers became good friends. Nin found Miller to be "so different from his brutal, violent, vital writing. . . . He is a man whom life intoxicates, who has no need of wine, who is floating in a self-created euphoria."[13] Miller found everything

[125]

about Nin and her house charming. He talked with her brother about his music and "went to shake my mother's hand." He browsed through the bookcase, explored the garden, savored the dinner and the wine.

Nin told her diary after the visit, "Emotionalism and sensibility are my quicksands. I am fascinated with the 'toughness' of Henry. . . . It is new to me."[14] She had immediately been overwhelmed by a desire to nurture Miller, and had sent him away from that first meeting with a set of Proust, railroad tickets to visit her again, and her typewriter (which he later pawned to buy his friends a round of drinks).

Miller and Nin began to meet and talk frequently, and much of Miller's talk was about his wife June. A beautiful dancer, she had captured his imagination by enveloping herself in mystery. "She told him several versions about her childhood, birthplace, parents, racial origins," Nin wrote.[15] Each version was romantic and imaginative, involving gypsies or "a magician" or Don Juan.

Then June came to visit her husband in Paris, and on December 30, 1931 Nin met her for the first time. Nin was immediately as fascinated and obsessed with this "most beautiful woman on earth" as was Miller himself, and, though she said her attraction was not sexual, fell so deeply in love with June she could think or write of little else during the entire two months of her visit.

During this time, Miller was writing *Tropic of Cancer*, an autobiographical work in which he portrayed his relationship with June. In April 1932, Nin began her own book about the woman, a work in the "surrealistic way." "The phrase which fired me and made me begin to write on June was Jung's 'to proceed from the dream outward,'" Nin told her diary.[16] Miller, in writing a new novel, was portraying June "so realistically, so directly. I felt she could not be penetrated that way. I wrote surrealistically. I took her dreams, the myth of June, her fantasies. But certain myths are not mysterious, undecipherable."[17]

By turns Miller and Nin argued aesthetics and read each

[126]

other passages from their works-in-progress. Out of this dialectic came two very different fictions, Miller's first published book, *Tropic of Cancer*, and Nin's first published novel, *House of Incest*.

Miller had begun *Tropic of Cancer* after an abortive attempt to revise *Crazy Cock* and get it published. "I grew so desperate I finally decided to explode—I did explode—I didn't write a piece of fiction: I wrote an autobiographical document, a human book. . . . I wanted to reveal myself as openly, nakedly and unashamedly as possible."[18] Nin, on the other hand, was not exploding so much as imploding, going into the subconscious world of the dream to discover a deeper reality in that inner space.

Much of Nin's interest in dreams stemmed from her experiences with psychoanalysis during this time. In order to "get cured of a lack of confidence in my womanly charms,"[19] she had begun to see an analyst, Dr. René Allendy, who interpreted her dreams for her in the classic Freudian manner. Nin became fascinated with the world of dreams and the subconscious, and began to analyze other people's dreams, including Miller's, in the same way. Writing, for her, was an art much like analysis, which delved into the subconscious mind to discover truths no "realistic" writing could portray.

With Nin's financial help and encouragement, Miller finished the first draft of *Tropic of Cancer* by mid-1932. She was willing to pay for publication of *Tropic* herself, if this should become necessary, but it looked for a while as if it would be published without Nin's subsidy. Miller gave his manuscript to literary agent William Bradley, who showed it to Jack Kahane, proprietor of Obelisk Press, a small Paris publishing firm. Kahane specialized in publishing "somewhat controversial, somewhat salacious books in English, mostly for the tourist trade,"[20] but he had always hoped to discover and publish an important literary work. When Kahane read *Tropic of Cancer*, he felt strongly he had at last made such a discovery, and he was eager to publish it. In October 1932, he offered Miller a contract on the book, which the writer

[127]

signed. However, Kahane's printer, M. Servant, was also a financial partner in Obelisk, and when he read the manuscript he was hesitant.

No doubt part of the reason was fear of prosecution. The French authorities who had for years ignored the English-language novels, such as *Ulysses*, being published within their borders, had begun to take notice when Titus brought out *Lady Chatterley's Lover* and scandalized even the liberal-minded French. They had confiscated Titus's stock of the books and only released them in response to the pleas of some French intellectuals. Servant had other reasons for not wanting to publish the book, according to Hugh Ford, who chronicled Kahane's publishing career in *Published in Paris:*

> To the practical-minded Servant, "literary" connoted "obscurity and unsaleability." What people wanted, he instructed Kahane, was "a clever description of underclothes . . . with plenty of spicy references to their contents." . . . Furthermore, Servant went on, Miller was unknown and probably a "down-and-out Montparnasse reject" who would demand advances on royalties and make scenes because his book was not selling a thousand copies a week.[21]

While he haggled with Servant, Kahane convinced Miller to write a "brochure" on D. H. Lawrence which would help establish Miller's reputation as a man of letters and so improve the chances of *Tropic*'s being taken seriously. As this delay stretched into a two-year wait, Nin's offer to pay for the publication of *Tropic* became more and more attractive to Miller.

Finally, in March 1934, Miller's discouragement with Kahane's delays in publishing *Tropic of Cancer* reached a head. "Jack Kahane has failed in business as well as in true loyalty to Henry," Nin told her diary in March.[22] "Bradley has lost interest in him. Rather than see him frustrated again, I will pay for publication of *Cancer*." The attitude of the agent and publishers, who had been so enthusiastic about Miller's writing, amazed Nin. "None will go all the way with him. We

[128]

felt free. They all worry about money, fear of risk, etc."

The next month Nin went to London "to see what I can do for *Tropic of Cancer*" with publishers there. Before leaving, she "won Kahane by a marvelous speech, and he will publish Henry, only I pay for the printing."[23] This done, she sat down to write a preface to Miller's book, calling it "a vitalizing current of blood" in "a world grown paralyzed with introspection and constipated by delicate mental meals."[24]

Meanwhile, Miller's agent Bradley became interested in Nin's writing. In March 1933, she had showed him her childhood diary, and Bradley was so enthusiastic he tried to persuade Alfred Knopf to publish it. Bradley preferred the style of the diary to the stylized, symbolic writing of *House of Incest,* and urged Nin to write a "direct narrative."

In May 1933, Nin arranged a reunion with her father, whom she had not seen since he deserted the family when she was eleven. This rediscovery of the man for whom she had started the diary so long ago was exhilarating, and soon Nin was as obsessed with him as she had been with June Miller the year before. During the summer of 1933, Nin began writing a story about this reunion, much of it taken from her diary. She called the book *Winter of Artifice,* and worked on it while revising *House of Incest.* As she worked she was assailed with self-doubts. In October 1933, she told her diary:

> Henry tries to restrain my extravagance in writing, while yet allowing himself complete exuberance. Why? It may be I am not good at my craft yet. My style suffers when I seek freedom, when I feel too strongly. My writing will have to learn to support the weight of my vitality. I guess I'm still a little young, in writing.[25]

This lack of confidence in her writing made Nin extremely sensitive to the comments of others to whom she showed it. "I break down under criticism," she wrote in the diary in February 1934.[26] "Cannot take it." After completing a first version of *Winter* and showing it to Miller, she went home and "broke up the whole book and made a different plan for Part One, which Henry did not like."

[129]

Although they had discussed the aesthetic principles behind her fiction in great detail, Miller did not fully understand the work itself. Nin was attempting "a telescoping, a condensation in words" much like the condensation of images in dreams. "Talk in the dream was only a phrase issuing from a million thoughts and feelings, only a phrase, now and then, formed out of a swift and enormous flow of ideas."[27]

Her trouble was that she had tried "unsuccessfully to weld the fantastic and the real, the plain and the enameled style. Failed because I castrated the poetry and made the plain writing sound false." Miller urged her to "combat the world, to face the resistance to *House of Incest* (on the part of Bradley and others). . . . To obey my own integrity, to fuse the two aspects of myself which I insisted must be kept apart."

Miller's encouragement roused Nin's "fighting spirit and . . . strength," but she still found the act of formulating her experience into art an ordeal. In the next month she rewrote *Winter of Artifice* two more times. Meanwhile, an argument with her father over several lies he had told disillusioned Nin and ended her earlier hopes of "a deep understanding between my father and me."[28] She finished the third version of *Winter* "ironically," but continued adding material to the work during the spring of 1934, even as she was rewriting and adding to *House of Incest*.

By June 1934, *Winter of Artifice* was finished and Bradley showed it to Alfred Knopf. The publisher had flattering words for Nin's story, but rejected it. The technique of condensation Nin used in her fiction was still being criticized by Bradley and others, but Nin defended herself, saying, "I believe in Japanese painting. . . . I hate stuffing."[29]

Her experiences with publishers helped lead Nin to the decision at about this time to become an analyst. "I want to earn my living by psychoanalysis, so that I may always write as I wish to, never make concessions" she told her diary.[30] She began to study psychology with Otto Rank at the Cité Universitaire, but soon began to feel the same as she had

[130]

about her high school classes in New York. "The intellectual nourishment was null," she told her diary after class one day.[31] "Everyone interrupted Rank, asked obvious questions, and created such a nursery ambiance that it made me furious." The university experience did, however, bring Nin into closer contact with "the monstrous reality *outside*, in the world":[32]

> I saw families broken apart by economic dramas, I saw the exodus of Americans, the changes and havocs brought on by world conditions. Individual lives shaken, poisoned, altered. Rank suddenly ruined financially, losing his home, moving, forced to go to America. The struggle and instability of it all. I was overwhelmed. And then, with greater, more furious, more desperate stubbornness I continued to build my individual life, as if it were a Noah's Ark for the drowning. I refused to share the universal pessimism and inertia.[33]

This was to remain Nin's stance in the argument of art versus action for the rest of her life. As world conditions disintegrated into war, many of her café friends and other intellectuals would begin to take sides in the political fray. Most became Socialists or Communists, and to them literary experimentation and writing about dreams seemed almost shameful in a world so much in need of action. The late thirties was a time when many intellectuals became activists, published tracts and political newspapers, or went to fight in the Spanish Civil War, and later World War II.

Nin, however, continued to insist on the need for individual art to preserve beauty in a world gone mad. Though her sympathies were with the Socialists, she quickly saw that there was much in their political movement which was just as destructive of the individual as the fascism they opposed. In a letter reproduced in her diary[34] in November 1936, she wrote, "If Proust had delivered speeches, written propaganda and talked all night with his comrades, he would have accomplished less for the destruction of false values than he did by satirizing a decadent society." Dreams and art were needed to

[131]

provide nourishment to the soul when the world outside offered only despair.

But Nin's dreamlike writing did not make her popular with the commercial publishers of her day. As Miller rose to a modest prominence after the publication of *Tropic of Cancer* (which Nin worked hard to distribute and promote), she met with rejection. In December 1936, she told her diary, "I promised Henry he would not be a failure, that I would make the world listen to him, and I kept my promise. Much that I have wanted for myself did not come true, but I suppose the day the creator wants something for himself, his magic ends."[35]

Nin's Marxist friend Gonzalo interpreted the neglect of her work by the commercial press as proof that the artist must work to change the world. Nin told him, "I worked obstinately to build an individually perfect world." He answered:

"Yes, but there comes a moment when this perfect world is destroyed by what happens in the bigger world. Now you cannot go any further. You are blocked. Your work cannot be published because it outrages bourgeois ideals."[36]

Nin admitted this was true. "Somewhere, at a certain point, my individual world touches the walls of reality." Still, however, she refused to allow "the artist in me" to be killed by the capitalistic world. She told her diary, "Limitations, defeats, come from within. I am fully responsible for my own restrictions."[37]

Despite this realization, Nin could not ignore the many defeats she suffered at the hands of publishers. Her first publication, the study of D. H. Lawrence, "was but partially distributed, not sent to reviewers" by Edward Titus, who divorced Helena Rubenstein a few months after the book was published, and then went bankrupt. Nin never received royalties on the book, not even in the form of copies for herself.

In June 1935, Jack Kahane agreed to publish her *Winter of Artifice*, but did not actually do so until 1939, and then only because her friend, fellow writer Lawrence Durrell, paid for the printing. In the meantime, Nin tried unsuccessfully to place it with other publishers, including Jonathan Cape of London. She gave *House of Incest* to Miller's agent Bradley, but he misunderstood the story's very stylized prose and was unenthusiastic about finding a publisher for it. When Kahane finally published the book, it appeared one week before the outbreak of World War II, and received no reviews.

Several commercial and alternative publishers were interested in publishing Nin's diaries, but again, nothing came of their overtures. In July 1936, Nin met Denise Clairouin, a literary agent who read the diaries and offered to find a publisher for them, calling them "a Proustian work."[38] She showed them to Faber & Faber (the British commercial publisher for whom T. S. Eliot was an editor). Faber kept the diaries several months and asked to see more of them, but ultimately rejected them "with a great deal of reluctance" because

> we cannot see how to shape the material into book form which could be published in England. Much of what we should wish to use for the integrity of the book, we should be prevented from using by the restrictions on books in England.[39]

In November 1937, Clairouin showed Maxwell Perkins of Scribner's the diaries. "What a curious, extraordinary woman," he said,[40] and he asked to see an abridged version. Nin set to work on the abridgment, but nothing came of this, either.

Meanwhile, Nin tried on her own to get the diaries published. In 1937 the *Criterion* published an essay by Miller in which he said Nin's diary "would take its place beside the revelations of St. Augustine, Petronius, Abélard, Rousseau, Proust." The editors of the *Nouvelle Revue Française* read the essay and asked to see the book in October 1937, but they, also, were unable to publish the work. Next, Henry Miller decided to publish it himself and sent out a circular to get subscriptions. The response was discouraging, and he finally dropped the plan. In November 1937, James Cooney of Woodstock, New York, wrote that he wanted to print "all the diaries on his hand press, one by one."[41] This scheme proved impossible.

After her return to New York during World War II, Nin showed her diary to several publishers there. Duell, Sloan & Pearce turned it down in September 1940. "Charles Pearce . . . said it was marvelous, but could only be published in a limited edition."[42] In 1941, a friend, Dorothy Norman, published seven pages out of the manuscript of the first diary volume in her little magazine, *Twice A Year*. Nin herself translated the pages from French to English. That October, Veronica Jennings at the *Saturday Review of Literature* told Nin her diary had "no universal quality."[43] Not until 1966 would the adult diaries finally begin to be published, and then their universality quickly made them a basic document of the women's movement.

Such bad experiences with publishers spurred Nin to take her publishing fate into her own hands, and twice she organized a press with the idea of bringing out her books, only to turn around and let other people take over the press, on the promise that they would publish her books for her. This ploy succeeded little better than her dealings with established publishers.

Nin bought her first press in 1935. She was still living at Louveciennes, and for several months had been toying with the idea of buying a press and publishing her own books. *Winter of Artifice* was still incomplete; *House of Incest* had met with so much misunderstanding and rejection that Nin was beginning to lose all hope of finding a publisher for it. Even Miller, who had gained some fame with the publication of *Tropic of Cancer* two years before, had now become discouraged with commercial publishers. "He cannot bear rejections," Nin wrote,[44] "the silence of conventional publishers, formal rejection slips from magazines, obtuse comments of people." Soon Nin, Miller, and Alfred Perles, Miller's neighbor at the Villa Seurat, began to eye the old barn next to Nin's house in Louveciennes. "Everybody loves the idea of setting up a printing press there, and to become independent of publishers."[45]

[134]

No sooner was the idea conceived than "Fraenkel came, appropriated the printing press project." Michael Fraenkel was an American writer who had come to Paris in 1926 with a fortune rumored to be nearly $100,000, which he had acquired selling encyclopedias. He had proceeded to spend everything he had on a publishing venture (Carrefour) dedicated to the idea that all writing should be published anonymously. By 1932 the money was gone, and Fraenkel went to the Philippines and sold encyclopedias again for two years, then returned to Paris with $50,000, upon which he lived and published until the outbreak of World War II. In 1931, Fraenkel's partner in Carrefour, Walter Lowenfels, had introduced him to Miller, who was at that time looking for a place to live. Miller moved in with Fraenkel at the Villa Seurat, and the two writers became friends.

Now, after being invited to spend the day as Nin's guest Fraenkel "dominated Louveciennes, talked uninterruptedly all day and far into the night. The ego!" Instead of leaving at the end of the evening, Fraenkel "moved in." When Nin fled to her room and tried to write, he barged in to interrupt her work so he could talk about his. "After this incident I told Henry I thought the printing press should be set up at the Villa Seurat," Nin wrote.[46]

Alfred Perles "baptized the press Siana, reversing the spelling of my name. Fraenkel makes a list of books we will publish and omits me," Nin wrote in her diary.[47] Ultimately, they agreed to publish Miller's *Scenario* first, and then Nin's *House of Incest*.

With the move of the press to the Villa Seurat, however, Nin lost all control over the publishing enterprise. Miller, Fraenkel, and Perles were sending long philosophical letters back and forth which they planned to publish as the *Hamlet* correspondence. "Something takes place at the Villa Seurat which I cannot share," Nin told her diary in October 1935. "The doors are closing on me. . . . I cannot start publication because Fraenkel would dominate it." Her only choice seemed to be a return to her career as an analyst. In January

[135]

1936, she returned to New York to resume her work with Rank. This, however, did not open doors in her life as she had hoped it would.

After a "short but vivid" trip to Morocco, she returned to Louveciennes in May 1936, feeling she had at last rid herself of "the cancer of introspection." In her absence, Miller, Fraenkel, and Perles, to whom she had abandoned her Siana Press, had not yet made good on their promise to publish *House of Incest*. Fraenkel had, as predicted, taken over Siana's day-to-day operations. He loaned Nin the money to have *House of Incest* printed and promised to distribute it as her publisher. When the book arrived from the printers, however, Fraenkel "lost interest in it . . . and did not distribute it as he had promised."[48] A few days after the book came out, he had a falling out with Miller and left for Spain.

There were no reviews to greet the publication of *House of Incest*. Nin had to be content with the reactions of her friends, which were generally good, and to see that the book reached bookstores herself. In the book she had referred to a dancer she had seen in a small theatre in Paris. Not long after the book was published Nin met this woman, Helba, and her husband Gonzalo. Helba was going deaf and was unable to dance. Her husband, a disinherited Peruvian aristocrat who wanted to be a writer, had always lived on Helba's income and was now unable to support her. Nin quickly became a close friend and benefactress of Gonzalo and Helba.

Gonzalo had a talent for conviviality but not, it seemed, for any sustained work. He was deeply concerned about the political situation in the world, however, and became committed to Marxism as he saw the Spanish republic come under attack by Franco's Fascist army. He talked about going to fight in Spain, but allowed Nin and Helba to dissuade him. He received aid from the Spanish legation for stamps, paper, and printing facilities to publish a series of manifestos in support of the Republic, but then his own lack of discipline defeated this effort.

Meanwhile, much of the allowance Nin was given to live on

[136]

went to pay Helba's medical expenses and Gonzalo's rent. In June 1937, in order to awaken his energy and pride as well as to give Gonzalo a chance for financial independence, Nin bought him a printing press:

> We went to buy the machine together. We danced around it. It lies flat on a table like a proof-making machine. Henry wanted it, but does not really need it. His work is published and accepted. Gonzalo needs it and can earn his living with it. . . . Afterwards I thought a little regretfully that I would have liked the press for myself, to do with as I liked, but I can never do this while those I love have a greater need. I was enjoying Gonzalo's joy.[49]

This scheme never worked out as it was supposed to. By August, Gonzalo had plenty of orders to keep him busy, but delayed hiring an assistant and delayed buying the paper to print on. Nin kept offering her help with the work, but Gonzalo procrastinated. "If I had kept the press for myself," Nin lamented in her diary,[50] "I would be producing, printing, publishing."

Then, two of Gonzalo's former friends among the Marxists accused Gonzalo of being a Fascist spy, and pointed out that his life had suddenly become easier financially, that he had been given his own press by Anaïs Nin, the daughter of a Spanish aristocrat. As a result, Gonzalo asked Nin to stay away from him and the press. Six months after she had bought Gonzalo the press, Nin told her diary:

> I see that the press, in Gonzalo's hands, has contributed little to the cause of Spain, . . . and I could have printed a book on it. . . . Gonzalo had promised before we bought the press: "I will print all your work."[51]

Still, Nin's compulsion to give things to needy friends overshadowed her need to take care of herself. In January 1938, she listed seven things she would do if she were rich. At the bottom of the list, below a visit to a sanatorium for Helba, a set of rare Chinese art books for Henry Miller, a radio-phonograph for a third friend, pensions for two others, and a subsidy for "all Henry's publications," she wrote that she would "buy a press for myself."

The outbreak of World War II dispersed Nin's circle of friends. Miller and the Durrells fled to Greece, Fraenkel to Mexico, Nin's father to Cuba. Jack Kahane was found dead in his apartment two days after the outbreak of the war, and William Bradley died a few days later. In September 1939, Nin and her husband returned to the United States, followed by Gonzalo and Helba.

Nin had already sent all her copies of *House of Incest* to Frances Steloff at the Gotham Book Mart in New York and placed her diaries in a bank vault for safekeeping in case of war. In New York she visited Steloff at the Gotham Book Mart and found her "busy among her books, boasting not of learning so much as of her love for them. She welcomes those who stand for hours browsing, she welcomes unknown magazines, unknown poets."

Steloff had made her bookshop the headquarters for the avant-garde writers of the twenties and thirties, had welcomed not only James Joyce's and D. H. Lawrence's books, but Miller's and Nin's. "She gives tea parties for authors on publication . . . ," Nin wrote. "The place is filled with photographs: Virginia Woolf, James Joyce, Whitman, Dreiser, Hemingway, O'Neill, D. H. Lawrence, Ezra Pound."[52]

Nin had brought with her copies of *House of Incest*, which had been published with Lawrence Durrell's backing as the last book to issue from Jack Kahane's Obelisk Press. Now that Kahane was dead and Europe embroiled in war, Nin was left to try to distribute *Winter* as best she could in the United States. "A few copies . . . have escaped censorship and are selling," she wrote in the winter of 1939.[53] In February 1940, she recorded that "Alfred Perles writes the best interpretation of *Winter of Artifice* in an English magazine, and Ralph Utley the most obtuse in a Washington paper."[54]

Caresse Crosby, who had run a small press in Paris during the twenties and thirties, was now living in a mansion in Bowling Green, Virginia, and talking about resuming her

[138]

publishing activities. Nin visited her at Hampton Manor in Bowling Green, and "we sat around and discussed the idea of setting up a press at Hampton Manor."[55] Nin was one of the writers Caresse wanted to publish, along with André Breton, Kay Boyle, and Miller.

Crosby had other house guests, including Henry Miller, who had come from Greece when the war reached there, and Salvador Dali and his wife. According to Nin, Mrs. Dali soon organized the household so that everything was functioning for the well-being of Dali, and Miller became irritated by her manipulations. Soon the atmosphere at Hampton Manor became hostile, the enchantment vanished, and with it disappeared the group's enthusiasm for a publishing venture. "Caresse did not have the money for the initial cost. John [Dudley] did not want to do all the work. I could not come often enough to be useful," Nin wrote.[56]

Meanwhile, Nin was running short of money, and was still supporting Helba and Gonzalo, along with contributing to Miller's support. Miller, however, was trying to move toward financial independence. His return to the United States had brought him back into contact with his parents, who were now impoverished, and Miller, feeling guilty at having lived only for himself all his life, vowed to support them in their old age. One means at his disposal was to write erotica for a private collector who would pay him by the page.

Soon Nin was helping Miller with the erotica, and getting part of the money. Then Miller left on a promotion tour and Nin took over the erotica business entirely, farming some of the work out to other needy writers who soon flocked around her, and thus helping them to support themselves. The only drawback to this "job" was that the collector, who refused to meet his writers face to face, would not pay for stories which weren't written as he wanted them written. "Concentrate on explicit sex," he told them. "Leave out the poetry."

So a remnant of writers exiled from Paris sat around thinking up plots for erotic stories. "Everyone is writing up their sexual experiences," Nin reported in December 1940.[57] "In-

[139]

vented, overheard, researched from Krafft-Ebing and medical books. . . . All of us need money, so we pool our stories." And they wondered about the anonymous "old man" who had such an appetite for "literary aphrodisiacs":

> One day when he has reached saturation I will tell him how he almost made us lose interest in passion by his obsession with the gestures empty of their emotions, and how we reviled him, because he almost caused us to take vows of chastity, because all that he wanted us to exclude was our own aprodisiac—poetry.[58]

(Nin had the last laugh. In the 1970s, when her erotica was published—the poetry intact—as *Delta of Venus*, it became a nationwide bestseller.)

But in the early 1940s, not only the "old man" rejected Nin's poetic writing. Though some of her short stories had been accepted by little magazines in the United States, Nin's efforts to find a publisher for her diaries or someone to bring out reprints of *House of Incest* and *Winter of Artifice* met with repeated failure. By April 1941, Nin was at the point of despair. Literary agent John Slocum told Nin he could do nothing for her work with publishers, and she wrote in her diary, "I felt America did not want my writing."[59] At the same time, Nin recognized that "being published would have been a bridge between myself and American life":

> In being deprived of publication I am deprived of existence, forced back into solitude, disconnected from life. . . .
> That night I felt unable to live if deprived of expression as a writer. The bridge. It was my first bridge. To reach my father. To reach Europe. To keep the people I loved from vanishing. Writing against loss, against uprooting, against destruction. Writing against erasing. Time erases. . . . Writing against death, separation. And now silenced. Books created my world. How will I create worlds without them? Without them my world is small and silent. Enclosed. Remote.[60]

Like the "old man," America's commercial publishers were happy to give Nin advice on how to write to please them, and

[140]

so get her work published. Of her "adventures with American publishers" she wrote in her diary:

> One of them called me up after reading *Winter of Artifice* and said I was a skillful writer, a fine writer, but could I write for him a novel with a beginning, a middle, and an end? Could I write something like *The Good Earth*?[61]

Nin recounted this advice to a friend during a walk through Chinatown. "The idea of my writing something like *The Good Earth* made us both laugh so hard we could not stop." An agent told Nin: "Put away your European work. It doesn't go here. Read *Collier's, Saturday Evening Post*, see how they do it, and go ahead."[62]

Meanwhile, "A would-be publisher promised to publish *Winter of Artifice;* he collects orders even though the book is not printed yet."[63] After several months, this "so-called publisher" did nothing with Nin's book, so she took it back. "Now Seon Gibben and Wayne Harris want to do it," Nin wrote in November 1941.[64] "Seon was working for Gotham Book Mart. She met Harris there, a wealthy young man. They want to go into publishing together."

With this new promise of publication, Nin set about revising *Winter* yet another time. She was beginning to see ever more clearly how important it was to her to publish her work:

> Without my books I would often turn my back upon adventure and become a recluse. With my books I feel I have a task. I am an explorer. I must visit the lands I am to describe. When I write the book I use the book like dynamite, to blast myself out of isolation.[65]

By December 1941 she had found a literary agent who believed in her work. At the same time she realized that "Wayne Harris and Seon Gibben are dreamers," and that she had wasted another year waiting for the promises of these "would-be" publishers to materialize:

[141]

There is no protection for the writer. Anyone can come and say he will publish it, keep it in a drawer for a year, and then return it. Meanwhile I am bound not to show it to anyone. The book is advertised as coming out, people send in checks, interest is aroused, then nothing happens. When it is mentioned again it seems like a hoax. And I am left to explain what happened.[66]

One might expect that after these experiences with alternative possibilities of publishing, Nin would give in and start tailoring her writing to the desires of the commercial houses, but this she would not. "I still have faith in *Winter of Artifice*," she wrote. She saw nothing but danger in commercializing one's writing:

How to murder a writer.
He writes a spontaneous book. He is sent for. He is asked to write something to order, something like the last best seller, *The Good Earth*. After a few forced books, he becomes impotent. The falsity sterilizes him. I wonder how many good American writers were murdered in this way. Second method: Ply them with gold. The money throws them off course, off the atmosphere they know, and feel in tune with. They are thrown into false situations, become rootless. They dry up emotionally.[67]

After Pearl Harbor was bombed and the United States entered the war, Nin once again was faced with the question of how she could indulge her private dreams in a world so beset with the threat of destruction. She wrote:

Imperturbably I get my typewriter cleaned for more work because to me that means if the world loves war and destruction I won't go along with it. I will go on loving and writing until the bomb falls. I am not going to quit, abdicate, and play its game of death and power.[68]

At this point there was only one course left for Nin's publishing career. People were asking for her books at the Gotham Book Mart, but both *Winter of Artifice* and *House of Incest* were out of print. She had given up on the small presses of her friends. She refused to tailor her writing to the needs of

[142]

commercial publishers, but at the same time she refused to give up writing for an audience. The only alternative left to her was to publish her own books.

The month before, she had asked Dorothy Norman, her wealthy friend who had published excerpts from Nin's childhood diary in her magazine *Twice A Year*, for $200 to buy a press. The idea was to provide Gonzalo a chance to work at a craft he loved—printing and book design—as well as to publish Nin's books. Norman had refused to loan her the money. She then took her request to Frances Steloff. Nin had seen secondhand presses for $75 and $100:

> One of them operated like an old-fashioned sewing machine, by a foot pedal. The inking had to be done by hand. The man said we could turn out Christmas cards on it, but not fine books. Gonzalo was sure it would work. We would have to find one hundred dollars for type and trays.[69]

Steloff agreed to advance Nin $75 on the promised books, and she borrowed $100 from another friend, Thurema Sokol.

After several days of searching for a place to set up the press, Nin found the perfect spot, a sky-lit loft, three flights up on the top floor of an old house at 144 MacDougal Street:

> It was old, uneven, with a rough wood floor, painted black, walls painted yellow. There was a very small kitchenette. It was all a little askew, it had character, like the houseboat [on which she had lived in Paris during the late thirties.] It had a fireplace. Past tenants had left a big desk and a couch. Thirty-five dollars a month. I took it immediately.[70]

As the nation rushed to prepare for war, Nin and Gonzalo

> went in quest of paper. . . . We bought type. . . . The press was delivered. We borrowed a book from the library on how to print. Gonzalo would run the press, I would set type. I started to learn typesetting. It took me an hour and a half to typeset half a page.[71]

Although Nin would later turn the profits of the press over

[143]

to Gonzalo, this time she remained a full partner in the day-to-day operations. Gonzalo might use the press for political tracts later, but first they would print *Winter of Artifice*. Still, Gonzalo was unreliable and the work was physically hard. Nin tried to interest Robert Duncan and George Barker in making it a communal press. "We would all do the work together and bring out all the books we wrote."[72] Barker dropped by with a manuscript of his poems, but "volunteered no help and soon made his escape. Robert had worked with the Cooneys on their magazine, and did not seem interested in manual labor." Nin, however, loved the work:

> The creation of an individual world, an act of independence, such as the work at the press, is a marvelous cure for anger and frustration. The insults of the publishers, the rejections, the ignorance, all are forgotten. I love the studio. I get up with eager curiosity. The press is a challenge.[73]

Gonzalo had a friend who was an engraver, William Hayter. He had lived and worked in Paris, then emigrated to New York when the war broke out. Here Hayter had set up Atelier 17, a studio for artists and engravers, where he taught an engraving process which had been invented by poet and artist William Blake in England 150 years before.

Blake, like Nin, had been an unpopular, uncommercial writer, and had published his own poetry by engraving it on copper plates. That this method had come to Blake in a dream no doubt appealed to Nin. Blake, whose poetry was symbolic and difficult to understand, had been more or less neglected as a writer until literary modernism had promoted such qualities as virtues. Now a handful of intellectuals were rereading Blake and finding in his work prophecies of the apocalypse which had come upon the world in the form of World War II.

Identifying with Blake, Nin and her husband, Ian Hugo, decided to illustrate *Winter of Artifice* with engravings by Hugo, using Blake's engraving method. In so doing, they were

[144]

in effect saying to that handful of intellectuals who now regarded Blake as a prophet, "Here is a piece of visionary writing that has been rejected by the establishment, as Blake's writings were in his day; like Blake's it is something that the world cannot afford to ignore." And to make sure readers got the point, they printed an explanation on the back page of *Winter:*

> For the engravings on copper in the text and cover Ian Hugo has used the technique which William Blake called "revealed" because it was revealed to him by his brother in a dream. This is the first time this technique, as developed by S. W. Hayter, has been employed since Blake invented it.

The printing of the 156-page booklet took four months, until May 5. "We learned the hard way, by experience, without a teacher," Nin wrote in her diary.[74] "Testing, inventing, seeking, struggling." Friends who had some experience in printing dropped by to give tips. "We dreamt, ate, talked, slept with the press. We ate sandwiches with the taste of ink, got ink in our hair and inside our nails."

Nin and her husband worked seven and eight hours a day, and Nin was exultant to be able to see her world of dreams and sensations at last made concrete in metal type, actually to touch the pages she had written:

> Instead of using one's energy in a void, against frustrations, in anger against publishers, I use it on the press, type, paper, a source of energy. Solving problems, technical, mechanical problems. *Which can be solved.*
> If I pay no attention, then I do not lock the tray properly, and when I start printing the whole tray of letters falls into the machine. The words which first appeared in my head, out of the air, take body. Each letter has a weight. I can weigh each word again, to see if it is the right one.[75]

By March 4 their efficiency had increased to four pages a day. "Jim Cooney helps us for an hour a day. His lessons saved us much time. We are now up to page 44."[76] By April they were

[145]

nearing the end of the book, and Nin realized that "the writing is often improved by the fact that I live so many hours with a page that I am able to scrutinize it, to question the essential words."[77] "Typesetting is like film cutting. The discipline of printing is good for the writer."

The printing was finished on May 5, and after a search to find a binder who would handle the odd size of a five inches by seven inches book, it was delivered from the bindery on May 15. The finished product was a case-bound hardback, 156 pages long, containing two novellas: "Winter of Artifice," which took up 84 pages, and "The Voice," which took up 71. The boards were covered in paper, with a black-on-white cover engraving done by Ian Hugo in a style much like that used by Blake to decorate the margins of his poem engravings. Like many of the Blake engravings, Hugo's cover suggests rather than illustrates. It suggests a bearded figure, straining upward, perhaps through ice, holding a stick (or icicle?) above his head. "Winter of Artifice" and "Anaïs Nin," written in cursive handwriting, are incorporated into the cover design.

Inside, the book is no less distinctive. In his design, Gonzalo made no attempt to imitate the products of the commercial publishers, but created a book that was artistic and unique. The text (as reported in a note on the last page of the volume) was printed with 12 point Spartan type, a rather bold sans serif face seldom used for books. Here and there certain words and blocks of narrative were printed in Bernhard Gothic Light Italic type for special emphasis. For example, a five-page lyric essay in "Winter of Artifice" in which the narrator compares her relationship with her father to a concert ("Two boxes filled with the resonances of an orchestra"), is set off in this way, and the typography adds to the reader's sensation of having entered a different state of awareness in this section of the novella.

The text was printed on a heavier paper than was usual, copper engraving paper according to the note on the final page. It was illustrated with five more Blake-esque Hugo

[146]

engravings, including one dropped into the center of a page like a rock in a stream, with words flowing all around it. Another unusual artistic feature was the use of extremely large margins, over an inch at the top, an inch on both sides, and two inches at the bottom of each page. No running heads were used, and page numbers were centered at the bottom of the pages. The total cost of the five -hundred-copy edition, including the price of the press and type, was $400.

Once again, Frances Steloff came forward to help Nin with her publishing venture:

> The Gotham Book Mart gave a party for it. The book created a sensation by its beauty. The typography by Gonzalo, the engravings by Ian Hugo were unique. The bookshop was crowded. Otto Fuhrman, teacher of graphic arts at New York University, praised the book. Art galleries asked to carry it. I received orders from collectors, a letter from James Laughlin, offering me a review in *New Directions* by anyone I chose.[78]

Nin chose William Carlos Williams, but when the review appeared she regretted it. He misunderstood her book as a biography and Nin as a man-hater. She saw the review before publication and "wrote him gently about his misinterpretations," but he refused to rewrite the review. Still, the experience of being published at last was exhilarating:

> Harvey Breit praised it for its sensibility. Alemany said it was "profound, audacious." The publishers had said "not universal." No one would be interested in a novel taking place in Europe. Yet one woman after another identifies with [the characters] Djuna and Lilith. Without advertising or reviews, the entire edition sold.[79]

By summer the euphoria had worn off. Another reviewer, Paul Rosenfeld, wrote a "totally inaccurate" review which, like that of Williams, treated the story as biography. Harvey Breit "tried to write about the book but the new editor of the *New Republic* would not let him," Nin recorded.[80] "Complete silence from the New York *Times*, the *Tribune*. My underground success continues from person to person, fervent, secretly and quietly."

The *New York Herald-Tribune* actually did review the book, but not in glowing terms. *Winter* was "a little overfull of . . . people saying mystic things about themselves, about others, about life. It presents stories and conclusions that come before the fact. Over all this there is a rather piquant icing of good language."[81] Another review in the book pages of the *Nation,* however, was more appreciative: "Anaïs Nin's writing will come to be regarded as one of the most admirable of purely lyrical efforts."

Though she turned all the profits of the press after *Winter* to Gonzalo, this was not enough to support him and Helba, and Nin was beginning to realize it might never be. "The qualities the three of us share, spontaneity, fantasy, love of creation, are incompatible with commercial life."[82] To earn more money, they agreed to reprint a book published earlier by Caresse Crosby from her Black Sun Press. But printing someone else's work was noncreative, and simply tiring. To make matters worse, Helba's illness was keeping Gonzalo from coming to work until late in the day, and Nin was left with a greater burden than she was able to carry. Under the pressure she broke down, and for the third time in her life sought help from an analyst.

In analysis, she came to grips with her compulsion to give to needy friends, even when they misused her gifts, even when they kept demanding more and never reciprocated. She realized that she had to learn how to give to herself, too. "All that I needed, I gave away," she told her diary.[83] She realized, too, how much she had sacrificed her own creative impulses and career. "I considered Henry's writing far more important than my own . . . I have crippled myself. . . . I see strongly creative women crush their men. I fear this."[84]

Nin was quick to repent, and to learn how to accept gifts as well as to give them. Miller sent her a gift of money early in 1943. "I did two things with it," she wrote him in a letter of thanks,[85] "I took my radio out of the repair shop, and I bought

[148]

paper to print my short stories on. When I finish the book for Caresse, I will print the stories."

It took until June for work to begin on *Under a Glass Bell*, a collection of Nin's short stories written in Paris and the United States during the decade 1934–43, several of which had been published in little magazines. Gonzalo designed the new book, once again using Ian Hugo's engravings on the cover and throughout the text. Through the summer Nin rested, "gathering strength to print *Under a Glass Bell*,"[86] so that the actual printing did not begin until October 1943.

Once under way, the job progressed rapidly. As she set the type, Nin thought about the public's reception of the book. She was constantly having to defend her writing against those who criticized its lack of realistic details. Fantasy writing seemed frivolous, even shameful, in a world where so much had gone wrong. If one had to write instead of becoming involved in the war effort, people reasoned, one should at least write with the sort of realism that might help people understand world conditions.

In order to give her beautiful little book of fantasies and stories a chance in this hostile literary environment, Nin decided to print her defense as an introduction to *Under a Glass Bell*. The preface she came up with was more of an apologia, and left the distinct impression that Nin had been won over to the realists' stance:

> Because these stories were written before the Spanish war I had thought first of all to destroy them, and then I understood a truth which it might be good to state for others. The stories must be placed in their proper light for those who fail to see the relations between fantasy and reality, the past and the present. Everything is related and inter-active but at times we fail to see how, and consequently, fail to make a higher synthesis.
>
> These stories represent the moment when many like myself had found only one answer to the suffering of the world: to dream, to tell fairytales, to elaborate and to follow the labyrinth of fantasy. All this I see now was the passive poet's only answer to the torments he witnessed. Being ignorant of the causes and therefore of a possibility of change, he sought merely a balm-art, the drug. . . .

[149]

I did not stay in the world of the isolated dream or become permanently identified with it. The Spanish war awakened me. I passed out of romanticism, mysticism and neurosis into reality.

I see now there is no need to destroy the art that was produced under an evil social structure. But it is necessary to understand, to be aware of what caused the suffering which made such an opium essential and what this fantasy world concealed. And to this task I will devote the rest of my writing.

By the end of October, Nin and Gonzalo had already received fifty-six subscriptions for the book and had reached page thirty-five. By January 1944, they had reached page sixty-four, and once again Nin experienced the satisfaction that came with printing her own work:

Joy at achievement and a certainty that the stories are poetically valuable. The severe test of typesetting failed to dissolve them. The words are as pure, as unalloyed, as meaningful, after all the scrutiny, the concretization in lead.[87]

Meanwhile, word got around that Nin and Gonzalo were printing another beautiful little limited-edition book, and the Graphic Arts Society became interested in the press. When two members of the society came by to see the operation, however, they seemed disillusioned by the unprofessional atmosphere of the "print-shop" in the MacDougal Street loft.

By the end of January the job was finished. They had produced three hundred copies of *Under a Glass Bell*—an "exquisite piece of workmanship," Nin told her diary.[88] The world would soon agree with her assessment. Gonzalo's "gift for book designing" had flowered in this slender eighty-eight-page book. It was an unusual shape, eight-and-a-half inches long and less than five inches wide, a case-bound hardback. Once again the Blakean method of engraving had been used. "The cover and seventeen engravings by Ian Hugo have been printed in relief directly from the original copper plates," Nin explained in a note at the end of the book. No title or author appears on the cover, just a white-on-black engraving of figures suggesting a sailing ship, a bird-like fish,

[150]

plants that might be eels, or trees, or fingers.

The text is printed in 10-point Bernhard Gothic Light Italic type on a heavy paper, "watermarked Zurich Plate Finish Paper," according to the note at the end of the volume. The title page is bordered by an engraving of suggestive little figures, and each story begins and ends with an engraving, placed on the page so that the printed text seems to roll out of one engraving and into the other. Each story has a separate title page, and there are no running heads. Page numbers are spelled out — "one" and "two" — in the bottom center of each page, in tiny light italic type.

For the moment, Nin seemed to have repented of her "dream-world" writing, and let it be known she was about to join the ranks of the realists. Her diary, she announced in 1944,[89] would be converted "into a full, long novel of the thirty years between 1914 and 1940 — between the two wars." Among the themes would be "the transition from romanticism to realism" Nin saw herself as having made. (This transition apparently never took place, and all references to it were edited out of Nin's diaries when she prepared them for publication in the late 1960s.)

But meanwhile, *Under a Glass Bell* had won over a Marxist friend of Nin's to her original aesthetic theory. "Every word you write is pure poetry," the friend told her. "I feel that you represent our poetic soul, and I regret having talked to you last summer about objective writing." More conversations were to follow, as critics and readers delighted in a thing of beauty, and so warmed to this purely artistic little book.

There was a successful exhibit of the book at Wakefield Gallery. "Comments were warm and enthusiastic. Miss Decker, of the Graphic Arts Society, said it was marvelous," Nin reported.[90] Suddenly Nin had the feeling she had achieved something approaching fame:

First of all, Paul Rosenfeld mentioned me to Edmund Wilson, who went to the Gotham Book Mart, where Frances Steloff talked of me, and he went home with a copy of *Under A Glass Bell* and

[151]

wrote a review which appeared in *The New Yorker* of April 1.

The morning *The New Yorker* appeared I was being photographed by the photographer of *Town and Country* in a dress by Henry La Pensée. . . .

John Stroup wrote a review of *Under A Glass Bell* in *Town and Country*. This started a rumor that I have arrived! *The New Yorker* was lying there, with the review by Edmund Wilson, who is the highest authority among the critics. Telephone calls, letters.[91]

Wilson's review, which Nin and Gonzalo printed up on an advertising flier, was destined to win her the attention and admiration of many who had never heard of her before:

The pieces in this collection belong to a peculiar genre sometimes cultivated by the late Virginia Woolf. They are half short stories, half dreams, and they mix a sometimes exquisite poetry with a homely realistic observation. They take place in a special world, a world of feminine perception and fancy, which is all the more interesting for being innocently international.

. . . In Miss Nin's case, . . . the imagery does convey something and is always appropriate. The spun glass is also alive: it is the abode of a secret creature. Half woman, half childlike, she shops, employs servants, wears dresses, suffers the pains of childbirth, yet is likely at any moment to be volatilized into a superterrestrial being who feels things that we cannot feel.

But perhaps the main thing to say is that Anaïs Nin is a very good artist, as perhaps none of the literary Surrealists is. . . . this poet has no need to apologize [for presenting a dream-world when so many are suffering]: her dreams reflect the torment, too.

This review in the *New Yorker* was exceptional at the time and would be exceptional today. The magazine's literary editor, inundated with commercially published books to be considered for review, would automatically eliminate alternative press and self-published books from consideration without a second glance. Edmund Wilson had become a well-respected literary critic and was a regular contributor to the *New Yorker* at this time, and it was no doubt because of his by-line that the review of Nin's little book appeared.

This new connection with "a few people" out in the world

[152]

once more gave Nin the feeling of escaping the isolation in which she had lived. It seemed like "the breaking of a shell, a second birth, a becoming visible and tangible," she wrote.[92] "My feeling of being merely a mysterious influence upon others ceased. I felt out in the daylight."

From California, Henry Miller wrote to congratulate Nin on her success:

> The format, the paper, the type, the engraving, all are beautiful, striking.
> . . . Your name is already legendary. I had heard that you had lost faith in the publishing and printing of your own books. I hope that it is not so. It would be just the wrong moment. . . . I beg you, be firm. Part of the act of creating is discovering your own kind. They are everywhere. But don't look for them in the wrong places.[93]

Nin did not lose faith in self-publishing, but went on to write a new novel, *This Hunger,* of which she printed a deluxe edition of forty, and a "regular" edition in September 1945.

Miraculously, the *New Yorker* again printed an Edmund Wilson review of the self-published volume. "The episodes of *This Hunger* are somewhat less satisfactory as writing than the pieces in *Under a Glass Bell,*" Wilson said, "but Anaïs Nin is attempting something more original and more complex."[94] It was a long review, which called the book "a revelatory document" and left the impression Nin was an important writer with great potential. "This new book, like the one before it, has been published by Nin herself," Wilson concluded. "Anaïs Nin is at present a special cult, when she ought to have a general public."

Following the *New Yorker's* lead, the *Nation* also broke with tradition and published Diana Trilling's review of the book. Far less kind to Nin than Wilson, Trilling did join him in urging commercial publishers to take note of Nin's work, for she ended with the remark, "I wonder why a book like *This Hunger* could not receive commercial publication in these days when nothing sells like the sick psyche."[95] These

[153]

two reviews brought the commercial publishers to Nin's door. In October she told her diary "I am supposed to see Random House, Harper's, and Pascal Covici, of Viking. I am both happy and sad."[96]

Nin knew the dangers that commercial publication posed:

> After my lunch with Harper's I realized the most difficult part of my life is starting now. The struggle with money and the press is nothing compared with the more subtle struggle against accepting money for compromising. Harper's began today, like Mephistopheles with Faust: "Yes, we absolutely want you. You have great talent. But do you think the next book might be . . . more of a novel . . . according to orthodox forms?"
>
> "No," I said. "It will be done in my own way."
>
> "It is strange," the editor admitted. "Publishers think they can tell the writer what the public wants, and then along comes someone who does something different, like you, and it is very obvious the public wants you."
>
> "It is a question of sincerity," I said. "If you would let the writer be himself, then naturally his experience answers a real need, not a spurious one."[97]

She had much the same conversation with Pascal Covici of Viking Press:

> "Oh," he groaned, "can't you write a novel like everybody else, with a beginning and an end?"
>
> "No."
>
> "I admit you are evolving your own form."[98]

Meanwhile, Nin's "fame" was bringing her into contact with young writers. One was Gore Vidal, who at twenty was "the youngest editor at E. P. Dutton." Vidal got Dutton interested in Nin and in December 1945 came to her with the news that they were going to offer her an advance of $1,000 and a contract for all the novels, including the one she was then writing, *Ladders to Fire*.

At last, Nin had won, had gotten a commercial publisher without commercializing her work. The new novel was published by Dutton late in October 1946, and three hundred

[154]

people flocked to the Gotham Book Mart to fete Nin "as one dreams of being feted."[99] This was followed by three more parties, all of which proved to Nin "that the world for which I write is larger than publishers thought, and also of higher quality and of greater sincerity. The young writers to come," she predicted, "will waste less energy in battling, in printing, in talking for themselves."

This prediction never came true. Though experimental writing would regain the respect of critics and literary scholars after World War II, it would never become popular enough to attract commercial publishers, and a whole new generation of young writers would have to learn to conform, or spend their energies battling and printing if they were to be heard.

For Anaïs Nin, however, self-publishing had gained her a modest success. Lasting fame would not come to her until the 1960s and 1970s, with the commercial publication of her *Diary*. Through self-publishing, however, she first found an audience for her work, readers with whom she could share her visionary world. In the midst of world-wide destruction, she had created something beautiful, and so reasserted the validity of literature which was "merely" art, which could "only" nurture the human spirit.

VLADIMIR NABOKOV

. . . the work of art as a dirty book

5

On November 12, 1940, Edmund Wilson, then literary editor of the *New Republic,* received a letter from Vladimir Nabokov, a Russian émigré who had come to the United States from Europe a few months before. Nabokov had written several novels in Russian which had enjoyed some success among White Russians who had fled their country when the Bolsheviks took over in 1917. Wilson liked the book review Nabokov sent with his letter; this Russian seemed to have a very good command of English. There were, however, a few things Nabokov would have to learn if he were to sell his writing in the United States, and Wilson was glad to inform him of these. Wilson told the newcomer in a letter, ". . . do please refrain from puns, to which I see you have a slight propensity. They are pretty much excluded from serious journalism here."[1]

Wilson was the foremost American critic of his time, and when he said a thing was to be excluded from serious writing one was well-advised to pay attention, for as in the case of Anaïs Nin, he had the power to make a writer's reputation with a single review. Nabokov, however, would not be easily cowed by the eminent critic. Puns and word games were important to his art and were a part of his literary heritage, as Simon Karlinsky has emphasized in the introduction to his edition of *The Nabokov–Wilson Letters:*

[159]

Interest in paronomasia, in discovering the hitherto unperceived relationships between the semantic and phonetic aspects of speech, pursued not for the purpose of playing with words but for discovering and revealing hidden new meanings, was basic to the prose of Remizov, Bely and other Russian Symbolists. It was even more basic to the poetry of Mayakovsky, Pasternak and Tsvetaeva, the three poets whose work had some of the same roots as Nabokov's prose and with whom he shared the bent for verbal experimentation that at first puzzled and then delighted readers of his novels written in English.[2]

Wilson would play a great role in forwarding Nabokov's literary career, but he never learned to appreciate Nabokov's literary game-playing. Other critics would take up the challenge, however, and in doing so would help to popularize Nabokov's approach to literature, just as Wilson had helped to popularize the approach of the literary moderns with his review of *The Waste Land* in 1922.

Nabokov would gain these critics' respect because of *Lolita*, a novel he wrote in the early 1950s. Because of *Lolita*'s controversial subject matter, and because it involved just such wordplay, the book was disliked by Wilson and was rejected by five New York publishers before it went begging for publication to Paris. There a small publisher of a series of "dirty books" in English brought it out. Helped by the publicity of the controversy surrounding it, *Lolita* finally began to capture the attention of a wider circle of readers in England and America. By the time it was published in a regular trade edition in 1958, the book was famous—infamous—and it quickly climbed to the top of the best-seller charts. In this way it bypassed the establishment editors and critics who disliked such literary game-playing, and found its own audience, helping to popularize a new "post-modern" phase of English-language fiction.

When Nabokov emigrated to the United States in 1940, he was already a successful Russian writer. The son of a wealthy and influential Russian liberal political writer, he began his career in Russia at the age of fifteen. Forced into

[160]

exile with his family at the age of twenty, Nabokov continued to write at Cambridge, England, where he attended college, and then in Berlin, where he lived among other White Russians until the late 1930s.

In Berlin, he found himself in the midst of a community of émigré writers and intellectuals that included the cream of prerevolutionary Russia's writing and publishing establishment. Here Russian literature flourished in Russian-language journals, newspapers, and publishing houses.

As the son of an editor of the *Rudder*, the largest Russian newspaper in Berlin, Nabokov had little trouble getting his work published. His father's good friend and coeditor, Joseph Hessen, "allowed me with great leniency to fill his poetry section with my unripe lines."[3] In fact his poetry appeared in the *Rudder* "virtually every week for months at a time in the period between 1921 and 1925."[4] In being Vladimir Vladimirovich Nabokov, son of Vladimir Dmitrievich Nabokov, there was one drawback, however. Readers could be expected to confuse his writings with those of his already established father. Nabokov therefore adopted the penname "Vladimir Sirin" when he began to publish in the Russian émigré journals, and used it until his immigration to the United States in 1940.

In 1924 Nabokov turned his talents to writing serious fiction. Two years later, *Mashen'ka* was published by Slovo, a Russian-language publishing house in Berlin, which was run by Hessen. Nabokov's writing career proceeded at a steady pace following this first novel, and Hessen continued to publish his books under the Slovo imprint. *Korol', Dama, Valet* appeared in 1928, a collection of short fiction and poems called *Vozvrashchenie Chorba; Rasskazi i Stikhi* came out in 1930.

Although Berlin was an important center for Russian émigré writing during these years, an equally vital group of Russian writers lived in Paris where the most important journal of the Russian diaspora, *Contemporary Annals*, was

[161]

published by Ilya Fondaminsky. Nabokov's third novel, *Zashchita Luzhena* was serialized in *Contemporary Annals* in 1929–30, and his next work, a novella called *Soglyadataj*, appeared there later in 1930. In 1932 the book publishing arm of *Contemporary Annals* brought out Nabokov's fifth and sixth novels, *Kamera Obskura* and *Podvig*. In December that year, excerpts from a seventh Sirin novel began appearing in the *Latest News*. This novel, *Otchayanie*, was serialized in *Contemporary Annals* in 1934, and was published as a book by the Berlin firm Petropolis in 1936.

With each new publication, Sirin's reputation among exiled Russians grew. Although Nabokov would later report that his books never sold more than a few hundred copies, "they were read by a reasonable percentage of the three million Russian emigres."[5] In 1936, when he gave a reading of his work in Paris, he shared the program with the eminent poet and critic Vladislav Khodasevich. He read in an auditorium packed with "the Parnassus of Russian émigré poetry." Nabokov's reading was a rousing success, and it was followed by a champagne celebration at the La Fontaine café which lasted until three in the morning. At one point in the festivities, Mark Aldanov called Nabokov "the first writer of the emigration" (as Nabokov reported the next day in a letter to his wife) and demanded that Nobel laureate Ivan Bunin "take off his signet ring and give it to Nabokov as a token in recognition of his superiority."[6]

In 1936 the young Russian's fiction became available to English-language readers for the first time. Translated by Winifred Roy, and "insufficiently revised" by Nabokov, *Camera Obscura* was published by John Long in London in 1936. "A year later, on the Riviera, I attempted—not quite successfully—to English the thing anew for Bobbs-Merrill, who published it in New York in 1938) under the title *Laughter in the Dark*.[7] Nabokov's attempts to "English" *Camera Obscura* followed by a few months his translating *Otchayanie (Despair)* into English for a John Long publication in 1937. He was apparently intrigued with writing in the English

[162]

language as a result of doing these translations, and soon after began his first novel in English. This novel, *The Real Life of Sebastian Knight*, was completed before Nabokov emigrated to the United States in 1940, but was not published until New Directions brought it out in 1941.

Meanwhile, Nabokov continued to write and publish in Russian. Between 1935 and 1938 three more Sirin books appeared, *Priglashenie Na Kazn'*, *Dar*, and *Soglyadataj*. Then, with the outbreak of World War II in 1939, Nabokov's "Sirin" period ended, as did the entire era of Russian émigré literature. For Russians like Nabokov who could never accept life in a Communist Russia, all hope of seeing their homeland again had by now faded. America seemed the only place left to go.

When Nabokov arrived in the United States in May 1940, he was almost unknown on this side of the Atlantic, despite Sirin's fame in the cultural centers of the Russian diaspora. However, he had not been without publicity in this country. Albert Parry has written[8] of "Introducing Nabokov to America" in 1933, through a short article for the *American Mercury*.

Ivan Bunin was on the verge of receiving the Nobel Prize for Literature, and H. L. Mencken assigned Parry to report on "belles lettres among Russian emigres" in Europe. As Parry recalls: "Said Mencken, 'Just for the hell of it, make any chancy prediction you want about talents that may yet come out of that heap. Pick two or three dark horses and ride 'em.'"[9] Parry picked Nabokov, Mark Aldanov, and Nina Berveroba as three young Russian writers who "bear watching and deserve translation."[10] Alfred Knopf, who at that time was publisher of the *American Mercury*, saw the article and called Parry to his office to discuss the three Russian writers:

> "What about these three?" Knopf demanded. "Should I publish them?"
> I answered, yes, he should, particularly Nabokov, who I had read and admired since the latter 1920s. Knopf mused: "Well, nobody seems to know this fellow Nabokov except you."[11]

[163]

Parry urged Knopf to take a chance on Nabokov, and gave him the name and address of his Berlin publisher. Knopf agreed to think about publishing Nabokov, but of course never did.

Two years later in August 1935, as *Otchayanie* was appearing serially in *Contemporary Annals* in Paris, Alexander Nazaroff wrote an article on "Recent Books by Russian Writers" for the *New York Times Book Review* in which the Sirin book was spoken of in glowing terms:

> ... In the novel's first chapters Russian critics sensed the beginning of a work of unique importance. They were not mistaken. Now, after all of "Despair" had been published, most of the critics agree that it is a masterpiece of quite exceptional artistic power and originality. . . . One closes it with the feeling that our age has been enriched by the appearance of a great writer.[12]

When Bobbs-Merrill published *Laughter In the Dark* in the United States, the book was widely reviewed in generally favorable terms. During May and June 1938, reviews appeared in *Books,* the *New Republic,* the *New York Times,* the *New Yorker,* the *Saturday Review of Literature,* and *Time.*

By 1940, however, Nabokov was all but forgotten on this side of the Atlantic. Writes Karlinsky, "In America . . . there could hardly have been more than a hundred people who were aware of his literary achievement at the time of his arrival."[13] Edmund Wilson, who had recently become an avid student of Russian literature, had apparently not read any of Nabokov's works when he first wrote Nabokov in 1940.

As literary editor of the *New Republic,* Wilson was one of the most influential critics on the American literary scene. His rise to prominence had begun in 1922 when his review of *The Waste Land* in the December *Dial* prepared the way for that poem's acceptance by the emerging generation of critics and readers. Then, in 1928, Wilson's own reputation was established with the publication of his book *Axel's Castle,* defining the origins of literary modernism. Along with many other Western intellectuals, Wilson developed an interest in

[164]

Marxism and Soviet Russia during the 1930s. He studied Russian language and literature and visited Russia in 1935. That he might have been ignorant of V. Sirin's work is a bit surprising until one takes into account the feelings among Western intellectuals against White Russians during those years. (This attitude would reach such an extreme during the war that when the Book of the Month Club chose a Mark Aldanov novel in 1943, storms of protest arose and a boycott was organized.[14])

Whatever Wilson's own feelings about the White Russians, his misgivings about Nabokov would not surface until years later. In 1940, Wilson apparently welcomed him as a respected writer and congenial friend. It was this friendship, along with what Wilson had heard of Nabokov's émigré reputation, that prompted Wilson to sponsor the Russian writer in the United States. From the evidence of *The Nabokov—Wilson Letters* the two men seem to have been introduced through Nabokov's cousin Nicolas Nabokov, a composer, who knew Wilson and suggested Nabokov write to him. Nabokov did, and sent a book review which Wilson published in the *New Republic* in November 1940.

Nabokov and Wilson became close friends. On January 11, 1941, Wilson wrote, "I am going to write Laughlin [James Laughlin, founder and editor of New Directions publishing house] about bringing out your books."[15] This without yet having read any of them! Wilson did recommend Nabokov to Laughlin, and New Directions agreed to publish *Sebastian Knight*.

In October, Wilson finally read the book from the proofs sent him by Laughlin. He was enchanted by it, but criticized Nabokov's phonetic transliteration of Russian words "into which I fear you have been led by your lamentable weakness for punning." He also expressed his dislike of a play on the words "smuggled" and "smugness" in chapter nine.

The book appeared in late 1941. It was widely reviewed in major journals, and praised by a majority of its reviewers. This initial success was followed by others. On March 5, 1941,

[165]

Nabokov sent Wilson a "Sirin" short story which he had translated into English from the original Russian version published in *Russian Annals* in 1937. Wilson showed the story to the editor of the *Atlantic Monthly*, Edward Weeks, who published it in the June 1941 *Atlantic* and asked Nabokov for "some more little masterpieces."[16] During 1941, Nabokov went on to publish a story ("The Aurelian") and his first English poem ("The Softest of Tongues") in the November and December issues of *Atlantic Monthly*. On November 23, a book review article of his appeared in the *New York Times Book Review*. He wrote Wilson, "I also got 'we-are-interested' letters from a publisher or two. . . . I am wondering whether this pleasant little flurry is not due to your fine blurb which perhaps Laughlin has been sending around."[17] Wilson answered modestly:

> I don't think my blurb has anything to do with the attention you seem to be attracting. . . . I think that your rapid progress has been due to the merits of your writing. One of the strangest cases on record—especially in view of the fact that your vein does not fall into any of the current fashions.[18]

As a result of all this attention from publishers, Nabokov was encouraged to begin a new novel in English, *Bend Sinister*. During the five years which elapsed between the publication of *Sebastian Knight* and *Bend Sinister*, Nabokov published his critical biography of Gogol. His short fiction, essays, and poetry appeared regularly also in the *Atlantic Monthly* and the *New Yorker*.

To look at Nabokov's list of publications in highly regarded literary magazines, the relative ease with which he found publishers for his books, and the reviews which greeted them in all the well-known reviewing media, one might think he had arrived as a writer long before *Lolita* appeared in the mid-1950s. Certainly his friendship with Wilson and other eminent men and women on the literary scene suggest this assumption. However, fame eluded the writer in the 1940s

[166]

and early 1950s. Financially, he continued to struggle. His annual salary at Wellesley College was apparently only $3,000 in 1946.[19] His books never sold well despite the many reviews with which they were greeted. They almost seem to have gotten lost among the hundreds of other well-reviewed, commercially published books during these years.

Nabokov expressed his frustration in a letter to Wilson in June 1951:

> I have decided to welcome all kind and manner of publicity from now on. I am sick of having my books muffled up in silence like gems in cotton wool. The letters from private individuals I get are, in their wild enthusiasm, ridiculously incommensurable with the lack of interest my inane and inept publishers take in my books.... I am completely in the *deche* [completely broke], am in miserable financial difficulties, see no way out of academic drudgery (ill-paid to boot) and so on.[20]

The reviews of Nabokov's books suggest that his writing was considered good but not "important" among members of the literary establishment in the 1940s and 1950s—before *Lolita*. The problem seems to have been that Nabokov's books were whimsical in tone, with word games, puzzles, and tricks which undermined the emotional impact of the narratives. Wilson and other prominent literary critics found these word games "IN UNSPEAKABLY SILLY BAD TASTE," as Wilson wrote Nabokov about such tricks in *Bend Sinister*.[21]

Wilson was a leading advocate of historical criticism, which examines works on the basis of their picture of or potential impact upon society. He could never quite approve of Nabokov's interest in language as a medium for creating exquisite mental puzzles. To Wilson, such game-playing did violence to the serious purpose of the literary work. Though he was quick to recognize Nabokov's considerable talent, Wilson often disapproved of the way in which it was applied. The more Nabokov explored the possibilities language held for puzzles and tricks, mirror-images and deceptions, the more disapproving his friend Edmund Wilson became.

The day was coming, of course, when Nabokov's literary game playing would be taken quite seriously by students of contemporary literature; but this was years away—after *Lolita*. In the 1940s and early 1950s, Nabokov had his fans among the readers of the *New Yorker* and *Atlantic*, but he had yet to have any real influence on the American literary culture. Ironically, it would take a scandalous small-press publication to make this writer one of the most discussed and studied novelists of the post-World War II era.

In April 1947, a few weeks after Wilson had written re-iterating his dislike of "those tricks you expound" in *Bend Sinister* and in a new Nabokovian short story, "Professor O," Nabokov told his friend:

> I am writing two things now 1. a short novel about a man who liked little girls—and its going to be called *The Kingdom by the Sea*—and 2. a new type of autobiography—a scientific attempt to unravel and trace back all the tangled threads of one's personality—and the provisional title is *The Person In Question*.[22]

Over the next seven years the autobiography would emerge as *Conclusive Evidence* and then *Speak, Memory*, while the short novel would evolve into *Lolita*. That the two books developed somewhat simultaneously is interesting for the literary historian, because the autobiography is among other things a commentary on Nabokov's method and purpose as a writer. The perceptive reader can learn from *Speak, Memory* the reasons why Nabokov did not take Wilson's advice and abandon puns and games for a more serious approach in his fiction.

In chapter 6 (titled "Butterflies" when it was first published in the *New Yorker*, June 12, 1948), Nabokov discusses the "artistic perfection" with which many species of caterpillar and moth mimic leaves, wasps, or other creatures in their environment. Utilitarian scientific theories of natural selection, he argued, could not fully explain why mimicry was carried to a point of subtlety and exuberance "far in excess of a predator's power of appreciation. I discovered in nature the

[168]

nonutilitarian delights that I sought in art. Both were a form of magic, both were a game of intricate enchantment and deception."[23]

Chapter 14 of the memoir seems a very clear statement and example of what Nabokov was up to in writing *Lolita*. Neatly emphasized at the culmination of Nabokov's discussion of Russian émigré writers is the admission that "the author that interested me most was naturally Sirin. He belonged to my generation." This is followed by an intriguing assessment of Sirin's work and its reception by critics and readers in the Russian enclaves of Berlin and Paris between the World Wars. Only a few of Nabokov's American readers in *Partisan Review* would have been well enough acquainted with Nabokov's career prior to his coming to this country to know that Sirin was the penname Nabokov used during this period.

This bit of leg-pulling is quite typical of Nabokov—the ignorant are the butt of a joke the sophisticated are privileged to share. At the same time, embedded in this discussion are important clues as to how one should go about reading a Nabokov (or Sirin) novel. "Russian readers who had been raised on the sturdy straightforwardness of Russian realism and had called the bluff of decadent cheats, were impressed by the mirror-like angles of his [Sirin's] clear but weirdly misleading sentences and by the fact that the real life of his books flowed in his figures of speech, which one critic has compared to 'windows giving upon a contiguous world . . . a rolling corollary, the shadow of a train of thought.'"[24]

There follows an entire section about the delights of composing chess problems. What does this have to do with the Russian exile, one wonders. Nothing, of course. The reason for its placement immediately following the discussion of the writings of young Sirin comes through only in parentheses and figures of speech:

It should be understood that competition in chess problems is not really between White and Black but between the composer and

[169]

the hypothetical solver (just as in a first-rate work of fiction the real clash is not between the characters but between the author and the world), so that a great part of a problem's value is due to the number of "tries"—delusive opening moves, false scents, specious lines of play, astutely and lovingly prepared to lead the would-be solver astray. But whatever I can say about this matter of problem composing, I do not seem to convey sufficiently the ecstatic core of the process and its points of connection with various other, more overt and fruitful, operations of the creative mind, from the charting of dangerous seas to the writing of those incredible novels where the author, in a fit of lucid madness, has set himself certain unique rules that he observes, certain nightmare obstacles that he surmounts, with the zest of a diety building a live world from the most unlikely ingredients—rocks, and carbon, and blind throbbings.[25]

A statement made in relation to a particular chess problem in the next paragraph of the essay serves as a warning to the future readers of Nabokov's fiction:

> It was meant for the delectation of the very expert solver. The unsophisticated might miss the point of the problem entirely, and discover its fairly simple, "thetic" solution without having passed through the pleasurable torments prepared for the sophisticated one.[26]

When the novel *Lolita* was completed early in 1954, Nabokov was distressed to find that before his literary puzzle could reach the hands of "expert solvers" among the reading public, it had to pass publishers who tended to "miss the point of the problem entirely." Part of the reason was that readers were not used to novels of this type, except perhaps in the murder-mystery genre.

Lolita can, of course, be read "straight" as a story about a man who pursues, seduces, then loses a prepubescent girl. Reading with just this in mind, one experiences the poignancy of Lolita's lost childhood, as well as the depth of Humbert's obsession, which becomes in Nabokov's hands something akin to aesthetic bliss. In the process, the ordinary reader can also enjoy the parody of America's middle-class

[170]

culture in all its delightful "tackiness," such as this account of a motel-room notice:

"We wish you to feel at home while here. *All* equipment was carefully checked upon your arrival. Your license number is on record here. Use hot water sparingly. We reserve the right to eject without notice any objectional person. Do not throw waste material of *any* kind in the toilet bowl. Thank you. Call again. The management. P.S. We consider our guests the Finest People of the World."[27]

By reading *Lolita* as a straight narrative, however, one must also read through much elaborate detail placed there solely for the benefit of the literary game player. One of the mysteries of the narrative, the solution to which is hinted at many times, beginning with the spurious John Ray "Foreword," is the identity of the man in the Aztec Red convertible who pursues Humbert and Lolita, and with whom she finally disappears. At one point, Humbert's pursuit of his rival's identity in motel registers, an exercise replete with literary allusions and anagrams, takes an entire five-page chapter. In another place, a hint that the rival is Clare Quilty occurs in a bilingual pun: "Remember? *Ne manque pas de dire a ton amant, Chimène, comme le lac est beau car il faut qu'il t'y mène.* Lucky beau! *Qu'il ty'y* — What a tongue-twister!"[28] If the reader is not playing the game, this elaboration seems pointless and boring. If, however, the reader is trying to add up the clues and "solve" the puzzle ahead of time, and if the reader is predisposed to enjoy the literary allusions and the "shadow of a train of thought" they evoke, the second part of the book provides the delight of a very sophisticated crossword puzzle.

Nabokov does much to encourage readers to take up the challenge of his literary puzzle. In the twenty-ninth chapter, when Humbert finally finds Lolita, married and pregnant, he begs her for the man's name. When at last she tells him, Nabokov hides the answer in a description which only the very astute could possibly understand:

[171]

> She said really it was useless, she would never tell, but on the other hand, after all—"Do you really want to know who it was? Well it was—"
> And softly, confidentially, arching her thin eyebrows and puckering her parched lips, she emitted, a little mockingly, somewhat fastidiously, not untenderly, in a kind of muted whistle, the name that the astute reader has guessed long ago.[29]

What the "astute reader" has guessed, of course, is the name "Quilty." But that is not stated here, so that ordinary readers must read on, mystified, for many more pages before they can finally gather this answer to the riddle. For those expecting some serious purpose in a novel, *Lolita*, with its constant parodies, its elaborate tangle of clues, and its ludicrous B-movie ending could not have been anything but a disappointment.

As a published author and a regular contributor to top magazines, Nabokov might still have found a commercial publisher for *Lolita* had his book not posed one further problem. As Nabokov later reported in "On A Book Entitled *Lolita*,"[30] "The four American publishers, W, X, Y, Z, who in turn were offered the typescript and had their readers glance at it, were shocked by *Lolita*. . . ." In July 1954, Nabokov wrote Wilson of his difficulties:

> The novel I had been working at for almost five years has been turned down by the two publishers (Viking and S[imon] & S[huster]) I showed it to. They say it will strike readers as pornographic. I have now sent it to New Directions but it is unlikely they will take it. I consider this novel to be my best thing in English, and though the theme and situation are decidedly sensuous, its art is pure and its fun riotous. I would love you to glance at it some time. Pat Covici [senior editor at Viking Press] said we would all go to jail if the thing were published. I feel rather depressed about this fiasco.[31]

A week later Nabokov wrote his agent in Paris, Douissa Ergaz, and told her "about my troubles," as Nabokov recounted in 1966 in an article for the *Evergreen Review*.[32] "She

[172]

had arranged the publication in French of some of my Russian and English books; I now asked her to find somebody in Europe who would publish Lolita in the original English."

But three days later Wilson wrote offering new hope for an American publication. "By all means, send me your book," he told Nabokov. "I'd love to see it, and if nobody else is doing it, I'll try to get my publisher, Straus, to."[33] On September 5, Nabokov thanked Wilson for writing Farrar & Straus about his book and added, "I am very anxious for you to read it, it is *by far* my best English work."[34]

When the *Lolita* manuscript reached Farrar & Straus it was read by Roger Straus, who apparently misunderstood the book and was not prepared to participate in solving Nabokov's literary puzzle. The first part of the book, up to Lolita's "capture" by Humbert was exciting, he told Wilson, but "the second half drags." Wilson agreed. He wrote a frank letter to Nabokov expressing his dislike of the book:

> I like it less than anything else of yours I have read. The short story that it grew out of was interesting, but I don't think the subject can stand this very extended treatment. Nasty subjects make fine books; but I don't feel you have got away with this. It isn't merely that the characters and the situation are repulsive in themselves, but that, presented on this scale, they seem quite unreal. The various goings-on and the climax at the end have, for me, the same fault as the climaxes of *Bend Sinister* and *Laughter in the Dark:* they become too absurd to be horrible or tragic, yet remain too unpleasant to be funny. I think, too, that in this book, there is—what is unusual with you—too much background, description of places, etc. This is one thing that makes me agree with Roger Straus that the second half drags. [35]

Wilson passed on to Nabokov two other opinions of the book, one from his former wife, the novelist and critic Mary McCarthy, and one from his present wife, Elena Wilson. McCarthy (who didn't get to finish the book before returning it) seems to have understood less about what was going on in *Lolita* than Wilson, but she was more willing to give Nabokov the benefit of the doubt. She wrote Wilson:

[173]

I don't agree with you that the second volume was boring. Mystifying, rather, it seemed to me; I felt it had escaped into some elaborate allegory or series of symbols that I couldn't grasp. Boyden [McCarthy's new husband] suggests that the nymphet is a symbol of America, in the clutches of the middle-aged European (Vladimir); hence all the descriptions of motels and other U.S. phenomenology (I liked this part, by the way). But there seems to be some more concrete symbolism, in the second volume; you felt all the characters had a kite of meaning tugging at them from above, in Vladimir's enigmatic empyrean. . . .

On the other hand, I thought the writing was terribly sloppy all through, perhaps worse in the second volume. It was full of what teachers call *haziness,* and all Vladimir's hollowest jokes and puns. I almost wondered whether this wasn't deliberate—part of the idea.[36]

Elena Wilson came closer than either Wilson or McCarthy to reading and appreciating the book as it was intended:

The little girl seems very real and accurate and her attractiveness and seductiveness are absolutely plausible. The hero's disgust of grown-up women is not very different, for example, from Gide's, the difference being that Gide is smug about it and your hero is made to go through hell. The suburban, hotel, motel descriptions are just terribly funny.

. . . Unfortunately, my opinion is very unimportant. . . .
                    Elena
In other words, I couldn't put the book down and think it is very important.

Though Wilson disliked the book he didn't hesitate to suggest other possible publishers:

I have . . . written about it to a man named Weldon Kees, a poet, who has just written me that he is associated with a new publishing venture in California. . . . I have also talked about it to Jason Epstein at Doubleday.[37]

Epstein, a twenty-six-year-old editor at Doubleday, had gone to work for the publishing company fresh out of Columbia University in 1951, and soon persuaded Doubleday editor-

[174]

in-chief Ken McCormick to let him start Anchor Books, a line of quality paperbacks. "This has been a huge success," Wilson wrote, "and I have been making money out of the two books of mine they have published." About Epstein Wilson added, "He's a highly intelligent boy, very well read and with a good deal of taste."[38] As Epstein remembers his first encounter with the book:

> I don't recall the date on which I first saw the manuscript of *Lolita*, but I do recall that Edmund Wilson gave it to me at his house in Wellfleet on Cape Cod . . . probably on the Thanksgiving weekend. The manuscript that Wilson gave me was in two black binders. He said it was "repulsive" but that I should read it anyway. . . .[39]

Epstein liked *Lolita* and wanted to publish it, as did others at Doubleday:

> There was considerable enthusiasm among the Doubleday editors for *Lolita*, though we were all apprehensive about possible legal consequences. As I recall, Ken McCormick, the editor-in-chief at the time, would have agreed to publish the novel if Douglas Black, the president of the company, authorized it. But Black was so strongly opposed that he refused even to read the manuscript. This was irritating since Black thought of himself as a defender of the First Amendment and liked to make speeches on the subject.[40]

Two years later, Nabokov summarized these publishers' reactions to *Lolita* in an essay, and added:

> . . . one reader suggested that his firm might consider publication if I turned my Lolita into a twelve-year-old lad and had him seduced by Humbert, a farmer, in a barn, amidst gaunt and arid surroundings, all this set forth in short, strong, "realistic" sentence ("He acts crazy. We all act crazy, I guess. I guess God acts crazy." Etc.).[41]

"Doubleday has of course returned the MS and I have now shipped it to France," Nabokov wrote Wilson on February 19,

[175]

1955.[42] Nabokov had written Ergaz three days before, suggesting that Sylvia Beach "might perhaps be interested if she still publishes."[43] This was not followed up, no doubt because Ergaz knew that Beach had steadfastly refused to publish any books other than James Joyce's since 1922.

In his February 19 letter to Wilson, Nabokov included a prophetic statement concerning *Lolita*'s fate. "I suppose," he wrote, "it will be finally published by some shady firm with a Viennese-Dream name—e.g., 'Silo.'" He likely had in mind Jack Kahane's Obelisk Press which had been part of the Paris publishing scene during Nabokov's residence there in the late 1930s. Kahane had died in 1939, but his son Maurice Girodias had revived Obelisk after the war and also inaugurated Les Editions du Chêne, a series of fine art books. In 1950, having "expanded my business too quickly without paying the least attention to the notion of money," Girodias admits in his introduction to *The Olympia Reader*,[44] his operations were taken over by one of his creditors and he was "expelled from my own firm."

Embittered by this "piece of classical capitalistic maneuvering," Girodias began the Olympia Press in 1953. Though basically commercial in nature, Olympia was far from being an establishment press. According to Girodias he began the operation not only "as a desperate move on my part to escape complete social and economic annihiliation," but also out of an "urge to attack the Universal Establishment with all the means at my disposal."[45]

Setting up shop in "a small room at the back of a rundown bookstore at 13 rue Jacob," with a "staff of myself and a part-time secretary,"[46] Girodias proceeded to publish erotic novels of all sorts, some of recognized literary value but most simply "violently extravagant and outrageous. . . . Those literary orgies, those torrents of systematic bad taste were quite certainly instrumental in clearing the air, and clearing out a few mental cobwebs," Girodias asserts.[47] Some of his books, like *Lolita*, came to him complete, but most of his publications fell in the category of works made-for-hire. As he recalls:

[176]

I usually printed five thousand copies of each book, and paid a flat fee for the manuscript, which, although modest, formed the substance of many an expatriate budget. My publishing technique was simple in the extreme, at least in the first few years: when I had completely run out of money I wrote blurbs for imaginary books, invented sonorous titles and funny pen names (Marcus van Heller, Adbar del Piombo, Miles Underwood, Carmencita de las Lunas, etc.) and then printed a list which we sent out to our clientele of booklovers, tempting them with such titles as *White Thighs, The Chariot of Flesh, The Sexual Life of Robinson Crusoe, With Open Mouth,* etc. They immediately responded with orders and money, thanks to which we were again able to eat, drink, write, and print. I could again advance money to my authors, and they hastened to turn in manuscripts which more or less fitted the descriptions.[48]

Not all of Girodias's publications were of erotica, but he made no attempt to distinguish the respectable books from the "infamous Travellers Companion series, the green-backed books once so familiar and dear to the eagle-eyed inspectors of the U.S. Customs," as Alfred Appel, Jr., writes in his introduction to *The Annotated Lolita.*[49] Girodias explains:

That confusion was deliberate, as it made it easy to sell the higher class of literature: the d.b.'s (short for dirty books) fans were as fascinated by the ugly plain green covers as the addict by the white powder, however deceptive both may prove to be. The confusion was also meant to keep the police at bay, as I had soon become the object of their special attention.[50]

In April 1955, Ergaz received the typescript of *Lolita* and telephoned Girodias to offer him the book. When he read *Lolita* Girodias seems to have had much the same reaction his father had had on reading Henry Miller's *Tropic of Cancer* some twenty years before:

I was struck with wonder, carried away by this unbelievable phenomenon: the apparently effortless transposition of the rich Russian literary tradition into modern English fiction. . . . I sensed that *Lolita* would become the one great modern work of

[177]

art to demonstrate once and for all the futility of moral censorship, and indispensable role of passion in literature.[51]

Girodias quickly accepted the book for publication, expressing his hope that "it might lead to a change in social attitudes toward the kind of love described in it,"[52] and on May 13, Ergaz wrote Nabokov with this news. According to Nabokov, she did not mention that Girodias's specialty was erotica, and he had no way of knowing how nearly Olympia Press fit his prophesied "shady firm with a Viennese-Dream name." As Nabokov recalls his first acquaintance with Girodias:

> . . . before Madame Ergaz mentioned his name, I was totally ignorant of his existence, or that of his enterprise. He was recommended to me as the founder of The Olympia Press, which "had recently published, among other things, *Histoire d'O*" (a novel I had heard praised by competent judges) and as the former director of the "Editions du Chene" which had "produced books admirable from the artistic point of view."
> . . . I have pondered the painful question whether I would have agreed so cheerfully to his publishing *Lolita* had I been aware in May, 1955, of what formed the supple backbone of his production. Alas, I probably would, though less cheerfully.[53]

Girodias also indicates that Nabokov was at first "reluctant to let the book appear under his own name," and that Ergaz "had to use all her influence to make him change his mind." Indeed, as the writing of the book was nearing completion in 1953, Nabokov had written Wilson that he was finishing the book "in an atmosphere of great secrecy." And when he again wrote Wilson about *Lolita* in 1954 he repeated "all this is a *secret.*"

In his 1966 article Nabokov attributed this secrecy to his connection with Cornell University, which he asked Girodias not to mention in publicity about the book. As Nabokov explained:

[178]

By signing *Lolita* I had shown my complete acceptance of whatever responsibility an author has to take; but as long as an unhealthy flurry of scandal surrounded my innocent *Lolita*, I certainly was justified in acting as I did, lest a shadow of my responsibility fall on the university that had given me unbelievable freedom in conducting my courses ... nor did I care to embarrass the close friend who had brought me there to enjoy that true academic freedom.[54]

Despite his ignorance of Girodias's reputation, Nabokov seems to have been suspicious of the publisher almost immediately. "From the very start I was confronted with the peculiar aura surrounding his business transactions with me, an aura of negligence, evasiveness, procrastination, and falsity."[55] Perhaps it was this aura which led to one unusual aspect of *Lolita*'s publication—the fact that Nabokov seems to have written his own contract. As Girodias recalls:

I bowed to all the terms imposed on me, paid an advance much larger than I could afford at the time, and did not even insist on reserving for my firm a share of the eventual film rights, as is the usual practice.[56]

With an author's pride, Nabokov quotes "in strophic form" portions of the "Memorandum of Agreement" dated June 6, 1955, between himself and Olympia Press:

8
In the event of the Publishers
Going bankrupt
Or failing to make accountings and payments
As herein specified,
Then in either event the present agreement
Becomes automatically null and void
And the rights herein granted
Revert to the Author.

[179]

9
The Publishers shall render statement
Of the number of copies sold
On the 30th June and 31st December
Of each year
Within one month from these dates
Respectively
And shall make payment to the Author
At the time of such rendering of account.[57]

Nabokov had reserved for himself the copyright and was anxious to make sure the book was properly registered in the United States, so that it could not be pirated here as had been the fate of *Ulysses* and other foreign publications. In order to do this, he had to enter the exact date of publication on the copyright application forms. Several times during August and September 1955, Nabokov wrote asking Girodias when he would be publishing *Lolita,* but received no answer. "On October 8, 1955, I received, at last, a copy of the published book, but only on November 28, after some more 'entreaties,' did I learn that *Lolita* had been published on September 15, 1955."[58]

When he opened his copy of *Lolita* to the copyright page, Nabokov found there the phrase "Copyright 1955 by V. Nabokov and the Olympia Press." This threatened to complicate Nabokov's rights to his book, as he relates:

> On January 28, 1956, I learned from the copyright Office in Washington that this matey formula (for which I had not given my permission) might cause trouble at re-publication in the U.S. which had to take place within five years. I was advised to get an "assignment or quitclaim" from Mr. Girodias, and this I at once asked him to send me. I got no reply . . . , wrote to him again and again, but only on April 20 (*i.e.,* three months later) got from him what I asked.[59]

Of the financial terms, Nabokov reports, "My benefactor had agreed to pay me an advance of 400,000 "*anciens*" francs

[180]

(about a thousand dollars), one half on signature of the agreement (dated June 6, 1955), and the other half on publication." According to Nabokov, Girodias was a month late with the first payment, and did not pay the second half of the money until December 27, over three months after the September 15 publication.

Nor did the statements of the number of copies sold and royalty payments arrive semiannually when they were due. Nabokov should have received the first such statement on December 31, 1955, but did not. "I had to wait till March 21, 1957, and when it came the statement did not cover the entire period for which it was due." The next statement was due on July 31, 1957. When it didn't arrive by October 5, Nabokov notified Girodias that all rights to *Lolita* had reverted to him under the terms of the contract. Girodias "promptly paid up (44,200 *anciens* francs), and I relented."[60]

By this time the rights to *Lolita* were worth a great deal, because the book was somewhat famous, and several American publishers were interested in taking a chance on bringing out the American edition. This fame was brought about by events not in the United States or Paris, but in London.

When *Lolita* was first published in September 1955, Graham Greene "bought it in the Olympia Press edition and enjoyed it enormously," as he recalls. "I and other authors are invited every year around Christmas to name three books which we have most enjoyed during the year and on this occasion I nominated *Lolita*."[61] In January 1956, John Gordon, columnist for the popular Sunday *Express*, wrote expressing his shock. *Lolita*, he declared, was "sheer unrestrained pornography." Greene responded by sending a letter to the *Spectator* proposing the formation of the "John Gordon Society" in recognition of "the struggle he has maintained for so many years against the insidious menace of pornography. . . ."[62]

Harvey Breit, of the *New York Times Book Review*, picked up the story in the February 26 issue, identifying the book in question as "'Lolita,' a long French novel about nymphets." This item produced "a flurry of mail—some of the corre-

[181]

spondents wanting to know more, some contributing information."[63] In a column amplifying the earlier piece, Breit quoted several of the informative letters, although he didn't say who wrote them, or even how many there were. All of the quotes defended *Lolita* from the charge of obscenity, and, in the process, eulogized the novel in a way Nabokov's books had seldom been praised before.

> The novel is much less detailed in its descriptions and far more decorous in its vocabulary, than many novels on recent best-seller lists. . . . It shocks because it is great art, because it tells a terrible story in a wholly original way. It is wildly funny, coarse, subtle and tragic, all at once. . . . The actual theme of the book — which has long held a powerful appeal for our most important writers — is the corruption of innocence, as now envisioned through the imagination of a European intellectual in quest of his private America. . . . Something of its bedazzlement might be suggested by a composite impression of *Daisy Miller* and *The Possessed* — or perhaps, again of *The Captive* and *Tender Is the Night.*

Meanwhile, back in London, on Tuesday, March 6, the first and only meeting of the John Gordon Society was held in a London pub. According to Greene ". . . John Gordon was invited as a guest."[64] Gordon attended, along with some sixty other people. Judging from a report of the meeting which Greene wrote for the *Spectator* of March 9, 1956, discussions at this event were more concerned with dirty books in general than with *Lolita* in particular, but Girodias seems to be referring to this meeting when he says that an "absurd and comical exchange — including even a very drunken public debate"[65] followed Gordon's attack of Greene. Says Greene of the meeting, "John Gordon certainly wasn't drunk nor was I or the other officers of the Society, but Randolph Churchill [son of Sir Winston] made a rather drunk interruption."[66]

In the United States, Nabokov's novel quickly took on the aura of a suppressed masterpiece. As had happened with *Ulysses* thirty years before, Americans traveling in Europe bought copies to smuggle home in their suitcases. Two such copies of *Lolita* were confiscated by the U.S. Customs in 1956, "then released after a few weeks, without any explanation."[67] After this, the book was free to circulate legally in this country. In 1956, however, it seems to have been generally believed that *Lolita* had been banned from the United States by the authorities, when in truth it had only been exiled by commercial publishers who feared the authorities. One example of this misconception is a letter to the *New York Times* by Howard Nemerov.[68]

> In the course of efforts to procure a copy of Vlidimir Nabokov's new novel "Lolita," which is published in Paris, I learned today that the law forbids the importation of this book into our country. I have become so used to being governed for my own good that for twelve hours after receiving this news I did not realize that I felt outraged.
> No doubt the law is a splendid law, and does much to save us from ourselves. Yet it may be that by the mere corruption of taste, and by the ample provision of substitutes for literature, our society is already so well protected against good writing that Mr. Nabokov's new book might be allowed to enter the United States without occasioning the fear of any general deterioration of morals or improvement of minds.

Soon reviews of *Lolita* began to appear in little magazines in the United States. Louis Simpson, writing in the *Hudson Review*,[69] labeled *Lolita* as farce, "at the far extreme from . . . the so-called realistic novel, the form in which so many contemporary heavyweights have labored," and took several digs at "realism" which must have warmed Nabokov's heart. A few months later the *Partisan Review*, a leftist journal which also, somewhat strangely, favored literary modernism, printed a three-page review calling *Lolita* "an extended trope on the pathetic fallacy, in which verbal hocus-pocus makes the obsessive object light up, in intellectual neon, everywhere."[70]

Interest in *Lolita* might well have died out at this point had not Doubleday's Jason Epstein intervened in Nabokov's behalf. Despite his employer's opposition, Epstein was deter-

[183]

mined to be the first to publish *Lolita* on this side of the Atlantic, and when it became obvious that he would not be allowed to do it as a book, he found another route. As editor in charge of the Anchor series, Epstein was also in charge of the *Anchor Review*, a literary journal published in the form of a paperback book. He recalls:

> . . . I knew Customs had admitted the Olympia edition into the United States and that this reduced the risk for the *Anchor Review*. Even so, there was some discussion at Doubleday about the propriety of publishing excerpts in the *Review*. . . . I do recall telling Melvin Lasky, the editor of the *Anchor Review*, that it would be a good idea if we published parts of *Lolita*. He seemed to have some doubts but succeeded in overcoming them.[71]

Meanwhile, Epstein was in the process of editing Nabokov's newest book, *Pnin*. This novel appeared in March 1957, at a time when the *Lolita* number of the *Anchor Review* was in the final stages of preparation. Epstein apparently took advantage of *Pnin*'s appearance to publicize *Lolita* and vice versa, because several reviews of *Pnin* made reference to the anticipated *Anchor Review* publication. *Time* magazine, in fact, reviewed both books in a single article, quoting the as yet unpublished Nabokov comments from the *Anchor Review*.[72] Howard Nemerov reviewed both books in a single six-page article in *Kenyon Review*.[73] Here Nemerov made a reference to "the odd silence" around Nabokov's name, for which he did not know how to account, and asserted (in a prediction which seems quite humorous today) that *Lolita* was bound to deepen that silence.

Then in early June, the summer issue of the *Anchor Review* appeared, containing 112 pages devoted to *Lolita*—thirteen-page preface by F. W. Dupee, a seven-page article "On a Book Entitled *Lolita*" by Nabokov (his first published comment on his controversial book), and ninety pages of *Lolita* excerpts.

It is rare when a piece of magazine fiction draws reviews in other magazines, but the *Lolita* number of the *Anchor Review* drew at least three of them—in addition to the March review in *Time*. R. W. Flint, writing in the *New Republic*,[74] set the tone of *Lolita's* reception saying, ". . . this first American edition of Vladimir Nabokov's novel is a major literary event, worth all the attention we can spare." George Baker's article on the events leading up to the *Anchor Review* publication appeared in the June 22 *Saturday Review*,[75] and reported that copies of the complete Olympia edition, when they could be obtained, were selling in New York bookshops at $12.50 a copy. (The original two-volume book sold for 900 francs.)

Part of the reason for the scarcity of the Olympia edition in 1957 was that it had been banned in France by the French government on December 20, 1956. This ban, according to Girodias, was due to "pressing demands . . . made on the Ministry of the Interior in Paris by the British Home Office"[76] and his own failure to pay a bribe to a police inspector of the French vice squad.[77]

Thus, at the time the *Anchor Review* "Lolita" hit the newsstands in the United States, the earlier edition was in the ironic position of being banned in traditionally libertine Paris, but legal in Boston, New York, etc. This interesting angle led to more publicity for the book in the U.S. press. According to George Baker, "The obvious result of all this: the American public, intrigued by the French ban (and unable to buy any American editions of the novel because no American publisher . . . has thus far thought it worthy of publication), is willing to pay exorbitant prices for 'Lolita.'"[78]

The attitude of the commercial publishers was changing, however. The *Anchor Review* publication with Dupee's "brilliant article," according to Nabokov, "helped to make the idea of an American edition acceptable."[79] At this point, the difficulties between Nabokov and Girodias presented an obstacle to publication. In his "A Sad, Ungraceful History of *Lolita*" chapter of the *Olympia Reader* Girodias reported, "One publisher spontaneously offered a 20 per cent royalty to get the book, but was then apparently frightened away by Nabokov's attitude when he met him later in New York: and Nabokov's attitude had indeed changed quite substantially as

[185]

Lolita's glory expanded on the horizon."[80]

In *Strong Opinions*, "*Lolita* and Mr. Girodias," Nabokov recalls, "On September 14, 1957, the head of a distinguished American publishing house flew over to Paris to discuss matters with Mr. Girodias." Of Girodias's account he says:

> . . . it was not I who dissuaded this particular publisher, but his partner. . . . Mr. Girodias does not say who was to get most of the 20 percent. "I am prepared to accept this proposal," wrote Mr. Girodias to me (apparently under the impression that he had got a definite offer which was not the case), "if my share is assured at 12.5 percent. The advance would be shared in the same proportion. Would you accept 7.5 percent as your share? I consider my claim justified and fair." My agent wrote that she was "*outrée de ces prétentions*" [outraged by these pretentions]. (His contract had obliged him to pay me a 10 per cent royalty up to ten thousand copies and 12 percent after that.)[81]

According to Nabokov, Girodias threatened to bring out his own American reprint, but finally on November 30, 1957, dropped this threat as well as his claims to "a larger share of the proceeds" than agreed to in the contract, thus clearing the way to an American publication.

Meanwhile, *Lolita*'s fame spread. The *Reporter* gave *Lolita* rather royal treatment in its November 28, 1957, issue, printing a three-page article by Richard Schickel who called the book "in many ways the most remarkable — and certainly the most original — novel written in English in recent years . . . ." Schickel concluded, ". . . Nabokov has written nothing more or less than an American *Dead Souls*. At the moment a number of American publishers are circling nervously around the book, weighing its possible sales against the possibility of bannings and litigation."[82]

By this time, one of the circling publishers was Walter Minton, president of Putnam's, the venerable old New York firm. Minton had been unaware of *Lolita* and the controversy surrounding the book until an acquaintance, Rosemary Ridgewell, told him about the excerpts she had been reading in *Anchor Review*. Minton, who had assumed control of the firm in

[186]

1955 from his dying father, Melville Minton, had already shown his willingness to take a chance on controversial books when he published Norman Mailer's *Deer Park*. According to Charles A. Madison, ". . . Minton manifested a business acumen that combined intelligence with a predilection for books that excite and titillate." When Minton read *Lolita*, Madison writes:

> The story did not seem to him particularly immoral or indecent, and he did appreciate its clever writing. Moreover, he was quick to sense that, properly promoted, the book would interest a lot of people.[83]

Minton decided to publish *Lolita*. Ridgewell, described in *Time* magazine as "a tall (5 ft. 8 in.), slithery-blithery onetime Latin Quarter showgirl who wears a gold swizzle-stick around her neck . . ." got a cut of the *Lolita* profits for discovering the book. Her share was "the equivalent of 10% of author's royalties for the first year, plus 10% of the publisher's share of subsidiary rights for two years," according to *Time*.[84]

The publication date was set for August 1958. Meanwhile, the *New Republic* printed a lengthy assessment of Nabokov's writing by Conrad Brenner in its June 23, 1958, issue. Brenner opens his four-page article "Nabokov: The Art of the Perverse," with a statement about how Nabokov's reputation stood then, on the eve of the Putnam *Lolita*. "Vladimir Nabokov is best known, if he is known at all, as one of those ghostly heroes on the out-of-print register, fondly perpetuated by a mute coterie."[85]

Of course, the Nabokov coterie had been far from mute during the two years and nine months since the Olympia *Lolita* and by now was becoming a chorus. Benner did not hesitate to join this chorus, saying Nabokov "is wildly and liquidly sophisticated, and he writes as well as any man alive." *Lolita* he proclaimed a great novel, "The conscience behind it is supremely public, supremely 'topical,' and the art of it supremely lonely, special."[86]

[187]

It is hard to believe Benner is discussing the same book Edmund Wilson had found boring and "too absurd to be horrible, . . . too unpleasant to be funny" four years before. This diversity of opinion about *Lolita* was destined to continue following its Putnam publication. *Time* magazine reported on November 17:

> Frederic Babcock, editor of the Chicago *Tribune*'s Magazine of Books, proclaimed: "*Lolita* is pornography, and we do not plan to review it." Other abstainers: The *Christian Science Monitor* and the Baltimore *Sun* papers.[87]

But "most publications did brace themselves to review the book," *Time* continues, and the many vehement attacks on *Lolita* were answered by equally vehement praise. *Lolita* was reviewed in at least twenty national periodicals, with a more-or-less equal number of negative and positive assessments. Some reviewers praised it as a work of genius, while others vehemently damned it as obscene. In *Esquire* Dorothy Parker pronounced *Lolita* "a fine book, a distinguished book—all right, then—a great book," but Kirkus Reviews dismissed it as "very literate pornography." The *New Republic* ran a lead editorial to recant its earlier praise of the book, calling it an "obscene chronicle of murder and a child's destruction."

The defense of Nabokov's "banned masterpiece" by established British and American critics had elevated his reputation in those quarters from "good—for a Russian émigré" to "one of the greatest living writers—a classic," by the time *Lolita* finally found a regular commercial publisher. The now loud controversy surrounding the book brought it to the top of the best-seller lists, making Nabokov rich as well. He retired from teaching and took up residence in a grand hotel in Montreaux, Switzerland, where he lived and wrote for the next seventeen years, until his death in 1977.

In later years, Nabokov tended to denigrate his Paris publisher Girodias's role in the chain of events which lifted him to the pinnacle of literary success. In 1966 he wrote:

... I was (and am) deeply grateful to him for printing that book. But I must also point out to him that he was not the right person to undertake the thing; he lacked the means to launch *Lolita* properly—a book that differed so utterly in vocabulary, structure, and purpose (or rather abscence of purpose) from his other much simpler commercial ventures, such as *Debby's Bidet* or *Tender Thighs.*[88]

What Nabokov overlooks here is that *Lolita's* debut in her ignominious green covers added immensely to her allure as a forbidden fruit of English literature. The book was destined by its nature to be controversial, but had it been brought out by a legitimate New York publisher in the first place, that controversy would probably have been a great deal less heated, for as we have seen, the United States authorities found nothing objectionable about the book, even in its Travelers Companion form. Had New Directions or Viking brought out *Lolita* in 1955, had the book never been shunted off to Paris like *Ulysses* before it, it is unlikely the American literary arbiters would have been moved to proclaim *Lolita's* greatness in the process of defending it from suppression.

Still, one cannot speak with any certainty on a what-if proposition. We can, however, be certain that if Maurice Girodias, or an alternative publisher like him had not published *Lolita* in 1955, Nabokov's book would have languished unpublished years longer, and Nabokov's fortunes would not have taken the dramatic turn upward they did in 1958.

As it is, *Lolita,* with its emphasis on the novel as a self-contained world, a puzzle complete with puns and tricks, "meant for the delectation of the very expert solver," helped extend Joycean modernism and popularize Nabokov's whimsical approach to literature among literary critics.

Writing in the tradition of the Russian symbolists, Nabokov added a unique note to English-language literature. He was able to do this only because of the influence he gained through the fame of *Lolita,* which came to the world through the offices of a little Paris publisher of ill repute.

[189]

6

[ALTERNATIVE] PUBLISHING
. . . the handmaiden of literature

T. S. Eliot wrote his early work for his friends' little magazines and presses, without much thought to the demands of the commercial market; Virginia Woolf's self-publishing activities made possible her change from a commercial to an experimental writer; James Joyce's fictional experiments were expanded because of the freedom which his amateur publisher Sylvia Beach gave him. Anaïs Nin found an audience for her unusual writing through self-publishing, while Vladimir Nabokov gained respect for his literary games through the alternative publication of his controversial novel *Lolita*.

These five cases are not unique. A look at the history of English-language literature reveals that alternative publishing, far from being unusual, is the usual path to prominence for writers whose work does not fit the contemporary commercial mold.

This was true to some extent in earlier centuries. In England, the careers of Blake, Shelley, Byron, and many other writers owe much to alternative publishing. And in the United States, most of the nineteenth-century writers whom we now think of as important to the development of American literature published their own works. Washington Irving's *Sketchbook*, Poe's *Poems* of 1831, Hawthorne's early fiction, Whitman's *Leaves of Grass*, Thoreau's *Walden*,

Twain's *Huckleberry Finn,* and Melville's later works, after the commercial failure of *The Confidence Man,* were all self-published.

But the twentieth century, with its elaborate system of commercial publishing, presents literary historians with a unique scene. Never before have the odds against having one's work published commercially been so large. Meanwhile, the twentieth century has been an era in which experimentation in literature has been practiced and encouraged as never before. "Make it new," said Ezra Pound; "Last year's words belong to last year's language," said T. S. Eliot; and the pursuit of the new became one of the primary tenants of literary culture.

If the experiments were unpopular with everyday readers, writers were encouraged to take a "public-be-damned" attitude. "So far as I personally am concerned the public can go to the devil," Pound told Harriet Monroe in 1912,[1] and he was echoed by later experimenters in the 1929 "Revolution of the Word Proclamation" in *transition,* the twelfth point of which was "THE PLAIN READER BE DAMNED" (vol. 16/17).

The movements and schools—futurism, imagism, vorticism, dadaism, surrealism, etc.—came and went, revolutionizing literature in their wakes as they opened new possibilities and purposes for the written language. Along with this experimentation, enabling it to take place, was a great burst of publishing outside the elaborate establishment system which centered in New York and London. Experimental writers, finding the commercial publishers generally unresponsive to their needs, set up alternative systems of their own to serve them.

So intricately tied were avant-garde writing and alternative publishing that it is now impossible to imagine one without the other. Without *Poetry* and *Des Imagistes* there could have been no imagism, without *Blast* no "Vorticist Manifesto," without *transition* no "Revolution of the Word." The Hogarth Press was as important a part of the Bloomsbury movement as were the various weekly salons; the avant-

[194]

garde publishers were as vital to the Paris literary scene during the 1920s and 1930s as were the left bank cafés. Nor did this phenomenon end when the heyday of literary modernism was over; alternative methods of publication have grown with each passing year.

By its very nature, alternative publishing has posed problems for writers and readers alike, problems not generally encountered when dealing with commercial publishers. Obvious among these problems is distribution. The establishment press, with its network extending to libraries and shops in virtually every city and hamlet in the English-speaking world, offers a writer access to a much wider audience than can be reached through the localized alternative presses.

Another problem inherent in alternative publishing is that of instability. In many instances, noncommercial also means unprofitable. Little magazines and small presses usually exist hand-to-mouth, often needing subsidies and donations to stay in operation. Writers who entrust their manuscripts to such alternative presses always face the possibility that their publisher, having accepted a work, will hold it for months or years and finally go out of business before it is published; or else publish a book, then go out of business, so that the book will be out of print after the first edition, as happened time and again to Anaïs Nin.

In cases where writers eliminate this risk by becoming their own publishers, other problems almost always arise. Self-publishing means setting up a small business. Investment capital must be found to start with, then the writer must take time away from his or her writing to do the work of publishing and distributing the book, often being forced to learn the skills needed for successful publishing as he goes along. Few writers have been able to sustain a self-publishing operation over a very long period of time. As for any small publisher, a lack of funds and energy are constant spectres.

Copyrights have also been a source of frustration to writers who publish through the alternative presses. Alternative-press publications have been far more frequently pirated

[195]

because of a widespread lack of respect for their operations, or because alternative publishers have been less than business-like in their approach to copyrights.

Works ruled obscene in this country face a special copyright problem, even though they are published freely elsewhere. *Ulysses* is a case in point. This novel appears to be in the public domain now, and probably has been since its Random House publication in 1934, although this question has never been tested in a court of law. As we have seen, substantial portions were published in the *Little Review* in 1918–20, and then ruled obscene by a New York court. United States law forbids the copyright of an obscene work, and states that any work published without a legal copyright automatically goes into the public domain. Thus, the *Little Review* publication, because it was ruled obscene, would seem to place *Ulysses* in the public domain. Once in public domain, a work can never be copyrighted. Even though the famous 1933 Woolsey decision cleared *Ulysses* from the obscenity charge, the text is now, apparently, beyond the protection of the copyright laws. Random House has not publicized this fact, but has not bothered to take other publishers to court in the few instances in which they have brought out "pirated" editions. In 1970, for instance, an edition of *Ulysses*, issued by a publisher of pornography in Industry, California, came to the attention of Darcy O'Brien, who was teaching a course on Joyce at nearby Pomona College. The edition contained advertisements for condoms, dildos, and other exotica, according to O'Brien, and carried no copyright notice. Curious, he wrote Random House asking if they were aware of the pirated edition. They were, Random House lawyers wrote back, but there was nothing they could do to prevent copyright infringements on *Ulysses* since their own copyright might not be valid. They did not want the publicity a lawsuit against a pirate would bring, the lawyers told O'Brien, especially since they were not confident of winning.[2]

Another drawback to alternative publishing has been the stigma which has attended it throughout the century.

[196]

Despite the obvious importance of small presses and little magazines in the development of modern literature, the bias that only "bad" writers need resort to alternative publication exsts to this day. In his tongue-in-cheek defense of the New York literary establishment in Bill Henderson's *The Publish-It-Yourself Handbook* (1973), Gordon Lish, then literary editor of *Esquire,* hurled the taunt at writers: ". . . it goes to show you're as dumb as I've been hinting throughout, . . . because after all, here you are wasting time 'self-publishing' . . . when you might have better used what little life you have learning how to write good enough to get up there where a person of my eminence will want to toast your existence over the *plat de jour.*"[3] Lish surely knows better, but the general public—and many reviewers and literary scholars—have always believed that alternatively published works can be classed with "vanity" publications and dismissed out-of-hand. The result of this bias is that these works are generally not reviewed in the press unless some eminent critic—an Edmund Wilson or a Graham Greene—has first placed his stamp of approval on the work.

Despite these very serious problems, alternative publishing has continued to grow in importance as more and more writers find the commercial establishment unwilling to serve their needs. The impact of alternative publishing on literary culture since World War II has been even more important than previously, as a cursory look at recent history shows.

There is, for instance, the case of Allen Ginsberg's poem "Howl." As *The Waste Land* shocked the literary world of 1922 and announced the arrival of literary modernism, "Howl" shook the literary world of 1955 and announced the arrival of the much-ballyhooed "Beat Generation," forerunner of the wider anti-establishment movement of the 1960s. Like that of *Ulysses* before it, the print publication of "Howl" was preceded by a sensational reading, this one at the Six Gallery in Berkeley, California, organized by Kenneth Rexroth. The following year—like *Ulysses*—"Howl" was published in a volume (*Howl and Other Poems*) by a bookseller,

[197]

Lawrence Ferlinghetti of City Lights Bookstore in San Francisco. "Howl" aroused the wrath of the San Francisco Police Department, which arrested Ferlinghetti for publishing and selling obscenity. Ferlinghetti and "Howl" were tried and cleared of the charges when literary critics testified to the quality of the poem, and the publicity made *Howl* a bestseller with the then emerging generation. This alternative publication was part of an entire alternative West Coast literary movement in the United States.

Also published in 1956 were two collections of short stories by James Purdy, a thirty-six-year-old former college teacher. The world-view portrayed in these stories was bleak, the narrative bizarre. Publisher after literary publisher in the New York rejected the stories, so that Purdy finally persuaded friends to help him publish his work privately as *63: Dream Palace* and *Don't Call Me By My Right Name, and Other Stories*. Purdy sent copies to leading literary figures in London. Edith Sitwell responded with praise, and soon was joined by others. On Dame Edith's recommendation, Purdy's work was soon brought out by commercial publishers, and, although his writing has never sold well, Purdy is now widely recognized as an important contemporary writer.

Since the 1960s, alternative publishing has grown in both size and importance in the United States. Helped by the underground press movement of the late sixties which became the small press movement of the seventies, this alternative method of publishing is today more than ever the most important force operating to open our national literature to new modes and voices. In 1973, Bill and Nancy Henderson of Yonkers, New York, spent $3,500 to print, bind, advertise, and distribute *The Publish-It-Yourself Handbook*. Their publishing company was named "The Pushcart Press" to commemorate a group of authors who sold their own books from a pushcart on the streets of New York to protest the inefficient distribution methods of their commercial publishers. The *Handbook* became a bestseller as much by word-of-mouth as by the Hendersons' publicity efforts and is still in

[198]

print in a revised edition. According to Bill Henderson's "Preface to the Eighth Printing," the small press movement tripled in membership between 1973 and 1976.

Over the years, many university presses have seen the need to spend some of their limited publishing funds to help foster new poetry and fiction, as commercial outlets for these forms have become progressively scarcer. Most famous is the Yale University Press Younger Poets Series, which has brought out numerous important poets over the past fifty years. Since 1970 the University of Iowa Press has published annually a collection of short stories by a previously unpublished writer. The University of Illinois Press publishes four volumes of short stories each year, and other presses bring out new poetry regularly. Several university presses have published novels, and more are considering entering the field.

The growth of alternative publishing has been so great during the past twenty years that an entire support industry has grown up around it. In the mid-1960s Len Fulton began to index alternative presses in a directory for use by libraries, writers, and others interested in these outlets. The nineteenth edition of this work, the *1983–84 International Directory of Little Magazines and Small Presses,* edited by Fulton and Ellen Ferber and published by Dustbooks in California, lists 3,535 English-language small presses and some 200 book and magazine distributors to serve them.

Ferber's preface to the 1980–81 *Directory* gives an interesting assessment of alternative publishing's recent past and probable future:

> This directory enters its third decade of documenting a publishing phenomenon which seems to show no diminution in its growth. We have greater sobriety these days to be sure, the effect perhaps of six or so years of efforts to solve problems of distribution and promotion. But the impact of the small, independent publishers on the book publishing industry as a whole is greater than ever. And it is clearly destined to continue. . . .
> . . . Listings from new publishers for this directory arrive at the

[199]

Dustbooks office at the rate of about fifty per month throughout the year, and while it is true that many operations die or suspend publication, the ratio of births to deaths is easily ten to one, creating an expanding industry that offers the new writer extraordinary possibilities for publication. . . .

Whatever else you may predict about the 80's, the true growth in publishing in anything like its traditional and creative sense, will all take place in the independent publishing business.

"Small Press publishing," writes Ferber in the 1983–84 *Directory*, "has achieved a permanent and significant place in American literary life and culture. . . ."

Alternative publishing, always an important part of the literary publishing scene, has become in the twentieth century the "handmaiden of literature" that the commercial publishing establishment is no longer equipped to be. It has helped to shape our literature by presenting to the public new forms of writing and new ideas about the literary art. Any student of literature who seeks to understand fully what has happened in the twentieth century must take a good look at the role of alternative publishing in the careers of its most influential writers. And by the same token, any reader who would like to discover the important trends and writers of tomorrow would do well to look for them in today's alternative press.

NOTES

INTRODUCTION

1 Ezra Pound, *The Letters of Ezra Pound, 1907–1941*, ed. D. D. Paige (New York: Harcourt, Brace & World, 1950), p. 9.

2 Pound, p. 10.

3 Pound, pp. 10–11.

4 Wyndham Lewis, ed., *BLAST*, no. 2 (July 1915), p. 6.

5 Wyndham Lewis, ed., *BLAST*, no. 1 (20 June 1914), p. 4.

6 Ezra Pound, *Literary Essays of Ezra Pound*, ed. T. S. Eliot (New York: New Directions, 1968), p. 9.

7 Frederick J. Hoffman, Charles Allen and Carolyn F. Ulrich, *The Little Magazine: A History and Bibliography* (Princeton: Princeton University Press, 1946), p. 18.

8 Sheldon Meyer and Leslie E. Phillabaum, "What is a University Press?" *Scholarly Publishing*, XI, no. 3 (April 1980), 217–18.

9 Thomas Whiteside, "The Blockbuster Complex," *New Yorker*, 29 September 1980, 48–101; 6 October 1980, 63–146; 13 October 1980, 52–143.

10 Noel Stock, *The Life of Ezra Pound* (New York: Pantheon Books, 1970), p. 47.

11 Stock, p. 55.

12 Stock, p. 55.

13 Ezra Pound, Letter to Mrs. Mathews, 23 December 1921, fol. 1051–53, *The Archives of Elkin Mathews, 1911–1938* (Published on microfilm by Chadwyck-Healey, Ltd., 1973), University Archives in the Library, the University of Reading, Whiteknights, Reading.

14 Pound, *The Letters*, pp. 7–8.

1. ELIOT

1 Ezra Pound, *The Letters of Ezra Pound, 1907–1941,* ed. D. D. Paige (New York: Harcourt Brace & World, 1950), p. 40.

2 Charles Norman, *Ezra Pound* (New York: Macmillan, 1960), pp. 165–66.

3 Pound, pp. 40–41.

4 Pound, p. 41.

5 Pound, pp. 44–45.

6 Pound, p. 50.

7 Pound, p. 57.

8 Pound, p. 60.

9 Valerie Eliot, ed., *The Waste Land: A Facsimile and Transcript of the Original Drafts Including the Annotations of Ezra Pound* (New York: Harcourt Brace Jovanovich, 1971), p. ix.

10 Norman, p. 181.

11 Noel Stock, *The Life of Ezra Pound* (New York: Pantheon Books, 1970), p. 205.

12 Jane Lidderdale and Mary Nicholson, *Dear Miss Weaver: Harriet Shaw Weaver, 1876–1961* (New York: Viking Press, 1970), p. 79.

13 Lidderdale, p. 120.

14 Lidderdale, p. 121.

15 T. S. Eliot, "Keepsake Number 1," from Special Collections, McFarlin Library, University of Tulsa, 1978.

16 Valerie Eliot, p. xii.

17 Lidderdale, p. 138.

18 Donald Gallup, *T. S. Eliot: A Bibliography* (London: Faber & Faber, 1962), p. 3.

19 Bernard Bergonzi, *T. S. Eliot* (New York: Macmillan, 1972), p. 40.

20 Bergonzi, p. 40.

21 Clive Bell, *Old Friends: Personal Recollections* (New York: Harcourt, Brace, 1956), p. 119.

22 Clive Bell, p. 121.

23 Clive Bell, p. 122.

24 Leonard Woolf, *Beginning Again: An Autobiography of the Years 1911–1918* (New York: Harcourt, Brace & World, 1963), p. 242.

25 B. L. Reid, *The Man From New York: John Quinn and His Friends* (New York: Oxford University Press, 1968), p. 273.

26 Charles Allen Madison, *Book Publishing In America* (New York: McGraw-Hill, 1966), p. 324.

27 Reid, p. 273.

28 Reid, p. 279.

29 Valerie Eliot, p. xii.

30 Valerie Eliot, p. xiv.

31 Valerie Eliot, p. xiv.

32 Valerie Eliot, p. xvi.

33 Valerie Eliot, p. xvi.

34 Valerie Eliot, p. xvi.

35 Valerie Eliot, p. xvi.

36 Valerie Eliot, p. xvi.

37 Virginia Woolf, *The Diary of Virginia Woolf*, I, ed. Anne Oliver Bell (London: Hogarth Press, 1977), p. 210.

38 Woolf, *Diary*, I, p. 273.

39 Leonard Woolf, pp. 245–46.

40 Virginia Woolf, *The Letters of Virginia Woolf*, II, ed. Nigel Nicolson (New York: Harcourt, Brace, Jovanovich, 1976), p. 282.

41 Leonard Woolf, p. 243.

42 Leonard Woolf, p. 242.

43 Leonard Woolf, p. 243.

44 Woolf, *Diary*, I, p. 91.

45 Valerie Eliot, p. xviii.

46 Lyndall Gordon, *Eliot's Early Years* (Oxford: Oxford University Press, 1977), p. 143.

47 Gordon, p. 105.

48 Pound, p. 169.

49 Pound, p. 170.

50 Pound, p. 171.

51 William Wasserstrom, "T. S. Eliot and *The Dial*," *Sewanee Review*, 70, no. 1 (Winter 1962), 81.

52 Wasserstrom, 84.

53 Nicolas Joost, *Schofield Thayer and the Dial* (Carbondale, Ill.: Southern Illinois University Press, 1964), p. 159.

54 Joost, p. 159.

55 Joost, p. 160.

56 Joost, p. 160.

57 Joost, p. 160.

58 Reid, p. 534.

59 John Tebbel, *A History of Book Publishing in the United States,* II (New York: Harcourt, Brace & World, 1963), pp. 390–91.

60 Bennett Cerf, *At Random* (New York: Random House, 1977), p. 41.

61 Reid, p. 534.

62 Valerie Eliot, p. xxiii.

63 Valerie Eliot, p. xxiii.

64 Valerie Eliot, p. xxiii.

65 Valerie Eliot, p. xxiii.

66 Joost, p. 161.

67 Valerie Eliot, p. xxiv.

68 Reid, p. 537.

69 Reid, p. 538.

70 Reid, p. 538.

71 Reid, p. 538.

72 Valerie Eliot, p. xxvi.

73 Woolf, *Diary,* I, p. 171.

74 Woolf, *Letters,* II, p. 521.

75 Woolf, *Diary,* I, p. 178.

76 Leonard Woolf, p. 245.

77 Bergonzi, p. 78.

78 Wasserstrom, p. 88.

79 Joost, p. 162.

80 Joost, p. 41.

81 *London Times Literary Supplement,* 20 September 1923, p. 616.

82 Bergonzi, p. 78.

WOOLF

1 Robert Humphrey, *Stream of Consciousness in the Modern Novel* (Berkeley: University of California Press, 1962), p. 22.

2 Quentin Bell, *Virginia Woolf: A Biography,* I (New York: Harcourt Brace Jovanovich, 1972), p. 40.

3 Bell, *Biography*, I, p. 93.

4 Bell, *Biography*, I, p. 54.

5 Quentin Bell, *Bloomsbury* (London: Weidenfeld & Nicolson, 1968), p. 41.

6 Bell, *Biography*, I, p. 99.

7 Bell, *Biography*, I, p. 126.

8 Bell, *Biography*, I, p. 153.

9 Bell, *Biography*, I, p. 154.

10 Bell, *Biography*, I, p. 176.

11 Virginia Woolf, *The Letters of Virginia Woolf*, II, ed. Nigel Nicolson (New York: Harcourt Brace Jovanovich, 1976), p. 23.

12 Bell, *Biography*, II, p. 16n.

13 Virginia Woolf, *The Diary of Virginia Woolf*, I, ed. Anne Oliver Bell (New York: Harcourt Brace Jovanovich, 1977), p. 28.

14 Bell, *Biography*, II, pp. 26.

15 Bell, *Biography*, II, p. 28–29.

16 Leonard Woolf, *Beginning Again* (New York: Harcourt, Brace & World, 1963), p. 87.

17 Leonard Woolf, p. 233.

18 Leonard Woolf, p. 234.

19 Woolf, *Letters*, II, p. 150.

20 Woolf, *Letters*, II, p. 153.

21 Woolf, *Letters*, II, p. 156.

22 Woolf, *Letters*, II, p. 156.

23 Bell, *Biography*, II, p. 42.

24 Leonard Woolf, p. 236.

25 Leonard Woolf, pp. 236–37.

26 Bell, *Biography*, II, p. 43.

27 Woolf, *Letters*, II, p. 167.

28 Woolf, *Letters*, II, p. 168.

29 Woolf, *Letters*, II, p. 159.

30 Woolf, *Letters*, II, p. 255.

31 Woolf, *Letters*, II, pp. 259, 261, and 289.

32 Woolf, *Diary*, I, p. 271.

33 Woolf, *Diary*, I, 273.

34 Woolf, *Diary*, I, p. 276.

35 Woolf, *Diary*, I, p. 277.

36 Woolf, *Diary*, I, p. 280.

37 Bell, *Biography*, II, pp. 68–69.

38 Woolf, *Diary*, I, p. 314.

39 Bell, *Biography*, II, p. 42.

40 Woolf, *Diary*, II, pp. 13–14.

41 Woolf, *Diary*, II, pp. 35–36.

42 Woolf, *Diary*, II, p. 40.

43 Woolf, *Diary*, II, p. 67.

44 Woolf, *Diary*, II, p. 69.

45 Woolf, *Diary*, II, p. 86.

46 Woolf, *Diary*, II, p. 106.

47 Woolf, *Diary*, II, pp. 106–07.

48 Woolf, *Diary*, II, p. 118.

49 Woolf, *Diary*, II, p. 109.

50 Woolf, *Diary*, II, p. 125.

51 Woolf, *Diary*, II, p. 125.

52 Woolf, *Diary*, II, p. 161.

53 Woolf, *Diary*, II, p. 179.

54 Woolf, *Diary*, II, p. 186.

55 Woolf, *Letters*, II, p. 574.

56 Woolf, *Diary*, II, p. 208.

57 *TLS*, 26 October 1922, p. 683.

58 Woolf, *Diary*, II, p. 214.

3. *JOYCE*

1 Richard Ellmann, *James Joyce* (New York: Oxford University Press, 1959), p. 88.

2 James Joyce, *Letters of James Joyce*, I, ed. Stuart Gilbert (New York: Viking Press, 1957), p. 105.

3 James Joyce, *Letters of James Joyce*, II, ed. Richard Ellmann (New York: Viking Press, 1966), p. 144.

4 Ellmann, p. 250.

5 Ellmann, p. 272.

6   Ellmann, p. 320.

7   James Joyce, *Selected Letters of James Joyce*, ed. Richard Ellmann (New York: Viking Press, 1975), p. 197.

8   Joyce, *Letters*, II, p. 293.

9   Ellmann, p. 326n.

10   Joyce, *Letters*, II, p. 298.

11   Ellmann, p. 339.

12   Ellmann, pp. 339–40n.

13   Joyce, *Selected Letters*, p. 202.

14   Joyce, *Letters*, II, pp. 309–10.

15   Joyce, *Letters*, II, p. 313–14.

16   Joyce, *Letters*, II, p. 311.

17   Joyce, *Letters*, II, pp. 314–15.

18   Joyce, *Letters*, II, p. 315.

19   Ellmann, p. 344.

20   Joyce, *Letters*, II, p. 323.

21   Joyce, *Letters*, II, p. 324.

22   John J. Slocum and Herbert Cahoon, *A Bibliography of James Joyce* (New Haven: Yale University Press, 1953), p. 12.

23   *London Times Literary Supplement*, 18 June 1914.

24   Ellmann, p. 364.

25   *Egoist*, 15 July 1914, 267.

26   Ellmann, p. 413.

27   Jane Lidderdale and Mary Nicholson, *Dear Miss Weaver: Harriet Shaw Weaver, 1876–1961* (New York: Viking Press, 1970), pp. 108–9.

28   Ezra Pound, *Pound/Joyce: The Letters of Ezra Pound to James Joyce, with Pound's Essays on Joyce*, ed. Forrest Read (New York: New Directions, 1967), pp. 64–65.

29   Pound, *Pound/Joyce*, pp. 65–66.

30   Pound, *Pound/Joyce*, p. 63.

31   Pound, *Pound/Joyce*, p. 67.

32   Ezra Pound, *The Letters of Ezra Pound, 1907–1941*, ed. D. D. Paige (New York: Harcourt Brace & World, 1950), pp. 74–75.

33   Pound, *Pound/Joyce*, pp. 118–20.

34   Frederick J. Hoffman, Charles Allen and Carolyn F. Ulrich, *The Little Magazine: A History and Bibliography* (Princeton: Princeton University Press, 1946), p. 56.

[207]

35 Hoffman, p. 55.

36 Pound, *Letters*, p. 106–07.

37 Margaret Anderson, *My Thirty Years' War* (New York: Corvici, Friede, 1930), p. 158.

38 Joyce, *Selected Letters*, p. 227.

39 Anderson, p. 39.

40 Anderson, p. 40.

41 Anderson, pp. 175–76.

42 Joyce, *Letters*, I, pp. 118–19.

43 Lidderdale, p. 147.

44 Virginia Woolf, *The Letters of Virginia Woolf*, II, ed. Nigel Nicolson (New York: Harcourt Brace Jovanovich, 1976), p. 242.

45 Woolf, II, p. 134.

46 Lidderdale, p. 160.

47 Lidderdale, p. 170.

48 Anderson, p. 221.

49 Anderson, p. 226.

50 Richard A. Sullivan, "The Blindness of Homer: An Exploration of Cultural and Social Contexts for Joyce's Ulysses," Ph.D. diss., University of Tulsa, 1980, p. 163.

51 Sylvia Beach, *Shakespeare and Company* (New York: Harcourt, Brace & World, 1959), pp. 46–47.

52 Beach, p. 48.

53 Joyce, *Letters*, I, p. 162.

54 Sullivan, pp. 167–68.

55 Sullivan, p. 168.

56 Sullivan, p. 169.

57 Ellmann, p. 527.

58 Beach, p. 58.

59 Harry Levin, Introd., *James Joyce's Ulysses: A Facsimile of the Manuscript*, with biographical preface by Clive Driver (New York: Farrar, Straus & Giroux, 1975), p. 2.

60 Levin, p. 6.

61 Levin, p. 7.

62 Clive Driver, pref., *James Joyce's Ulysses: A Facsimile of the Manuscript*, with critical introd. by Harry Levin (New York: Farrar, Straus & Giroux, 1975), p. 24.

63 Levin, p. 5.

64 Levin, p. 7.

65 Levin, p. 5.

66 Levin, p. 6.

67 Ellmann, p. 535.

68 Sullivan, p. 170.

69 Sullivan, pp. 164–65.

70 Quotations from Larbaud's lecture are taken from *James Joyce: The Critical Heritage,* ed. Robert H. Deming (London: Routledge and Kegan Paul, 1970), pp. 252–62.

71 Beach, p. 74.

72 Beach, p. 85.

73 Lidderdale, p. 193.

74 Lidderdale, p. 193.

75 Lidderdale, p. 195.

76 Lidderdale, p. 199.

77 Ellmann, p. 546.

78 See Ellmann, p. 521n.

79 Slocum, p. 29.

80 Bennett Cerf, *At Random* (New York: Random House, 1977), p. 91.

81 Beach, p. 202.

82 Beach, p. 204.

83 Cerf, pp. 92–93.

84 Cerf, p. 93.

85 Cerf, pp. 94–95.

86 Ellmann, p. 705.

4. NIN

1 Anaïs Nin, *The Diary of Anaïs Nin,* III, ed. Gunther Stuhlmann (New York: Swallow Press and Harcourt Brace Jovanovich, 1969), p. 261.

2 Rose Marie Cutting, *Anaïs Nin: A Reference Guide* (Kent, Ohio: Kent State University Press, 1978), p. vii.

3 Anaïs Nin, *The Diary of Anaïs Nin,* I, ed. Gunther Stuhlmann (New York: Swallow Press and Harcourt Brace Jovanovich, 1966), pp. 4–5.

4 Nin, *Diary,* I, p. 5.

5   Nin, *Diary*, I, p. 5.

6   Nin, *Diary*, III, p. 128–29.

7   Matthew Josephson, *Life Among the Surrealists, A Memoir* (New York: Holt, Reinhart and Winston, 1962), p. 215.

8   Josephson, p. 217.

9   Henry Miller, *Letters to Anaïs Nin*, ed. Gunther Stuhlmann (New York: G. P. Putnam's Sons, 1965), p. ix.

10   Miller, pp. viii–ix.

11   Nin, *Diary*, I, p. 7.

12   Nin, *Diary*, I, p. 7–8.

13   Nin, *Diary*, I, p. 8.

14   Nin, *Diary*, I, p. 11.

15   Nin, *Diary*, I, p. 12.

16   Nin, *Diary*, I, p. 132.

17   Nin, *Diary*, I, p. 130.

18   Miller, p. xii.

19   Nin, *Diary*, I, p. 163.

20   Miller, p. xviii.

21   Hugh D. Ford, *Published In Paris: American and British Writers, Printers, and Publishers in Paris, 1920–39* (New York: Macmillan, 1975), p. 364.

22   Nin, *Diary*, I, pp. 319–20.

23   Nin, *Diary*, I, p. 321.

24   Anaïs Nin, Introd. to *Tropic of Cancer*, by Henry Miller (New York: Grove Press, 1961), p. xxix.

25   Nin, *Diary*, I, p. 267.

26   Nin, *Diary*, I, p. 315.

27   Nin, *Diary*, I, p. 306.

28   Nin, *Diary*, I, p. 319.

29   Nin, *Diary*, I, p. 328.

30   Nin, *Diary*, I, p. 328.

31   Nin, *Diary*, I, p. 328.

32   Nin, *Diary*, I, p. 331.

33   Nin, *Diary*, I, pp. 331–32.

34   Anaïs Nin, *The Diary of Anais Nin*, II, ed. Gunther Stuhlmann (New York: Swallow Press and Harcourt Brace Jovanovich, 1967), p. 146.

35 Nin, *Diary*, II, p. 149.
36 Nin, *Diary*, II, p. 154.
37 Nin, *Diary*, II, p. 156.
38 Nin, *Diary*, II, p. 107.
39 Nin, *Diary*, II, p. 206.
40 Nin, *Diary*, II, p. 268.
41 Nin, *Diary*, II, p. 274.
42 Nin, *Diary*, III, p. 47.
43 Nin, *Diary*, III, p. 156.
44 Nin, *Diary*, II, p. 28.
45 Nin, *Diary*, II, p. 43.
46 Nin, *Diary*, II, p. 44.
47 Nin, *Diary*, II, p. 46.
48 Nin, *Diary*, III, p. 259.
49 Nin, *Diary*, II, p. 204.
50 Nin, *Diary*, II, p. 238.
51 Nin, *Diary*, II, p. 264.
52 Nin, *Diary*, III, pp. 11–12.
53 Nin, *Diary*, III, p. 13.
54 Nin, *Diary*, III, p. 25.
55 Nin, *Diary*, III, p. 40.
56 Nin, *Diary*, III, p. 41.
57 Nin, *Diary*, III, p. 70.
58 Nin, *Diary*, III, p. 72.
59 Nin, *Diary*, III, p. 113.
60 Nin, *Diary*, III, p. 116.
61 Nin, *Diary*, III, p. 161.
62 Nin, *Diary*, III, p. 161.
63 Nin, *Diary*, III, p. 162.
64 Nin, *Diary*, III, p. 162.
65 Nin, *Diary*, III, p. 174.
66 Nin, *Diary*, III, p. 176.
67 Nin, *Diary*, III, p. 176.
68 Nin, *Diary*, III, p. 177.

69 Nin, *Diary*, III, p. 179.

70 Nin, *Diary*, III, p. 180.

71 Nin, *Diary*, III, p. 181.

72 Nin, *Diary*, III, p. 181.

73 Nin, *Diary*, III, p. 181.

74 Nin, *Diary*, III, p. 185.

75 Nin, *Diary*, III, p. 186.

76 Nin, *Diary*, III, p. 188.

77 Nin, *Diary*, III, p. 192

78 Nin, *Diary*, III, p. 196.

79 Nin, *Diary*, III, p. 196.

80 Nin, *Diary*, III, p. 205.

81 "Anaïs Nin," *Current Biography* (1944), pp. 494.

82 Nin, *Diary*, III, p. 206.

83 Nin, *Diary*, III, p. 248.

84 Nin, *Diary*, III, p. 258–60.

85 Nin, *Diary*, III, p. 264.

86 Nin, *Diary*, III, p. 291.

87 Nin, *Diary*, III, p. 303.

88 Nin, *Diary*, III, p. 307.

89 "Anaïs Nin," p. 494.

90 Nin, *Diary*, III, p. 308.

91 Nin, *Diary*, III, p. 312.

92 Nin, *Diary*, III, p. 312.

93 Nin, *Diary*, III, p. 309.

94 Anaïs Nin, *The Diary of Anaïs Nin*, IV, ed. Gunther Stuhlmann (New York: Swallow Press and Harcourt Brace Jovanovich, 1971), p. 84.

95 Nin, *Diary*, IV, p. 87.

96 Nin, *Diary*, IV, p. 103.

97 Nin, *Diary*, IV, pp. 103–04.

98 Nin, *Diary*, IV, p. 105.

99 Nin, *Diary*, IV, p. 163.

5. NABOKOV

1   Simon Karlinsky, ed., *The Nabokov–Wilson Letters: Correspondence Between Vladimir Nabokov and Edmund Wilson, 1940–1971* (New York: Harper Colophon Books, 1979), p. 29.

2   Karlinsky, p. 21.

3   Vladimir Nabokov, *Speak, Memory: An Autobiography Revisited* (New York: Capricorn Books, 1970), p. 281.

4   Andrew Field, *Nabokov: His Life in Part* (New York: Viking Press, 1977), p. 149.

5   Vladimir Nabokov, *Strong Opinions* (New York: McGraw-Hill, 1973), p. 5.

6   Field, *His Life in Part*, p. 194.

7   Nabokov, *Strong Opinions*, p. 82.

8   Albert Parry, "Introducing Nabokov To America," *Texas Quarterly*, 14, no. 1 (1971), 16–26.

9   Parry, "Introducing," 16.

10   Albert Parry, "Belles Lettres Among the Russian Emigres," *American Mercury* (July 1933), 319.

11   Parry, "Introducing," 18.

12   Alexander Nazroff, "Recent Books by Russian Writers," *New York Times*, 18 August 1935, sec. VI, p. 8, col. 4.

13   Karlinsky, p. 10.

14   See Karlinsky, p. 10.

15   Karlinsky, p. 37.

16   Karlinsky, p. 40.

17   Karlinsky, p. 53.

18   Karlinsky, p. 54.

19   Karlinsky, p. 173.

20   Karlinsky, p. 264.

21   Karlinsky, p. 187.

22   Karlinsky, p. 188.

23   Nabokov, *Speak, Memory*, p. 125.

24   Nabokov, *Speak, Memory*, p. 288.

25   Nabokov, *Speak, Memory*, pp. 290–91.

26   Nabokov, *Speak, Memory*, p. 291.

27   Vladimir Nabokov, *The Annotated Lolita*, ed. Alfred Appel, Jr. (New York: McGraw-Hill, 1970), p. 212.

[213]

28 Nabokov, *Annotated Lolita*, p. 225.

29 Nabokov, *Annotated Lolita*, pp. 273–74.

30 Nabokov, *Annotated Lolita*, p. 315.

31 Karlinsky, p. 285.

32 Nabokov, *Strong Opinions*, p. 270.

33 Karlinsky, p. 286.

34 Karlinsky, p. 287.

35 Karlinsky, p. 288.

36 Karlinsky, pp. 288–89.

37 Karlinsky, p. 288.

38 Karlinsky, p. 288.

39 Letters received from Jason Epstein, 23 February and 4 March 1982.

40 Letter received from Epstein, 23 February 1982.

41 Nabokov, *Annotated Lolita*, p. 316.

42 Karlinsky, p. 292.

43 Nabokov, *Strong Opinions*, p. 270.

44 Maurice Girodias, ed., *The Olympia Reader* (New York: Grove Press, 1965), p. 17.

45 Girodias, pp. 11–18.

46 Girodias, p. 18.

47 Girodias, p. 19.

48 Girodias, p. 19.

49 Nabokov, *Annotated Lolita*, p. xxiii.

50 Girodias, p. 20.

51 Girodias, p. 535.

52 Nabokov, *Strong Opinions*, p. 271.

53 Nabokov, *Strong Opinions*, pp. 270–71.

54 Nabokov, *Strong Opinions*, pp. 274–75.

55 Nabokov, *Strong Opinions*, p. 272.

56 Girodias, p. 535.

57 Nabokov, *Strong Opinions*, p. 269.

58 Nabokov, *Strong Opinions*, p. 273.

59 Nabokov, *Strong Opinions*, p. 274.

60 Nabokov, *Strong Opinions*, p. 274.

61 Letter received from Graham Greene, 9 March 1982.

62 Graham Greene, "The John Gordon Society," *Spectator* (10 February 1956), 182.

63 Harvey Breit, "Lolita," *New York Times Book Review*, 11 March 1956, p. 8.

64 Letter received from Graham Greene, 9 March 1982.

65 Girodias, p. 536.

66 Letter received from Graham Greene, 9 March 1982.

67 Girodias, p. 536.

68 Howard Nemerov, Letter, *New York Times*, 30 October 1956, p. 36.

69 Louis Simpson, "Fiction Chronicle," *Hudson Review*, XXI, no. 3 (Summer 1956), 302–09.

70 John Hollander, "The Perilous Magic of Nymphets," *Partisan Review*, 23, no. 4 (Fall 1956), 559.

71 Letters received from Jason Epstein, 23 February and 4 March 1982.

72 "Pnin & Pan," *Time* (18 March 1957), 109–10.

73 Howard Nemerov, "The Morality of Art," *Kenyon Review*, 9, no. 2 (Spring 1957), 313–21.

74 R. W. Flint, "Nabokov's Love Affairs," *New Republic* (17 June 1957), 18–19.

75 George Baker, "'Lolita': Literature or Pornography?" *Saturday Review* (22 June 1957), 18.

76 Girodias, p. 537.

77 See Girodias, p. 24.

78 Baker, p. 18.

79 Nabokov, *Strong Opinions*, p. 275.

80 Girodias, p. 538.

81 Nabokov, *Strong Opinions*, p. 276.

82 Richard Schickel, "A Review of a Novel You Can't Buy," *Reporter* (28 November 1957), 45–47.

83 Charles Allan Madison, *Book Publishing In America* (New York: McGraw-Hill, 1966), p. 414.

84 "The Lolita Case," *Time* (17 November 1958), 102.

85 Conrad Benner, "Nabokov: The Art of the Perverse," *New Republic* (23 June 1958), 18–21.

86 Benner, p. 21.

87 "The Lolita Case," 102.

88 Nabokov, *Strong Opinions*, p. 275.

[215]

6. *ALTERNATIVE PUBLISHING*

1 Ezra Pound, *The Letters of Ezra Pound, 1907–1941*, ed. D. D. Paige (New York: Harcourt, Brace & World, 1950), p. 13.

2 Personal interview with Darcy O'Brien, 5 April 1982.

3 Bill Henderson, ed., *The Publish-It-Yourself Handbook* (Yonkers, New York: Pushcart Book Press, 1973), p. 340.

BIBLIOGRAPHY

Anderson, Margaret. *My Thirty Years' War*. New York: Corvici, Friede, 1930.

Appel, Alfred, Jr., and Charles Newman, eds. *Nabokov: Criticism, Reminiscences, Translations and Tributes*. Evanston: Northwestern University Press, 1970.

Baker, George. "'Lolita': Literature or Pornography?" *Saturday Review* (22 June 1957): 18.

Beach, Sylvia. *Shakespeare and Company*. New York: Harcourt, Brace & World, 1959.

Bell, Clive. *Old Friends: Personal Recollections*. New York: Harcourt, Brace, 1956.

Bell, Quentin. *Bloomsbury*. London: Weidenfeld & Nicholson, 1968.

————. *Virginia Woolf: A Biography*. 2 vols. New York: Harcourt Brace Jovanovich, 1972.

Benner, Conrad. "Nabokov: The Art of the Perverse." *New Republic* (23 June 1958): 18–21.

Breit, Harvey. "Albion." *New York Times Book Review*, 26 February 1956, p. 8.

————. "Lolita." *New York Times Book Review*, 11 March 1956, p. 8.

Bergonzi, Bernard. *T. S. Eliot*. New York: Macmillan, 1972.

Cerf, Bennett. *At Random*. New York: Random House, 1977.

Cutting, Rose Marie. *Anaïs Nin: A Reference Guide*. Kent, Ohio: Kent State University Press, 1978.

Dupee, F. W. "A Preface To *Lolita.*" *Anchor Review* (Summer 1956): 1–13.

Eliot, T. S. "Keepsake Number 1." Special Collections, McFarlin Library, University of Tulsa, 1978.

Eliot, Valerie, ed. *The Waste Land: A Facsimile and Transcript of the Original Drafts Including the Annotations of Ezra Pound.* New York: Harcourt Brace Jovanovich, 1971.

Ellmann, Richard. *James Joyce.* New York: Oxford University Press, 1959.

Epstein, Jason. Letter to author (23 February 1982).

————. Letter to author (4 March 1982).

Field, Andrew. *Nabokov: A Bibliography.* New York: McGraw-Hill, 1973.

————. *Nabokov: His Life in Art.* Boston: Little, Brown,, 1967.

————. *Nabokov: His Life in Part.* New York: Viking Press, 1977.

Flint, R. W. "Nabokov's Love Affairs." *New Republic* (17 June 1957): 18–19.

Ford, Hugh D. *Published In Paris: American and British Writers, Printers, and Publishers in Paris, 1920–1939.* New York: Macmillan, 1975.

Fulton, Len and Ellen Ferber, eds. *The International Directory of Little Magazines and Small Presses.* Paradise, California: Dustbooks, 1980, 1983.

Gallup, Donald *T. S. Eliot: A Bibliography.* London: Faber & Faber, 1962.

Girodias, Maurice, ed. *The Olympia Reader.* New York: Grove Press, 1965.

Gordon, Lyndall. *Eliot's Early Years.* Oxford: Oxford University Press, 1977.

Greene, Graham, and John Sutro. Letter. *Spectator* (10 February 1956): 182.

Greene, Graham. "The John Gordon Society." *Spectator* (9 March 1956): 309.

————. Letter to author (9 March 1982).

[218]

Henderson, Bill, ed. *The Publish-It-Yourself Handbook: Literary Tradition and How-To.* Yonkers, New York: Pushcart Book Press, 1973.

Hoffman, Frederick J., Charles Allen, and Carolyn F. Ulrich. *The Little Magazine: A History and Bibliography.* Princeton: Princeton University Press, 1946.

Hollander, John. "The Perilous Magic of Nymphets." *Partisan Review,* 23 (1956): 557–560.

Humphrey, Robert. *Stream of Consciousness in the Modern Novel.* Berkeley: University of California Press, 1962.

James Joyce's Ulysses: A Facsimile of the Manuscript, with a critical introduction by Harry Levin and a biographical preface by Clive Driver. New York: Farrar, Straus & Giroux, 1975.

Joost, Nicholas. *Schofield Thayer and the Dial: An Illustrated History.* Carbondale, Ill.: Southern Illinois University Press, 1964.

Josephson, Matthew. *Life Among the Surrealists, A Memoir.* New York: Holt, Rinehart and Winston, 1962.

Joyce, James. *Letters of James Joyce.* Vol. I. Ed. Stuart Gilbert. New York: Viking Press, 1957.

————. *Letters of James Joyce.* Vols. II and III. Ed. Richard Ellmann. New York: Viking Press, 1966.

————. *Selected Letters of James Joyce.* Ed. Richard Ellmann. New York: Viking Press, 1975.

Karlinsky, Simon, ed. *The Nabokov–Wilson Letters: Correspondence Between Vladimir Nabokov and Edmund Wilson, 1940–1971.* New York: Harper Colophon Books, 1979.

Lidderdale, Jane, and Mary Nicholson. *Dear Miss Weaver; Harriet Shaw Weaver, 1876–1961.* New York: Viking Press, 1970.

Madison, Charles Allan. *Book Publishing In America.* New York: McGraw-Hill, 1966.

Miller, Henry. *Letters to Anaïs Nin.* Edited by Gunther Stuhlmann. New York: G. P. Putnam's Sons, 1965.

Miller, Henry. *Tropic of Cancer.* Introd. by Anaïs Nin. New York: Grove Press, 1961.

Nabokov, Vladimir. *The Annotated Lolita.* Ed. Alfred Appel, Jr. New York: McGraw-Hill, 1970.

[219]

————. "On A Book Entitled *Lolita.*" *Anchor Review* (Summer 1956): 105–12.

————. *Speak, Memory: An Autobiography Revisited.* New York: Capricorn Books, 1970.

————. *Strong Opinions.* New York, McGraw-Hill, 1973.

Nazaroff, Alexander. "Recent Books by Russian Writers." *New York Times Book Review,* 18 August 1935, sec. VI, p. 8.

Nemerov, Howard. Letter. *New York Times,* 30 October 1956, p. 36.

————. "The Morality of Art." *Kenyon Review,* 9, no. 2 (1957): 313–21.

"Nin, Anaïs," *Current Biography* (1944): 494.

Nin, Anaïs. *The Diary of Anaïs Nin.* Vols. I–IV. Ed. Gunther Stuhlmann. New York: Swallow Press and Harcourt Brace Jovanovich, 1966, 1967, 1969, and 1971.

————. *Linotte: The Early Diary of Anaïs Nin.* New York: Harcourt Brace Jovanovich, 1978.

Norman, Charles. *Ezra Pound.* New York: Macmillan, 1960.

Parry, Albert. "Belles Lettres Among the Russian Emigres." *American Mercury* (July 1933): 316–19.

————. "Introducing Nabokov To America." *Texas Quarterly,* 14, no. 1 (1971), 16–26.

"Pnin & Pan." *Time* (18 March 1957): 108–10.

Pound, Ezra. *The Letters of Ezra Pound, 1907–1941.* Ed. D. D. Paige. New York: Harcourt Brace and World, 1950.

————. *The Literary Essays of Ezra Pound.* Ed. T. S. Eliot. New York: New Directions, 1968.

————. *Pound/Joyce: The Letters of Ezra Pound to James Joyce, with Pound's Essays on Joyce.* Ed. Forrest Read. New York: New Directions, 1967.

Prescott, Joseph. *Exploring James Joyce.* Carbondale: Southern Illinois University Press, 1964.

Reid, B. L. *The Man From New York: John Quinn and His Friends.* New York: Oxford University Press, 1968.

[220]

Schickel, Richard. "A Review of a Novel You Can't Buy." *Reporter* (28 November 1957): 45–47.

Simpson, Louis. "Fiction Chronicle." *Hudson Review*, 21, no. 3 (1956), 302–9.

Slocum, John J., and Herbert Cahoon. *A Bibliography of James Joyce.* New Haven: Yale University Press, 1953.

Stock, Noel. *The Life of Ezra Pound.* New York: Pantheon Books, 1970.

Tebbel, John. *A History of Book Publishing in the United States.* Vol. 2. New York: R. R. Bowker, 1975.

"The Lolita Case." *Time* (17 November 1958): 102.

Wasserstrom, William. "T. S. Eliot and *The Dial.*" *Sewanee Review*, 70, no. 1 (Winter 1962).

Woolf, Virginia. *The Diary of Virginia Woolf.* Vols. I and II. Ed. Anne Oliver Bell. London: Hogarth Press, 1977, 1978.

―――. *The Letters of Virginia Woolf.* Vol. II. Ed. Nigel Nicolson. New York: Harcourt Brace Jovanovich, 1976.

Woolf, Leonard. *Beginning Again: An Autobiography of the Years 1911–1918.* New York: Harcourt Brace & World, 1963.

Whiteside, Thomas. "The Blockbuster Complex." *New Yorker* (29 September 1980): 48–101; (6 October 1980): 63–146; (13 October 1980): 52–143.

INDEX

Abélard, 133
Adelphi, 23
"Age d'Or" (Buñuel), 125
Agents, literary, 6, 92, 127, 133, 141, 172. *See also* Clairouin, Bradley, Ergaz, Pinker, Slocum
Aiken, Conrad, 18, 44
Albemarle Hotel, 34
Aldanov, Mark, 162–63, 165
Aldington, Richard, 19, 21–22
Alemany, 147
Allendy, René, 127
Alternative publishing: as an outlet for new writing, 3, 12, 193–200; bias against, 196–97; Blake and, 193; Boni & Liveright and, 38; Byron and, 193; defined, 3; development of all literary genres and, 5–6, 193–200; Eliot and, 17–18, 33–34; growth of, 197–200; handmaiden of literature, 200; Joyce and, 95–115; Nin's troubles with, 141–42; permanent part of literary scene, 3, 191–93, 199– 200; problems of, 195–97; reviewing media and, 32, 152–53; shaper of modern writing, 8, 12, 45, 192–93; Shelley and, 193;

Times (London) Literary Supplement and, 32; William Carlos Williams and, 12. *See also* Self-publishing
American Mercury, 163
Anaïs Nin: A Reference Guide (Cutting), 121
Anchor Books, 175, 184
Anchor Review, 184–86
Anderson, Margaret, 3, 96–98, 101–02
Anderson, Sherwood, 105
Annotated Lolita, The, 177
Antonini, A., 9–10
Appel, Alfred, Jr., 177
Aquitania, 113
Ara Vos Prec (Eliot), 32–33, 101
Arnold, Edward, 81
Art versus "realism" in writing, 119, 127, 149–50, 152–53, 155
Art, literature as, 2–3, 119–20, 127, 131–32, 155, 168–69
Art versus popularity in literature, 2–3, 8, 96–97
Atelier 17, 144
Athenaeum, 28, 33, 66
Atlantic Monthly, 1, 166, 168
Auguste Bartholdi, rue (Paris), 125

[223]

Augustine, Saint, 133
"Aurelian, The" (Nabokov), 166
Author's alterations, 107–08
Autobiography (Williams), 42
Avant-garde presses. *See*
  Alternative publishing
Avant-garde writing. *See* Ex-
  perimental writing
Axel's Castle (Wilson), 44, 164

Barker, George, 144, 185
Barnacle, Nora. *See* Joyce,
  Nora
Baudelaire, Charles-Pierre,
  110
Beach, Sylvia, 78, 95, 103–15,
  176
Beat Generation, 197
Beginning Again (Leonard
  Woolf), 30, 61
Bel Esprit, 36
Bell, Anne Oliver, 30
Bell, Clive: Bloomsbury and,
  52–54; Eliot and, 24; Woolf
  and, 30, 62, 66
Bell, Quentin, 51, 54, 66
Bell, Vanessa (née Stephen,
  sister of Virginia Woolf), 50,
  52, 53, 59, 60, 66; illustrates
  Kew Gardens, 63–65
Bély, 160
Bend Sinister (Nabokov), 166,
  167–68, 173
Bennett, Arnold, 68–69, 111
Bergonzi, Bernard, 24, 42, 44
Berkeley, California, 197
Berlin, Germany, 161
Berveroba, Nina, 163
Black Manikin, 122
Black Sun Press, 138, 148
Black, Douglas, 175
Blake, William, 144–45, 150, 193
BLAST, 20, 194
Bloomsbury group, 24, 25,
  51, 52–53, 111, 120

Bloomsbury (London), 30, 52
Bobbs-Merrill, 162, 164
Bodley Head, 10–11
Boni & Liveright, 17, 28, 101.
  See also Liveright
Boni, Albert, 20, 38
Book of the Month Club, 165
Bookstore, publishing: alter-
  native publishing and, 3;
  commercial publishing and,
  77–78; "Howl" and, 197;
  history of, 77; *Ulysses* (Joyce)
  and, 78, 95, 103–15; writer's
  control and, 77. See also
  Ulysses
Books, 164
Borzoi Books, 26, 33
Boston, Massachusetts, 185
Bowling Green, Virginia, 138–
  39
Boyle, Kay, 139
Bradley, William, 127–29, 130,
  133, 138
Breit, Harvey, 147, 181–82
Brenner, Conrad, 187–88
Breton, André, 123–24, 139
Bridgeport, Connecticut, 125
British Weekly, 70
Brooklyn, New York, 124
Buck, Pearl, 120
Bunin, Ivan, 162, 163
Buñuel, Luis, 125
Bunyan, John, 77
"Butterflies" (Nabokov), 168
Byron, Lord, 193

Cambridge University, 52, 53,
  161
Camera Obscura (Nabokov), 162.
  See also *Kamera Obskura*
Cantos (Pound), 37
Cape, Jonathan, 94, 133
Capitalism, 132
Carrefour, 135
Carrington, Dora, 61, 63

Carson, Pirie, Scott and Company, 96
Cather, Willa, 26
Catholic Anthology, 20, 22
Censorship, 3; English printers and, 80, 94, 98, 100, 101, 133; of Joyce's work, 78, 83–89, 94, 97–98, 101–02, 112–15, 182; of Lawrence's work, 94, 128; of Nabokov's *Lolita*, 172–89; of Travellers Companion series, 177
Central Hotel, Paris, 125
Cerf, Bennett, 38, 112–14
Chamber Music (Joyce), 81, 101
Champ de Mars, 125
Chicago Tribune, 125
Chicago, Illinois, 96
Child, Harold, 65
Churchill, Randolph, 182
Churchill, Sir Winston, 182
Cité Universitaire (Paris), 130
City Lights Bookstore, 198
Clairouin, Denise, 133
Colefax, Mrs. Sybil, 25
Columbia University, 174
Colum, Padraic, 43
Commercial publishers: Blake and, 144; Boni & Liveright as, 38; booksellers as, 77; coterie publishing and, 4–5; exile *Lolita*, 183; expatriate writers and, 124; experimental writing and, 1–3, 5–7, 9, 12, 193, 194–200; interested in Lolita, 185–89; Joyce's career and, 95, 114–15; Joyce's opinion of, 93; Knopf as a, 26; literary renaissance and, 1, 37, 100, 200; Miller and, 134; Nabokov and, 160, 167, 183, 185–89; Nin and, 120, 132, 133–34, 140–43, 151–55; popularize literary trends, 7; Pound tries with early work,

1, 9; size and complexity, 7, 194; story of, 7; survival depends on sales, 2, 7; *Ulysses* and, 95, 101, 107, 112–15; Woolf and, 49–51, 63
Communism, 120, 131, 163
Complete Press, 98, 99–100
Conclusive Evidence. See Speak, Memory
Confidence Man, The, 194
Conrad, Joseph, 26
Contact Editions, 6
Contemporary Annals, 161–62, 164
Cooney, James, 133, 144, 145
Copyrights, 125, 180, 195–96
Cornell University, 178–79
Cornhill, 54
Corvici, Pascal, 154, 172
Coterie publishing, 4
Crazy Cock (Miller), 124, 127
Crès, Georges, 98
Criterion, 41–43
Critic In Judgement, The (Murry), 64
Crosby, Caresse, 138–39, 148–49
Cuba, 138
Cummings, E. E., 29
Customs, English, 112
Customs, United States, 113–14, 177, 183–84
Cutting, Rose Marie, 121

Dadaism, 194
Daily News. See London Daily News
Dali, Salvador, 139
Dar (Nabokov), 163
Darantière, Maurice, 104, 105–06, 110, 111
Dead Souls (Gogol), 186
Delta of Venus (Nin), 140
Des Imagistes (Pound), 20, 194
Despair (Nabokov). See *Otchayanie*

Dial, 29, 34, 35–45, 70, 102, 164
Dial's prize for service to American Letters, 39–44
Diaries of Anaïs Nin: beginnings of, 120–21; excerpts published in *Twice A Year*, 134; "have no universal quality," 134; husband omitted from, 121; offered to Knopf, 129; placed in bank vault, 138; publication in series begins, 134, 155; publishers look at but reject, 133–34, 140; secrecy of, 122–23; realism edited out, 151
D. H. Lawrence: An Unprofessional Study (Nin), 122, 125, 132
Diary of Virginia Woolf, 30
Dickinson, Violet, 52, 55, 62, 63, 66, 72
Dijon, France, 104
Don't Call Me By My Right Name, and Other Stories (Purdy), 198
Doran Company, Publishers, 69
Double Dealer, 6
Doubleday and Company, Publishers, 26, 174–75, 183–84
Douglas, James, 111
Dreiser, Theodore, 138
Driver, Clive, 107
Du Maurier, Daphne, 5
Dubliners (Joyce), 79–92, 95, 96, 101, 102, 114–15; reviews of, 90–91; stories in: "Counterparts," 86, 88; "The Dead," 81; "An Encounter," 84, 86, 88; "Ivy Day in the Committee Room," 83, 86, 88; "Painful Case," 88
Dublin, Ireland, 79, 81, 84, 89, 108
Duckworth Publishers, 55, 57–58, 62–63, 66, 93–94

Duckworth, George, 50, 52, 53, 55, 62–63
Duckworth, Gerald, 50, 55, 58, 62–63, 72
Dudley, John, 139
Duell, Sloan & Pearce, 134
Dunkin, Robert, 144
Dupee, F. W., 184–85
Durrell, Lawrence, 132, 138
Dustbooks, 199–200
Dutton, E. P., 154

Editions du Chêne, 176, 178
Edward, King (of England), 83–84
Egoist, An Individualist Review: ceases publication, 33, 100; edited and supported by Harriet Weaver, 21–23; Eliot and, 22–23; Joyce's *Portrait* and, 92–93; Joyce's *Ulysses* and, 96, 99–101; Pound defends Eliot in, 21; Pound pays contributors in, 21; Pound reviews *Dubliners* in, 91
Egoist Press: exists on donations, 3; established, 23; Eliot and, 25; publishes *Prufrock*, 29; publishes *Portrait*, 94; *Ulysses* and, 98, 100–01, 103–105, 111–12
Eliot, Henry Ware, Jr. (brother of T. S. Eliot), 28
Eliot, Henry Ware, Sr. (father of T.S. Eliot), 27–28
Eliot, Mrs. Henry Ware, Sr. (mother of T. S. Eliot), 27–28, 32
Eliot, Thomas Stearns, 15–45; alternative presses and, 17–18, 37–45, 49, 193; begins writing, 18; commercial presses and, 17, 193; editor for Faber & Faber, 132; edits and writes

for *Egoist,* 22–23; involved in "coterie" publishing, 4, 193; Joyce's *Ulysses* and, 99; Knopf and, 26–29; Leonard Woolf and, 25, 99; *Little Review* and, 97; Lloyd's bank and, 22; meets Pound, 17; Milton Academy and, 35; needs encouragement as a writer, 21; new writing and, 194; Nobel Prize and, 18; Pound reads "Prufrock," 17, 18; reads *Waste Land* to Woolfs, 40–41; reputation as an innovator in poetry, 66; resides permanently in London, 20; studies at Harvard, 18; studies at Oxford, 17; Woolf and, 68–69, 70. *See also* works: *Ara Vos Prec; Poems by T. S. Eliot; Poems; Prufrock and Other Observations; Sacred Wood, The; Tradition and the Individual Talent; Waste Land, The;* "Boston Evening Transcript, The," 20; "Fire Sermon," 34; "Gerontion," 28, 29; "Hysteria," 20, 33; "Le Directeur," 33; "Le Spectateur," 33; "Love Song of J. Alfred Prufrock, The," 17, 18–20; "Miss Helen Slingsby," 20; "Ode," 33; "Portrait of a Lady," 20; "Preludes," 20; "Rhapsody on a Windy Night," 20

Eliot, Valerie (née Fletcher), 27, 28

Eliot, Vivienne (née Haigh-Wood), 20, 27

Eliot's Early Years (Gordon), 34

Ellmann, Richard, 83, 91, 105

Encounter, 22

Epstein, Jason, 174–75, 183–84

Ergaz, Douissa, 172–73, 176–78, 186

Ernst, Morris, 112–14

Erotica, 139–40, 176–78

Esquire, 188, 197

Establishment, literary, 160, 167 176, 189, 197. *See also* Commercial publishers

Euston Station, 11

Evergreen Review, 172

Excelsior Printing Supply Company, 59

Exiles (Joyce), 101

Expatriate writers, 123–24, 177

Experimental writing: alternative publication of, 2–3, 5, 6, 8, 194; commercial publication of, 6–7; Eliot and, 31, 33, 44–45, 49; Gotham Book Mart and, 138; Joyce and, 78–79, 95, 105, 108, 109, 110, 115; literary modernism and, 2–3, 119, 194; Liveright willing to publish, 38; Nabokov and, 166, 189; Nin and, 120, 154–55; out of fashion in 1940s, 119–20, 131; Paris as center for, 101, 109, 123; Russian writers and, 160; stream of consciousness narrative as, 49–50, 61, 72–73; Titus and, 122; unsaleability of, 2–3, 119–20, 128, 132, 194; Woolf and, 49–50, 61–62, 63, 65, 72–73

Exploring James Joyce, (Prescott), 108

Express, Sunday, 181

Faber & Faber, Publishers, 133

Fascism, 131, 136–137

Farrar & Straus, 173

Faulkner, William, 5

Ferber, Ellen, 199–200

Ferlinghetti, Lawrence, 198
Figaro (Paris), 109
Finnegans Wake (Joyce), 95, 108, 115
First Amendment, 175
Fitzgerald, F. Scott, 124
Fitzroy Square (London), 53, 65
Flaubert, Gustave, 110
Fleischman, Leon, 101
Flint, R. W., 185
Florence, Italy, 122
Fondaminsky, Ilya, 162
Ford, Ford Maddox, 19
Ford, Hugh, 128
Forster, E. M., 24, 44, 66
Forum, 43
Fraenkel, Michael, 135–36, 138
Franco, Generalissimo Francisco, 136
Freewoman, 21. See also *Egoist: An Individualist Review*
Fry, Roger, 30, 65, 70, 73
Fuhrman, Otto, 147
Fulton, Len, 199
Futurism, 194

Gallup, Donald, 23
Galway, Ireland, 84
Gardner, Erle Stanley, 5
Garnett, David, 62
Garnett, Edward, 55, 93–94
Garsington, 24
"Gas from a Burner" (Joyce), 89
George V, King (of England), 84
Gerontion (Eliot), 28
Gibben, Seon, 141
Gide, André, 105, 174
Ginsberg, Allen, 197–98. *See also* "Howl," *Howl and Other Poems*
Girodias, Maurice, 176–82, 185–86, 188–89
Gogol, Nikolai, 166
Gonzalo, 132, 136–39, 143, 144, 147, 148–50, 152

Good Earth, The (Buck), 120, 141–42
Gordon Square (London), 52
Gordon, John, 181–82
Gordon, Lydall, 34
Gotham Book Mart, 138, 141–42, 147, 151, 155
Gould, Gerald, 91
Grantwood, New Jersey, 20
Grant, Duncan, 52
Graphic Arts Society, 150–51
Greece, 138, 139
Greene, Graham, 181–82, 197
Greenwich Village, 124
Griffith (editor of *Sinn Fein*), 88
Guardian, 52
Guiler, Hugh (husband of Anaïs Nin), 121, 138, 144–47, 149–50

Haigh-Wood, Vivienne. *See* Eliot, Vivienne
Hamlet correspondence, 135
Hampton Manor, 139
Harpers, 2, 9, 154
Harris, Wayne, 141
Harvard University, 17–21, 34, 35
Hawthorne, Nathaniel, 193
Hayter, William, 144–45
Heap, Jane, 96–98, 101–02
Hecht, Ben, 98
Helba, 136–39, 148
Hemingway, Ernest, 5–6, 124, 138
Henderson, Bill, 197–99
Henderson, Nancy, 198–99
Hessen, Joseph, 161
Histoire d'O, 178
Historical criticism, 167
"Histrion" (Pound), 10
Hogarth House, 30, 56–57, 72, 73
Hogarth Press, 25, 29, 50; beginnings of, 29–31, 56–61; Bloomsbury group and, 194;

[228]

expansion of, 63, 66; first production of, 59–60; gives Woolf power over hurts, 70; innundated with orders for *Kew Gardens*, 65; publications of: see *Critic In Judgement, The* (Murry), *Jacob's Room* (Woolf), *Kew Gardens* (Woolf), *Monday or Tuesday* (Woolf), *Poems* (Eliot), *Prelude* (Mansfield), *The Waste Land* (Eliot), *Two Stories* (Woolf and Woolf); reasons for starting, 56–58; *Ulysses* rejected by, 99; Woolf's experimental writing and, 51, 70, 73

Holt (publishers), 38

Home Office, British, 185

Hone, Joseph, 83, 85

House of Incest (Nin), 127, 129–30, 133–36, 138, 140, 142

"Howl" (Ginsberg), 197–98

Howl and Other Poems, (Ginsberg), 197–98

Huckleberry Finn (Twain), 194

Huddleston, Sisley, 111

Hudson Review, 183

Huebsch, B. W., publishes *Dubliners*, 92; publishes *Portrait*, 94–95, 98, 115; *Ulysses* and, 101–02, 107, 113

Hueffer, Ford Maddox. *See* Ford, Ford Maddox

Hugo, Ian. *See* Guiler, Hugh

Hulme, T. E., 11

Hutchinson and Company, 81

Hutchinson, Mary (Mrs. St. John), 25, 30

Huxley, Aldous, 25, 42

H. D., 19

Illinois, University of, 199

Imagism, 194

Indiana, 9

Industry, California, 196

International Directory of Little Magazines and Small Presses, 199–200

"Introducing Nabokov to America" (Parry), 163–64

Iowa, University of, 199

Ireland, 78. *See also* Joyce, James

Irish Book Lover, 95

Irving, Washington, 193

Italy, 120

Jacob's Room (Woolf): begins writing, 67–68; Duckworth and, 72; experimental technique of, 49–50, 67, 68, 72–73; Leonard reads, 71; printing and binding of, 71–72; publication delayed, 71; published in 1922, 8, 49; "puffs" printed at the back of, 70; resolves to finish writing, 69; reviews of, 72–73; self-published, 50, 68; Woolf's predictions of success, 72; writing delayed by doubts, 69–70; writing delayed by illness, 70–71; writing finished, 71

Jacob, rue (Paris), 176

James Joyce's Ulysses: A Facsimile of the Manuscript, 106–07

Jennings, Veronica, 134

John Gordon Society, 181–82

Joost, Nicholas, 36, 39

Josephson, Matthew, 123–24

Joyce, James, 75–115; burning of *Dubliners*, 89; burning of *Ulysses*, 105, 112; deletes "objectionable" material from *Dubliners*, 80, 83–88; financial success of, 115; first book publication, 81; Gotham Book

Mart and, 138; Grant Richards and, 78–81, 83–86, 90; Ireland and, 78, 81–84, 89, 91, 95; Larbaud and, 103, 105, 109–10; legal action against publishers, 81, 83, 86, 112; *Little Review* and, 97–98; moves to Paris, 100–101; Pound and, 22, 26, 91–92, 94–97, 100–01; reputation in Paris, 109; self-publishing and, 84–85, 88–89; subsidizes publication of *Dubliners*, 89–92, 95, 115; Sylvia Beach and, 78, 95, 103–15, 176, 193; Weaver and, 23, 30, 92–95, 98–101, 103, 111–12; Woolf compared to, 66, 68–69. *See also* works: *Chamber Music; Dubliners; Exiles; Finnegans Wake; Portrait of the Artist as a Young Man; Stephen Hero; Ulysses;* "The Dead," see *Dubliners;* "Gas from a Burner." *See also* Censorship
Joyce, Nora (née Barnacle), 79, 83–84, 86–87
Joyce, Stanislaus (brother of James Joyce), 81, 84
Joyce, Stephen (son of James Joyce), 82
Jung, Carl, 126

Kahane, Jack, 127–28, 132–33, 138, 176
Kamera Obskura (Nabokov), 162
Karlinsky, Simon, 149–50, 164
Kees, Weldon, 174
Kenyon Review, 184
Kew Gardens (London), 65
Kew Gardens (Woolf), 31, 63–67, 73; reviewed, 65
Keynes, John Maynard, 52
Khodasevich, Vladislav, 162
Kingdom by the Sea. See Lolita

Kirkus Reviews, 188
Knopf, Alfred: commercial publishing and, 26; Liveright and, 38; Nabokov and, 163–64; Pound and, 26–29; publishes *Poems by T. S. Eliot*, 17, 26–29, 32, 38; publishes *The Sacred Wood*, 33; rejects *House of Incest*, 130; rejects *The Waste Land*, 29
Korol', Dama, Valet (Nabokov), 161
Koteliansky, 62
Krafft-Ebing, 140
Kreymborg, Alfred, 20

La Fontaine café, 162
La Pensée, Henry, 152
Ladders to Fire (Nin), 154
Ladies Home Journal, 1, 9
Lady Chatterley's Lover (Lawrence), 122
Lane, John, 29, 114
Larbaud, Valéry, 103, 109–10
Latest News, 162
Laughlin, James, 147, 165
Laughter in the Dark (Nabokov), 162, 173; reviews of, 164. See also *Kamera Obskura*
Laurie, T. Werner, 94
Lausanne, Switzerland, 34
Lawrence, D. H., 94, 122, 128, 132, 138
Leaves of Grass (Whitman), 193
Legion of Honor, 103
Levin, Harry, 106–08
Lewis, Wyndham: edits *BLAST*, 2, 20; meets Eliot, 19; Pound and, 22, 26, 97
Lidwell, George, 86
Life Among the Surrealists (Josephson), 123–24
Lish, Gordon, 197
Literary Review, 43
Little magazine publishing, 3, 6,

[230]

140. *See also* Alternative publishing

Little Review, 96–98; existed on donations, 3, 36; obscenity trial of, 101–03, 109, 196; Pound and, 22, 96–97; *Ulysses* and, 96–98, 105, 196

Liveright, Horace, 28, 38, 102, 107; publication of *The Waste Land*, 38–45

Lloyd's Bank of London, 22, 30, 34, 37

Lolita (Nabokov), 168–89; banned in France, 185; bestseller, 188–189; completed, 170; contract for, 179–81, 186; controversial subject of, 160; copyright of, 180; evolved from short story, 168; as a chess problem, 169–170; fame of, 181, 183–89; Greene and, 181–82; Nabokov is secretive about, 178–79; Nabokov's reputation before, 166–67; Paris publication of, 160; published alternatively, 8; radical in purpose, 8; rejected by New York publishers, 160, 172–75; reviews of, 181, 183–89; royalty payments for, 181, 185–88; story line of, 170–71; Wilson and, 160; word play and puzzles in, 160, 168–72, 173–74. Editions of: Olympia, 180–87, 189; *Anchor Review*, 183–86; Putnam, 186–89

London Daily News, 70

London Evening Standard, 10

"London Letter" to *Dial* (Eliot), 36

"London Letter" to *Vanity Fair* (Huxley), 42

London Mercury, 67

Long, John, 81, 162

Louveciennes, France, 121, 134–36

"Love Song of J. Alfred Prufrock, The" (Eliot), 17–20

Lowenfels, Walter, 135

Lume Spento, A (Pound): bookstores sell, 10–11; Pound's calling card in London, 10; printing of, 1, 9, 10, 12; promotion of, 10; reviews of, 10

McAlmond, Robert, 105

McCarthy, Mary, 173–74

McCormick, Ken, 175

MacDougal Street, 143, 150

Madison, Charles A., 187

Magazines, general circulation, 6, 7

Mailer, Norman, 187

Maison des Amis des Livres, 109

Mandel Brothers, 96

Mansfield, Katherine, 25, 30, 63, 66, 99

Margate, 34

"Mark on the Wall, The" (Woolf), 60–61, 62, 63, 66, 67

Marsden, Dora, 22

Marshall, Simpkin, 84

Marxism, 132, 136–37, 151, 165

Mashen'ka (Nabokov), 161

Mathews, Elkin: Bodley Head and, 10–11; Lane and, 10–11; offered Joyce's *Dubliners*, 89–90; Pound's early career and, 10–12; publishes *Catholic Anthology*, 20; publishes Joyce's *Chamber Music*, 81; rejects Eliot's *Prufrock*, 23

Mathuen & Company, 33

Maunsel & Company, 81–89

Mayakovsky, Vladimir Vladimirovich, 160

Melville, Herman, 194

[231]

Melymbrosia, 54. See also,
  Voyage Out, The
Mencken, H. L., 18, 92, 163
Meurice, Hotel, 39
Mexico, 138
Michigan, Lake, 96
Miller, Henry, 124–30, 132,
  133–39, 148–49, 153. *See also*
  works: *Crazy Cock, Scenario,*
  Tropic of Cancer
Miller, June, 124, 126, 129
Milton Academy, 35
Milton, John, 77
Ministry of the Interior,
  French, 185
Minton, Melville, 187
Minton, Walter, 186–87
Modern Library, 38
Modernism, literary: Blake and,
  144; bumper crop in 1922, 8;
  critical theory and, 119; *Dial*
  and, 35–36, 39–40; *Egoist*
  and, 100; Eliot and, 17, 25, 31,
  35, 39–45; experimentation
  and, 2–3, 7, 119; heyday ends,
  195; Joyce and, 78–79, 105,
  108, 109–10, 189; Nabokov and,
  189; *Partisan Review* and, 183;
  popularized by commercial
  publishers, 7; published by
  new publishers, 6; stream of
  consciousness narrative and,
  49; the art of literature and,
  119, 197; unpopularity of in
  the 1930s and 1940s, 119–20;
  Wilson and, 160, 164; Woolf
  and, 49, 73
Moeller, Philip, 101–02
Monday or Tuesday (Woolf), 67,
  69–70
Monnier, Adrienne, 104, 109
Monologue intérieur, 111
Monroe, Harriet: editor of
  Poetry, 29; Eliot's "Prufrock"

and, 17–19, 20; Pound and, 1–2,
  23, 194; starts *Poetry* with
  donations, 1
Monro, Harold, 17, 18
Montparnasse, 110, 123, 128
Montreux, Switzerland, 188
Moore, George, 36
Moore, G. E., 52
Morell, Lady Ottoline, 25
Morell, Philip, 25
Morley College, 53
Morocco, 136
Mrs. Dalloway (Woolf), 49, 67,
  73
Murry, Middleton, 25, 33, 64,
  66, 111

Nabokov, Nicholas (cousin of
  Vladimir), 165
Nabokov, Vladimir Dmitrievich
  (father of Vladimir), 161
Nabokov, Vladimir Vladi-
  mirovich, 157–89; alternative
  publishing and, 8, 9; as a Russian writer, 160–63; Berlin
  career, 161; chess problems
  and, 169–170; commercial
  publishers and, *see* Commercial publishers; Cornell and,
  178–79; early publicity about
  in U.S., 163–65; emigrates to
  United States, 160–61, 163; exiled from Russia, 161; financial plight before *Lolita,* 167;
  Girodias and, 176–82, 185–86,
  188–89; reluctant to put name
  on *Lolita,* 178–79; reputation
  before *Lolita,* 166–67; Sirin
  and, 161–62, 169; studies at
  Cambridge, 161; success after
  Lolita, 188–89, 193; Wellesley
  and, 167; Wilson and, 159–60,
  164–68, 173–76, 178; writes
  poetry, 161. *See also* works:

Mashen'ka; Korol', Dama, Valet; Vozvraschenie Chorba; Rasskazi i Stikhi; Dar; Zashchita Luzhena; Soglyadataj'; Kamera Obskura; Podvig; The Real Life of Sebastian Knight; Priglashenie Na Kazn'; Otchayanie; Bend Sinister; Nikolai Gogol; Conclusive Evidence; Speak, Memory; Lolita; Pnin; Strong Opinions; "On a Book Entitled *Lolita*"; "The Aurelian"; "The Softest of Tongues"; "Professor O"; "Butterflies"

Nabokov-Wilson Letters, The, 159–60, 165

National City Bank, 125

Nation, 43, 111, 148, 153–54

Nazaroff, Alexander, 164

Nemerov, Howard, 183, 184

New Directions, 147, 165, 172, 189

New Freewoman, 21. See also *Egoist: An Individualist Review*

New Republic, 147, 165, 185, 187–88

New Statesman, 24, 70, 91

New writing. *See* Experimental writing

New York Herald-Tribune, 98, 147–48

New York Society for the Suppression of Vice, 98

New York Times Book Review, 164, 166, 181–82

New York Times, 43, 98, 147, 164, 183

New York University, 147

Night and Day (Woolf), 60, 63, 66

Nin, Anaïs, 117–54; begins diary, 120–21; buys first press, 134; buys second press, 136; buys third press, 143; childhood, 120; "deprived of existence," 140–41; education, 121; fame comes to, 150, 155; flees to New York in WWII, 138; Fraenkel and, 135–36; marriage, 121; Miller and, 124–30, 132, 133–39, 148–49, 153; Perles and, 134–36; prints *Under a Glass Bell,* 149–51; prints *Winter of Artifice,* 143–46; problems with publishers, 195; realism and, 131–32, 149–52; rejections by commercial publishers, 120, 133–34; born in Paris, 120; reviewed in commercial press, 152–54; Seana and, 134–36; self-publishing and, 8, 120, 134–55, 193; visits Morocco, 136. *See also* works: *Delta of Venus; Diaries; House of Incest; This Hunger; Ladders to Fire; Under a Glass Bell; Winter of Artifice;* "The Voice"

Nin, Joaquin (father of Anaïs), 120, 129–30, 138, 140

Nobel Prize for Literature, 18, 120, 162, 163

Norman, Dorothy, 134, 143

Northern Whig (Belfast), 84

Nouvelle Review Français, 103

Novels, 6, 7, 73. *See also* Stream of consciousness

Obelisk Press, 127–28, 138, 176

Obscenity: copyrights and, 196; *Howl* and, 198; *Little Review* and, 101–03, 109, 198; *Lolita* and, 157, 160, 172–73, 181–82; *Ulysses* and, 101–03, 109, 112–14, 198

[233]

Observer, 111
Olympia Press, 176, 178–81, 183–89
Olympic Reader, The (Girodias), 176, 185–86
"On a Book Entitled *Lolita*" (Nabokov), 172, 184
Osborn, Richard, 125
Otchayanie (Nabokov), 162, 164
Others: A Magazine of New Verse, 20
Our Women (Bennett), 68–69
Ovid Press, 32–33, 101
Oxford, 17, 19, 35
O'Brien, Darcy, 196
O'Neill, Eugene, 138

Paradise Lost (Milton), 77
"Paris Letter" in *Dial* (Pound), 36
Parker, Dorothy, 188
Paronomasia, 160
Parry, Albert, 163
Partisan Review, 169, 183
Pasternak, Boris, 160
Pavannes and Divisions (Pound), 28
Pearce, Charles, 134
Pearl Harbor, 142
Pelican Press, 100
Perkins, Maxwell, 133
Perles, Alfred, 124, 134–36, 138
Person In Question, The. See *Speak, Memory*
Personae (Pound), 11–12
Petronius, 133
Petropolis, 162
Philosophy Club, Harvard, 19
Pilgrims Progress (Bunyan), 77
Pinker, J. B., 92–93, 100, 113
Pnin (Nabokov), 184
Podvig (Nabokov), 162
Poems by T. S. Eliot, 26–29, 32, 38; reviews of, 29
Poems of 1831 (Poe), 193

Poems (Eliot), 29–32, 33, 64
Poetry and Drama, 18
Poetry, 1, 2, 36, 194
Poetry: 5, 11, 35–36; *Waste Land*'s effect on, 42, 44
Poet's Club, 11
Poe, Edgar Allan, 193
Pomona College, 196
Popular literature, opposed to new writing, 2
Pornography. *See* Obscenity, Censorship
Portrait of the Artist as a Young Man, A (Joyce), 23, 79, 96, 101, 115; writing bogs down, 80–83; publication of, 92–95; reviewed, 95
Post Office, United States, 112
Post-modernism, 160
Pound, Dorothy (née Shakespear), 11, 23
Pound, Ezra Loomis: begins writing, 9; commercial publishers and, 1–2, 9; edits *Catholic Anthology*, 20; edits *Des Imagistes* anthology, 20; edits Eliot's *Waste Land*, 34–35; Eliot's *Prufrock* and, 23; encourages Harriet Monroe to start *Poetry*, 1; "Good art can't possibly be palatable all at once," 2; in Italy, 120; introduces Eliot in London literary circles, 19–20; involved in "coterie" publishing, 4; is "on verge of starting a quarterly," 2; Joyce and, 79, 91–92, 94–95; Joyce's *Ulysses* and, 96–97, 101, 105; leaves for Europe, 9; leaves Paris, 120, 124; *Little Review* and, 96–97; "Make it new," 194; modern literary renaissance and, 1, 9, 96;

moves to Paris, 34; "permanent books," 103; pays contributors in *Egoist*, 21; picture of at Gotham Book Mart, 138; promotes Eliot's career, 17, 37; promotes Eliot's "Prufrock," 18–20; "TO HELL WITH HARPERS," 2; *Waste Land* publication and, 35–45. *See also* works: *Cantos*, 37; *Lume Spento, A*, 1, 9–12; *Lustra*, 26; *Pavannes and Divisions*, 28; *Personae*, 11–12; *Quinzaine For This Yule, A*, 11–12; "Possibility of a Poetic Drama," 36

Powys, John Cowper, 102

Prelude (Mansfield), 30, 31, 63, 99

Prescott, Joseph, 108

Priglashenie Na Kazn' (Nabokov), 163

Princeton University, 103

Prix Goncourt, 103

"Professor O" (Nabokov), 168

Proletarian literature, 8, 120

Proust, Marcel, 126, 131, 133

Prufrock and Other Observations, 23–26, 29; reviews of, 24–25

"Prufrock." *See* "Love Song of J. Alfred Prufrock, The"

Public domain, the, 196

Published in Paris (Ford), 128

Publish-It-Yourself Handbook, The (Henderson), 197–99

Puns. *See* Word games

Purdy, James, 198

Pushcart Press, 198

Putnam's, 186–88

Quarterly Review, 20

Quinn, John, 23, 25; Joyce and, 79; *Little Review* and, 97, 101–02; Liveright and, 38; *Poems by T. S. Eliot* and, 26–29; *Prufrock* and, 26–29; *Ulysses* and, 101–02, 105; *Waste Land* and, 32

Quinzaine For This Yule, A, (Pound), 11–12

R & R Clark Printers, 72

Rainbow, The (Lawrence), 94

Random House, 112–14, 154, 196

Rank, Otto, 130–31, 136

Real Life of Sebastian Knight, The (Nabokov), 163, 165–66

Realism, 119, 127, 131–32, 149–52, 169, 173, 175, 183

"Recent Books by Russian Writers" (Nazaroff), 164

Regent Street, 19

Regional publishing, 4

Reid, B. L., 25, 26, 40

Reporter, 186

"Revolution of the Word Proclamation," 194

Rexroth, Kenneth, 197

Rezimov, 160

Rhymers Club, 10–11

Richards, Grant, 79–81, 83–86, 90, 93, 94–95, 102

Richmond (London), 59, 72

Ridgewell, Rosemary, 186–87

Rivers, Alston, 81

Roberts, George, 82–89

Rodker, John, 32–33, 101, 111–12

Romanticism, 151

Rosenfeld, Paul, 147, 151

Rothermere, Lady, 41

Rousseau, 133

Royal University, Dublin, 82

Roy, Winifred, 162

Rubenstein, Helena, 122, 132

Rudder (Berlin), 161

Russell, Bertrand, 24

Russell, George, 85

Russian Annals, 166
Russian émigré literature, 159, 161–63, 169, 177
Russian Symbolists, 160, 189
Russians, White, 159, 161, 165
Rutherford, New Jersey, 12

Sacred Wood, The (Eliot), 27, 33
Saint Bride's school of printing, 58
Saint James's Gazette, 10
Saintsbury, George, 43
Samizdat publishing, 3
San Francisco Police Department, 198
San Francisco, California, 198
Saturday Evening Post, 6
Saturday Review of Literature, 134, 164, 185
Scenario (Miller), 135
Schickel, Richard, 186
Schmitz, Ettore, 82
Scholarly publishing, 4
Scribners, 6, 10, 38, 133
Seana, 135–36
Sebastian Knight. See Real Life of Sebastian Knight
Secker, Martin, 89, 93
Seldes, Gilbert, 37, 40–43
Self-publishing, 3, 8; Blake and, 144; Hawthorne and, 193; Irving and, 193; Joyce and, 84–85, 88–89; Lawrence and, 122; Melville and, 194; Miller and, 124; Nin and, 120, 144–46, 149–55; Poe and, 193; Pound and, 1, 9–12; problems with, 195; Thoreau and, 193; Twain and, 194; Whitman and, 193; Woolf and, 49–75. *See also* Alternative publishing
Servant, M., 128
Sewanee Review, 35
Shakespear, Dorothy. *See* Pound, Dorothy

Shakespear, Olivia, 11
Shakespeare and Company, 78, 103–15
Shakespeare, William, 77
Shaw, Bernard, 11
Shelley, Percy, 193
Short stories in popular magazines, 5–6
Simon and Shuster, 172
Simpson, Louis, 183
Sinn Fein (Dublin), 84, 88
Sirin, Vladimir. *See* Nabokov, Vladimir Vladimirovich
Sitwell, Edith, 198
Six Gallery, 197
63: Dream Palace (Purdy), 198
Sketchbook (Irving), 193
Slocum, John J., 112, 140
Slovo, 161
Small press publishing, 3, 6, 8, 198–200. *See also* Alternative publishing
Smart Set, 18, 92
Smythe, Ethel, 60, 67
Socialism, 131
Society of Authors, 81
"Softest of Tongues," 166
Soglyadataj (Nabokov), 162–63
Soho, 17, 22
Sokol, Thurema, 143
Southport, England, 99
Soviet Russia, 165
Spanish Civil War, 119
Spanish Republic, 119, 136
Speak, Memory (Nabokov), 168–70
Spectator, 181–82
Sporting Times, 111
Steloff, Frances, 138, 143, 147, 151
Stephen Hero. See Portrait of the Artist as a Young Man, A
Stephen, Adrian (brother of Virginia Woolf), 52, 53
Stephen, Julia (mother of Virginia Woolf), 50

[236]

Stephen, Leslie (father of Virginia Woolf), 50, 52
Stephen, Thoby (brother of Virginia Woolf), 52, 53
Stephen, Vanessa. *See* Bell, Vanessa
Stephen, Virginia. *See* Woolf, Virginia
Strachey, Lytton, 25, 52, 62, 65, 66, 70, 99
Straus, Roger, 173
Stream of consciousness narrative, 49–50, 61, 72–73, 110, 111
Strobel, Marion, 29
Strong Opinions (Nabokov), 186
Stroup, John, 152
Subsidy publishers, 4
Suffragettes, 21
Sullivan, Richard, 103, 109
Sunday Express, 111
Surrealism, 121, 123–24, 125, 126, 152, 194
Svevo, Italo. *See* Schmitz, Ettore
Sydney-Turner, Saxon, 52
Symons, Arthur, 81

Tebbel, John, 38
Telemachia (Joyce), 97, 106. See also *Ulysses*
Thayer, Schofield, 29, 35–39, 101–02
Theatre Guild, 102
This Quarter, 122
Thoreau, Henry David, 193
"Three Jews, The " (L. Woolf), 60–61
Three Mountains Press, 6
Times (London) Literary Supplement: effect on *The Waste Land*, 32; Eliot writes for, 33. Reviews in: of *Ara Vos Prec*, 33; of *Dubliners*, 91; of Eliot's *Poems*, 31–32; of *Jacob's Room*, 72; of *Kew Gardens*,

65; of *Monday or Tuesday*, 69, 70; of *Night and Day*, 66; of *Prufrock and Other Observations*, 24; of *The Waste Land*, 44; Woolf writes for, 54, 61
Time Magazine, 164, 184–85, 187–88
Titus, Edward, 122, 128, 132
To the Lighthouse (Woolf), 49
Town and Country, 152
Tradition and the Individual Talent (Eliot), 22
Transition, 194
Travellers Companion series, 177, 189
Trevelyan, Bob, 60
Trieste, 79, 83, 84, 89
Trilling, Diana, 153–54
Tropic of Cancer (Miller), 126–29, 132, 134; Nin pays for publication of, 127–29
T. S. Eliot (Bergonzi), 24
Tsvetaeva, 160
Tulsa, University of, 25
Twain, Mark, 194
Twice a Year, 134, 143
Twickenham, England, 56
Two Stories (Woolf), 30, 59–63
Tynan, Katherine, 85

Ulysses, 5, 30, 95–111; advertising about, 105, 109, 111; alterations easily made in, 5, 95; banned in England, 112; bookstore publication of, 78, 95, 197; burning of, 105, 112; censorship of, 97–98, 101–02, 110, 112–15, 189; contracts for, 100, 104–05, 107; copyright problems with, 196; Eliot praises to Woolf, 68; French translation, 109; landmark of modernism, 7, 78; *Little Review* serializes, 97–98, 103, 105; published in 1922, 8, 96,

110; reading and lecture in bookstore, 109–10, 197; reviews of, 98, 111, 113; revision of on proofs, 105–09; smuggling of, 112, 114, 182; writing of, 96, 105–09. Chapters in: "Aoelus," 106; "Circe," 102, 105, 107, 108; "Cyclops," 108; "Eumaeus," 102; "Hades," 100; "Nestor," 100; "Penelope," 108, 109; "Proteus," 100; "Telemachus," 98; "Wandering Rocks," 100. Editions of: first, 110; Egoist, 111–12, 114; second, 112; third through tenth, 112; pirated, 112, 180, 196; Random House, 112–14; John Lane, 114

Under a Glass Bell (Nin), 8, 149–52; reviews of, 151–54

Underground press movement, 198–99

University of Illinois Press, 199

University of Iowa Press, 199

University of Pennsylvania, 9

University press publishing, 3, 199

Unsolicited manuscripts, 6

"Unwritten Novel, An" (Woolf), 67–68, 73

Upward, Allen, 21

Utley, Ralph, 138

Vanity Fair, 42

Vanity publishing, 4, 197

Venice, Italy, 9

Venus de Milo, 94

Victoria, Queen (of England), 83

Vidal, Gore, 154

Vienna, Austria, 39

Vigilance Committee, 85, 90

Vigo Street, 10–11

Viking Press, 154, 172, 189

Villa Seurat, 134–36

"Voice, The," (Nin), 146

Vorticism, 194

Vorticist Manifesto, 194

Voyage Out, The (Woolf), 54–55, 57–58

Vozvraschenie Chorba; Rasskazi i Stikhi (Nabokov), 161

Wakefield Gallery, 151

Walden (Thoreau), 193

Wasserstrom, William, 35

Waste Land, The: as a response to *TLS* review of *Prufrock* and *Poems,* 32; begins writing, 34; contract for publication of, 40–41; copyright of, 40; delays work on, 33; *Dial* publication of, 35–45; editing complete, 38; effect on Eliot's career, 34; Eliot's first major poem, 39–40; fragmentary nature of, 35; Knopf rejects, 29, 38; landmark of modernism, 7, 42, 197; plans to write, 32; Pound arranges publication of, 34–40; Pound edits, 33–35; published in 1922, 8, 41–42; reviews of, 43–45; shocked literary world, 197; Wilson's review of, 160, 164

Waterlow, Sydney, 64

Watson, James Sibley, 35–39

Waugh, Arthur, 20

Weaver, Harriet Shaw, 3; Communist party and, 120; edits and supports *The Egoist,* 21–23; Eliot and, 22–23, 25; Joyce and, 92–95, 98–101, 103–05, 111–12, 114–15; repays Pound for Eliot's *Prufrock,* 23; Woolfs and, 30

Weeks, Edward, 166

Wellesley College, 167

Wells, H. G., 93

West Coast literary movement, 198

Westminster Gazette, 24

West, Rebecca, 21, 22

Whiteside, Thomas, 7

Whitman, Walt, 138, 193

Williams, William Carlos, 12, 20, 42, 147

Wilson, Edmund: *Axel's Castle,* 44, 164; historical criticism and, 167; literary modernism and, 160, 164; Nabokov and, 159–60, 164–68, 173–76, 178, 188; *New Republic* and, 159, 164; reputation as a critic, 159, 164, 197; reviews Nin's *Under a Glass Bell,* 151–52; reviews *The Waste Land,* 43, 44, 45, 164; visits Russia, 165

Wilson, Elena (wife of Edmund), 173–74

Winter of Artifice (Nin), 8, 134; commercial publishers reject, 140–42; Kahane and, 132; Nin distributes, 138; Nin prints and publishes, 144–48; reviews of, 147–48; writing of, 129–30

Woodstock, New York, 133

Woolf, Leonard: Bloomsbury Group and, 52; Eliot and, 25, 29–32, 41–42, 68; Hogarth Press and, 29–31, 51, 56–57, 58, 60–61, 66; marries Virginia Stephen, 54; reads *Jacob's Room,* 71; reads *Kew Gardens,* 64; returns from Ceylon, 52; Woolf (Virginia) compares herself to, 68–69

Woolf, Virginia, 49–73; conventional writing, 49, 193; death of, 51; education, lack of, 52, 53; Eliot and, 29–32, 41–42, 68–69, 70, 99; ex-perimental writing, 50, 51, 65, 66–68, 69, 70, 193; illness and fears of failure, 50–51, 54, 55–57, 69, 70–71; involved in "coterie" publishing, 4; Joyce's *Ulysses* and, 98; marriage to Leonard Woolf, 54; molested by George Duckworth, 50; moves to Fitzroy Square, 53; moves to Gordon Square, 52; picture of at Gotham Book Mart, 138; reputation as an innovator in fiction, 66; reviews for the *Times Literary Supplement,* 54; self-publishing and, 66, 69–70, 72–73, 193; starts Hogarth Press, 25, 29–31; suicide attempts, 51, 55; teaches at Morley College, 53; tours Greece, 53. *See also* Hogarth Press; *Jacob's Room; Kew Gardens; Monday or Tuesday; Mrs. Dalloway; Night and Day; To the Lighthouse; Two Stories; Voyage Out, The;* "Mark on the Wall"; "Unwritten Novel, An"

Woolsey, Judge John M., 114, 196

Word games & puns: *Lolita* and 171–72, 183, 189, 193; Nabokov's Russian heritage and, 159–60; Nabokov's "weakness" for, 165; Wilson's attitude toward, 167– 69

World War II: apocalypse of, 144; attitude toward White Russians during, 165; literature after, 155, 168; magazines after, 6; outbreak of, 133–35, 138–42

Yale University Press Younger Poets Series, 199

[239]

Yeats, John, 1–12, 20, 89, 92
Yonkers, New York, 198

Zaschita Luzhena (Nabokov), 162

Z
231.5
.L5
D47
1984

Dennison:
[Alternative]
literary publishing:
five modern histories

DEMCO